Shortcuts to Songwriting for Film & TV

114 Tips for Writing, Recording, & Pitching in Today's Hottest Market

ROBIN FREDERICK

TAXI MUSIC BOOKS™
Los Angeles, California

Published by:
TAXI Music Books, a division of MicroMini Media, Inc.
5010 Parkway Calabasas #200
Calabasas, CA 91302

Visit TAXI Music Books at www.SongwritingBooks.com.

TAXI Music Books
Publisher: Michael Laskow
Executive Editor: Robin Frederick

TAXI Music Books and TAXI Books are trademarks of
MicroMini Media, Inc.

MicroMiniMedia®

Cover Design by LeeAnn Nelson for Nelson Design
Page Design by Lynn M. Snyder for Nosy Rosy Designs

ISBN-13: 978-0-9820040-2-9
ISBN-10: 0-9820040-2-8

Acknowledgments

My very special thanks to Michael Laskow whose ongoing belief in my books has opened up exciting new vistas for me. Without his support and generosity, this book would not have been possible. I am indebted to the talented, experienced people who generously shared their time and knowledge with me both in the interview section of this book and on background: Tanvi Patel, Chris Mollere, Stephan R. Goldman, Paul Antonelli, Peter Greco, Marianne Goode, Pat Weaver, and Charlyn Bernal.

Thanks to Ronny S. Schiff, Rachel Laskow, Ted Myers, and Bethany Rubin whose eagle eyes catch my mistakes and to Andrea Brauer, Esq. for her diligence in making sure I got the business concepts right. To LeeAnn Nelson of Nelson Design and Lynn Snyder, my deep appreciation for contributing to the look and readability of this book.

This book is dedicated to the songwriters and artists who make such beautiful music and to the music supervisors, editors, producers, directors, and all those who blend pictures with music and lyrics to create the memorable moments that move us all!

Robin Frederick
Los Angeles, CA
September, 2010

About the Author

Robin Frederick is the author of *Shortcuts to Hit Songwriting: 126 Proven Techniques for Writing Songs That Sell.* She has written and produced hundreds of songs for television, music albums, musical theatre, and audio products. While Director of A&R and Production for a division of Rhino Records, Robin was responsible for the creation of more than sixty albums. As head of the A&R/Screener Team at TAXI, she has overseen the work of top music industry experts and offered songwriting advice to TAXI's thousands of members. She has served on the board of the Recording Academy (the GRAMMY organization) and is past president of Los Angeles Women in Music. Through her books, articles, and workshops, Robin has shared her insights into song craft with hundreds of thousands of people.

Also by Robin Frederick:

Shortcuts to Hit Songwriting: 126 Proven Techniques for Writing Songs That Sell

Shortcuts to Songwriting for Film & TV:

114 Tips for Writing, Recording, & Pitching in Today's Hottest Market

What Film & TV Can Do for You

Part One: The Quick Start Manual

Part Two: Know Your Film & TV Opportunities

PART THREE: **Build Film & TV Songs on a Strong Foundation**

PART FOUR: **Shortcuts to Music for Film & TV Songs**

PART FIVE: **Shortcuts to Lyrics for Film & TV Songs**

PART SIX: Shortcuts to Song Production for Film & TV

PART EIGHT: **Shortcuts to Getting Placements in Film & TV**

PART NINE: Get It from a Pro

Foreword

When was the last time you enjoyed a sequel as much or more than the original? I just finished reading *Shortcuts to Songwriting for Film & TV* and my face hurts—literally! Why? Because I found myself smiling more and more as I went page-to-page, topic-to-topic, and Shortcut-to-Shortcut.

Robin Frederick has written the perfect sequel to her best-selling first book, *Shortcuts to Hit Songwriting*.

When Robin and I brainstormed topics for her second book, we couldn't find anything on the market specifically about songwriting for film and TV placements. Frankly, we were surprised as film and TV licensing has clearly become the target for so many songwriters and artists today. As the publisher for the *Shortcuts* series, it was obvious to me that Robin would be the ideal author for this book as she's had hundreds of placements with *her* songs.

I'll admit to being a little worried about matching the quantity and *quality* of information in our first book. By all accounts, it set a new standard and the reviews have been nothing short of unanimous in their praise. Could Robin do it again?

I'm proud to report that the answer is "Yes!" As with her last book, reading Robin's *Shortcuts to Songwriting for Film & TV* makes you feel like you're hanging out with your best friend who just happens to know everything one could ever *need* to know about the subject. This is not a dry, laborious textbook. This isn't one of those books about someone else's experiences designed to inspire you but falling short of giving you actionable steps.

No, *this* book will show you all the possibilities you've probably never realized are out there for your music. *This* book will help you create songs that are true to your muse, but *also* crafted for today's hottest market. *This* book will show you how to get your songs placed, make sure you understand how to track the income you deserve, and how to build a long-term career with your songwriting skills.

As the founder and CEO of TAXI, this streamlined, easy-to-read book, with its common sense, down-to-earth approach and actionable steps, dovetails perfectly with my personal philosophy of helping musicians earn their living doing what they love. TAXI has been a true pioneer in getting thousands of independent songwriters' music placed in movies and TV shows since 1992—*long* before it became fashionable.

Members of the uber-cool A&R community laughed at me for being the first to help independents like you back then. They aren't laughing any more! I'm pretty sure they will be reading this book so they can coach *their* songwriters and artists to achieve more success in this burgeoning market. I'm glad you're reading it first. Long live independent songwriters and artists. Long live Robin Frederick and her excellent books that I will always be proud to publish!

To your success,
Michael Laskow
FOUNDER & CEO, TAXI

Introduction

How to Get the Most From This Book

In many ways, writing for the film and television market is easier than pursuing that big radio hit song. There are many more opportunities in a far wider range of styles than in mainstream commercial radio. However, the film and TV market makes its own unique demands on a song. Unlike hit radio where the song is the focus of attention, in film and television uses, the song must support what's happening on the screen.

Whether it's a film scene in a honky-tonk with a jukebox playing just the right, gritty dance song, or a TV drama that ends with a close-up of a character's tear-stained face as a song conveys her feelings, or a commercial that uses a song to evoke the lighthearted happiness of a brand-name product, the song is there to support the emotion, create atmosphere, or add energy to the visual. The Shortcuts in this book will show you how to craft songs that will enhance these scenes, adding to their impact and memorability for viewers. That's what the film and TV market needs from you!

Watch the scenes. Listen to the song examples.

In this field, your eyes and ears are the most important learning tools you have. It's important to *watch and listen* to the song examples in this book so you can understand the techniques in the Shortcuts and see how they're applied in the industry.

<= Do this. It will really help!

There are many song examples, films, and TV shows referenced throughout the book. See the Resources section on page 307 for inexpensive, easy ways to stream, rent, or buy them. While you can listen to the songs simply as songs, watching them in conjunction with the visual media will help you understand their effect and why they were chosen.

On page 310, you'll find the "Film & TV Song List." This list includes all the songs referred to in the book, along with the title of the movie, TV show, or commercial in which you can see how the song is used. You can locate the song within the film or TV show by using the "at time" information.

Many of the songs I'll be referring to are not well known. Most are by independent artists whose work is not played widely on the radio. Sure, there are a few hit songs by established artists but, as you look through the "Film & TV Song List," you may see many names you don't recognize. Don't let that put you off. That's actually a good thing because *you* could be one of them!

Write and record as you go

You'll get the most from this book if you're actively writing and recording songs as you read. If you have unfinished or unrecorded songs, these will provide great raw material to use when reading the Shortcuts. Go ahead and try different ideas and techniques suggested by the book. If you don't like the results, go back to what you had and start again.

Feel free to skip around the Shortcuts, focusing on those areas you feel would be most useful for you, or write a song as you read through Part Three "Build Film & TV Songs on a Strong Foundation" and Part Four "Shortcuts to Music for Film & TV Songs." These will lead you through a process that will help you write a song based on mood, atmosphere, and energy level, something that has strong appeal in the film and TV market.

Basic song craft

In this book, I've assumed that you're already familiar with some basic song craft. When necessary, I'll try to briefly fill in some of this information but if you find yourself running into more than a few unfamiliar songwriting concepts, try reading my book *Shortcuts to Hit Songwriting: 126 Proven Techniques for Writing Songs That Sell.* You'll find all the basic information you need to write strong, commercial songs in all styles.

Song credits

The song examples are referred to by the song title and the name of the artist who recorded the version used in the film, TV show, or commercial. It's not my intention to slight the songwriter, if different from the artist, but it seems the best way to identify a song quickly and accurately.

For updates and new tips, visit www.robinfrederick.com.

What Film & TV Can Do for You!

The film and television market uses thousands of songs each year in movies, TV series, commercials, and more. These songs earn fees and royalties, boost CD sales, and create new fans for bands and artists. The market is hungry for new music… your music!

Shortcut #1

Film & TV Productions Need Your Songs!

This accessible, growing market uses thousands of songs.

More and more, today's music fans are turning to television shows and films as their best source for discovering new songs, artists, and bands. Because songs increase the appeal—and ratings—of a TV show or film, producers are adding more to their projects. Think about this: the young adult TV series *One Tree Hill* averages eight to ten songs per episode. There are 24 episodes in a six-month season so that show alone needs up to 240 songs each season. A series like *90210,* which is often carpeted with songs, uses even more.

In fact, there are currently around 35 prime-time drama series on network and cable television using an average of five songs per show. Let's do the math: In a single 24-episode season, these 35 shows will air 4,200 songs! Now think about this: MTV has nine reality-based TV series that use 20 or more songs per episode. Put a season of those nine shows into the mix and you have another 4,320 songs.

That's more than 8,500 songs needed by national and cable networks in a six-month period, and I haven't even included songs used in films, commercials, movie and TV show trailers, news programs, comedy series, daytime dramas, documentaries, and educational programming. In a single year, the industry can use 17,000 songs or more!

Thousands of songs are used each year...

Don't you think some of those thousands of songs should be yours? You're right... they should!

And the opportunities don't stop there. The film and television market uses more than eight million pieces of *instrumental* music every year. That's right, 8,000,000! If you make an instrumental mix of your song—a version without the vocal—you can pitch it as an instrumental music cue and have *millions* of opportunities to get your music into film and TV productions.

... and millions of instrumental tracks!

Your songs don't need to sound like hit records.

For this market, a simple, well-recorded song that evokes an emotion or creates a mood will work just as well as, or better than, an attention-grabbing hit. Many of the examples I'll be using in this book rely on stripped-down instrumental arrangements that feature piano or guitar. The vocals are unique and distinctive, depending on character and personality to convey the emotion in the lyric rather than the belt-it-out power of a Celine Dion.

How songs are used in film and TV

Some song uses are obvious. It's hard to miss the theme song of your favorite TV show or a song that plays when a character turns on a car radio or goes dancing in a nightclub. Many TV commercials use songs to give their product a human touch; these, too, are easy to pick out.

Read Part Two of this book for more info on song uses in film and TV.

But the largest and fastest growing use of songs may be the hardest to spot. Currently, songs are replacing the instrumental music or "underscore" that accompanies almost all scenes in movies and TV shows. Underscore is used to increase the emotional impact of a scene for viewers. When it's doing the job well, viewers feel it on an emotional level but don't consciously notice it. A song can perform the same job, increasing the emotional effect of a scene not just with music, but also with lyrics and vocal. Throughout this book, I'll be giving you many examples of this type of use, showing you how to listen for it and how to craft your songs to give them a competitive edge.

Like anything worth doing, writing for the film and TV market requires study, practice, and resources. All are within your reach. Best of all, because this field uses so much music, once you've got what they need, you can build an active catalogue of broadcast quality songs and instrumental tracks that will work hard for you over many years to come.

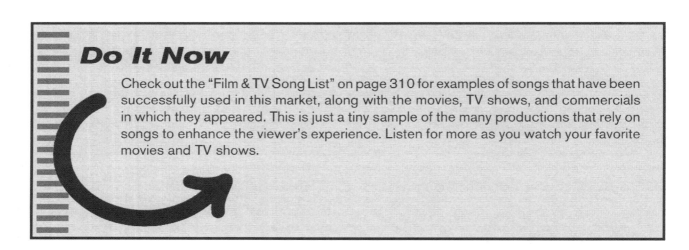

Do It Now

Check out the "Film & TV Song List" on page 310 for examples of songs that have been successfully used in this market, along with the movies, TV shows, and commercials in which they appeared. This is just a tiny sample of the many productions that rely on songs to enhance the viewer's experience. Listen for more as you watch your favorite movies and TV shows.

Shortcut #2

Build an Income That Will Pay Off for Years

Songs are used and re-used, generating fees now and royalties later.

Every time you hear a little-known song playing beneath a scene on *Grey's Anatomy*, each time an American Idol belts out a big Power-Pop ballad, whenever Sheryl Crow sings "Everyday Is a Winding Road" in a Subaru commercial or the *Gilligan's Island* theme song introduces the TV show for the umpteen-millionth time, every time one of those things happens, a song is earning money for its creator. According to ASCAP, songwriters now earn more royalties from television broadcasts than from radio airplay. In 2008, ASCAP paid out more than $265 million to its members for network, local, and cable TV broadcasts of their music in the United States.

I'll be honest with you: Will a big hit song on the radio earn more royalties than one, lone song placement in one TV show? Yes, it will. *But* the film and TV market is all about getting *many* songs into *many* shows. Remember, this market needs thousands of songs each year and those songs are replayed in summer reruns, on local stations, and in foreign markets. It's entirely possible that in a single year you could write a song that's used under a scene in a network TV series, another that's placed in a cable show, plus several pieces of music based on the instrumental tracks of your songs. You can even place the same song in more than one production. Once you begin racking up multiple placements your royalties will grow. A hit songwriter might write hundreds of songs and have one or two radio singles. In film and TV, once you know what the market is looking for, you can write dozens of songs and instrumental tracks and have *all* of them out there earning royalties for you for years!

While royalties offer long-term rewards, there's yet another income source that delivers a more immediate payoff: licensing fees. When a film, TV program, or commercial wants to use one of your songs, they must get permission and you can negotiate a fee for that use. Often, they'll also want to use your *recording* of the song; you can negotiate a second fee for that. Fees and royalties: money up front and money on the back end—it's a sweet deal!

Earn fees up front and royalties later.

How much can you make?

How much money your song can earn will vary depending on the type of use, how many people are likely to see and hear it, and how much the music user wants that song. For example, the licensing fees for a national commercial can be $100,000 and up, even for unknown songs by unsigned artists. A one-minute feature performance of your song on a major network during primetime can pay around $2,000 in performance royalties. When the show is repeated in the same time slot, say, in summer re-runs, you get paid another $2,000. When the show is aired on a cable channel or smaller network ("in syndication"), you earn around $750 each time the show is run, season after season, year after year. Popular TV series are aired in foreign countries and you'll receive royalties for that, too.

It all adds up. A single song placement in a primetime network TV show can earn $8,500 to $15,000 and more in fees and royalties over a five-year period, and it will keep on earning long after that. A placement in a national TV commercial can pay well over $100,000. But remember, this isn't a "single song" business. When you get 20 songs out there working for you plus instrumental tracks, then you're looking at a continual stream of earnings year after year, adding up to hundreds of thousands of dollars. While you, of course, continue to write and place more songs.

Focus on getting many placements. Build up your income stream.

And there's more...

There are other important income sources related to the use of your song in film and television, such as the sale of a soundtrack album and digital downloads of your song at online music sites like iTunes. Music sales may, in fact, turn out to be a major source of income. Each time your song is broadcast, it reaches millions of potential music buyers—far more than a single radio broadcast. Just one effective placement of a song by an unknown, unsigned artist can generate $60,000 or more in sales at iTunes, as Ingrid Michaelson did when her song "Keep Breathing" was used in a season finale of *Grey's Anatomy.* Christina Perri's song "Jar of Hearts" topped 100,000 downloads at iTunes after it was used on Fox's *So You Think You Can Dance.* This unsigned artist suddenly had a Top 20 single at iTunes, beating out well-established major label acts with big hits.

You'll find more information about royalties, fees, license agreements, and performing rights organizations like ASCAP and BMI in Part Eight of this book. As you read those Shortcuts, you'll begin building your knowledge base, organizing your business, and locating resources that can help you put your songs to work making money now and building an income for the future.

Few things are more fun than getting a royalty check in the mail. It feels like a wonderful birthday present that just appeared out of the blue—and it's not even your birthday! Of course, when you stop to think about it, you know it took an investment of time and money to earn it, but a good song placement or two will pay back that investment many times over!

Shortcut #3

You Don't Have to Be 18 or Famous or Live in L.A.

Get your songs into film and TV at any age from anywhere.

"Help wanted. Big entertainment company with many hit TV shows is looking for talented unknowns. No experience needed. Can work from anywhere in the world. Starting pay is negotiable but the sky's the limit!"

What if you saw an ad like this on the Internet or in your local paper? It sounds too good to be true, doesn't it? Maybe you'd just assume it was a scam and move on. But no, this ideal work is for real.

The songs that fill today's films, TV shows, and commercials come from bands, artists, and songwriters of every age and from everywhere. If you've got music that fits their needs, no one is going to ask where you live, how old you are, or whether you've done this before. It simply doesn't matter. In fact, if you're a "talented unknown" it can be a big plus! Intrigued? Let's take a closer look.

Not famous? Not a problem.

There are good reasons why a TV show or film would use a song by an unknown artist or songwriter rather than one by U2.

#1: Many TV series and movies cater to an audience looking for new music. They may offer a mix of well-known hits and intriguing new songs that viewers haven't heard before. In fact, a TV series like *Grey's Anatomy* prides itself on discovering new songs and artists that will give their episodes an edgy, fresh feel. As a result, an unknown can compete on the same footing as an established artist.

You're a new discovery and your songs are affordable.

#2: Famous artists are expensive! In fact, any established artist with a record label deal is going to cost a lot of money. A film with a low music budget or a primetime TV series that packs ten or more songs into a single episode will be looking for good material that fits their budget. They can't pay the big fees that major publishers and record labels charge for a song. *You* are an affordable alternative.

No Beverly Hills address? Who cares!

Let's say you live in Moose Breath, Wyoming. There are a number of ways to get your songs from Moose Breath to the people who will use them in film and TV productions. Not one of them involves a visit to Hollywood Boulevard. They won't even ask if you've ever been there!

> **Go directly to the music supervisor:**
> Every production has its own unique music pipeline, however, the "music supervisor" is most often the person who searches for and auditions songs, so this is the person you want to reach. Contact information for music supervisors is available in directories and online. An email with the right approach can get you heard. Find out more in Shortcut 97.

> **Get your songs into a music library:**
> These large collections of songs make life easier for busy music supervisors by pre-sorting and even pre-screening songs based on the supervisor's needs. There are several variations on the basic music library idea. They may call themselves artist catalogues, song brokers, film and TV reps, or film and TV publishers. They're always looking for strong songs and will do the pitching for you through their extensive contacts. Read Shortcut 98 to learn more about music libraries.

> **Use a pitching service:**
> An online pitching service like TAXI can help you strengthen your material, sharpen your pitches, and put you directly in touch with A-list music supervisors, music libraries, and more (Shortcut 99).

> **Create an Internet presence:**
> While it's not as common now, just a couple of years ago, most music supervisors actively search the Internet for interesting songs and bands. Ingrid Michaelson's music was discovered on MySpace with several songs ending up in *Grey's Anatomy*. You can put together an interesting, easy-to-navigate, informative website from anywhere!

Not an artist or band? Songwriters welcome.

What if you're a songwriter only—you don't perform your own material. That's not a problem, either. With the growth of home studio technology, affordable demo production services, and online recording resources, you can create broadcast quality recordings that are competitive in the market. Or consider collaborating on songs with someone who does perform, combining your strengths with theirs. Read Part Six, "Shortcuts to Song Production for Film & TV," to find out more about performance and production. The bottom line is this: If you pitch a song that fits the needs of the market, they're not going to ask you for a glossy photo or want to know your age or the size of your fan base, so don't worry.

Still love disco? Well...

Songs are very effective at evoking a time period or location. From Delta Blues to Big Band Jazz to Seattle Grunge, film and TV shows use them all. And, yes, a flashback to Studio 54 will require a really hot disco track to set the scene. If you've got it, they need it!

PART ONE

The Quick Start Manual

Impatient to get going?

Here are four essential Shortcuts

that will get you started writing songs

for the film and television market right now!

Shortcut #4

Craft Your Songs to Dramatically Increase Potential Film & TV Uses

The right approach to lyrics, music, and production can give your songs the edge!

For every song that's placed in a film, TV show, or commercial, many are auditioned—often hundreds—but only one is chosen. The song that will get the job is the one that most effectively heightens the impact and memorability of a scene for viewers. Is a character discovering real love for the first time? The song needs to evoke that feeling and enhance the sensation for the audience. Is the film set in a small town in the 1950s? The song should vividly recall the era. Always remember: *the song serves the needs of the project.*

With that in mind, it may seem a little strange that a majority of the songs that are placed in film and TV are written and recorded *first,* then pitched to these projects. Often, the songs are part of an artist's or band's CD. While they're being written, there's no way to know how these songs will eventually be used in a film or TV show. So, if you don't know how your song will be used, how can you craft it to increase your chances of a placement?

What makes a song effective?

➢ **Lyrics:**
   A good lyric for film and TV is universal enough to allow the song to be used in a variety of scenes while still maintaining integrity, originality, and focus. Of course, no song will work for every scene but some themes and situations occur more frequently than others—falling in love, breaking up, or overcoming adversity, for example. If you choose one of these, you're more likely to be successful. Watch a few TV episodes and notice the themes. Read Shortcut 45 for a list of common themes. Chances are you're already using many of them in your songs.

   Make your song usable for film/TV and still be true to your vision.

   Imagery, emotional detail, and a fresh approach to your theme will all add muscle to a universal lyric, making it more appealing to film and TV. On the other hand, too many specific physical details, like place names, proper names, and dates, will limit the uses. In Part Five of this book, you'll learn more ways to write a strong universal lyric.

➢ **Music:**
   Filmmakers have always used instrumental music to communicate mood, energy, and atmosphere to the audience, from soaring love themes to the high anxiety of a fast-paced action cue. As songs have grown in popularity with viewers, they're being used to replace some of that instrumental music. A song that works well for film and TV is one that, like an instrumental cue, uses melody, chords, tempo, and rhythm to evoke a single mood or energy level.

If you've written an uptempo song about a wild party or a slow song about lost love, you're already using tempo and rhythm to express energy. Songwriters often do this instinctively, unconsciously, but you can hone that ability for the film and TV market, making your music even more expressive and usable. Like a film composer, you can choose a tempo and groove that physically express the energy level you want, then back it up with chords melody, and lyrics. Learn more about building your song on a solid musical foundation in Parts Three and Four of this book.

Make "broadcast quality" recordings

To get your song placed in a TV show or film, you'll need a recording of it, one that can be used "as is." If you already have a commercially produced CD, you probably have broadcast quality recordings. However, you'll have the best chance of success in this field if you can continually create new recordings quickly and inexpensively. There are many ways to make a good recording on a budget. Try a simple arrangement with an intimate, personal sound. Record as much as you can in a home studio then use a more expensive commercial studio to add gloss to your mix. Hire an online session player or use an affordable demo production service. Read Part Six for more ideas that will save you time and money.

Watch, listen, and learn

Study songs in films and TV shows to see how they work.

Like an actor, a song in a film, TV episode, or commercial has a role to play. The theme, lyric language, musical feel, and singer's voice must work with and support an onscreen moment. Watch films and TV shows that use songs. (You'll find a list on page 310.) Notice how these songs underscore, reinforce, or deepen the viewer's experience of the characters or situation. At the same time, notice how the songs feature lyric and musical elements that are common to many songs, perhaps even some of your own. They can stand alone as songs, expressing the artist's creativity and message, yet they offer the film and TV industry what it needs. This is the sweet spot where you want to be. You've got good songs; now make them good *film* and *television* songs!

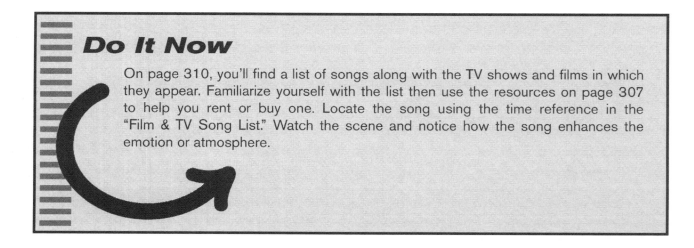

Do It Now

On page 310, you'll find a list of songs along with the TV shows and films in which they appear. Familiarize yourself with the list then use the resources on page 307 to help you rent or buy one. Locate the song using the time reference in the "Film & TV Song List." Watch the scene and notice how the song enhances the emotion or atmosphere.

Shortcut #5

Get Your Song to the Top of the Pile

Use the "sorting technique" to move to the head of the line.

Music supervisors play a crucial role in finding songs for movies and TV shows. They interpret the musical vision of the director or producer and then find songs that will realize that vision. The schedule is almost always tight and so is the budget. By understanding how music supervisors streamline this process, you can give yourself an advantage, making your song easy to find and, when they find it, right for the use.

Imagine that you're a music supervisor who just got a call from a trendy young film director. "Hey," he says, "my new indie picture could use a few songs. It's an action-adventure saga with a romantic love story in a doomsday scenario kinda thing. Lemme hear some songs ASAP."

Put yourself in the music supervisor's shoes!

You meet with the director to watch the nearly completed film. Together, you identify six scenes that could be enhanced with the addition of a song. You'll need to give the director at least three song choices for each of the six scenes and hope that one of the three will strike him as the *right* one—a song that will enhance the scene and make it more compelling for the audience. You've got a week to find the songs. Here's what you do:

First, you turn to your own collection of music, which is extensive. "Extensive" is an understatement! A music supervisor's library may run to thousands of tracks. Your lifeline is your music database, where these thousands of songs are categorized and labeled, roughly like this:

- Song title
- Music genre
- "In the style of..."
- Lyric theme and content
- Mood/Emotional feel/Tempo
- Artist name and contact information

Songs are categorized so they can be searched quickly.

➤ **Search by "in the style of":**
As the director filmed one of the big action scenes, he used a well-known Mainstream Rock song to give him a feel for how the final scene would look and sound. He loves the song but there's not enough money in the budget to license this hit, which could cost tens or even hundreds of thousands of dollars. So, you need to look for something more affordable that has a similar sound and feel.

To replace this song, you look under the "in the style of" heading in your database for a song that you've noted as being similar to the hit song in energy, feel, and style. You're in luck; there is one song. The music and vocal have a powerful, raw quality that's reminiscent of the hit. The structure shares the same sweeping dynamic build to the chorus. The lyrics communicate a comparable emotional urgency. No attempt was made to create a "sound alike," just a song that evokes the same overall feeling in the listener. Good!

> **Search by genre and song title:**
> Another scene in the film focuses on the moment when the romantic leads meet for the first time. The scene has a quirky, light-hearted feel. A Modern Pop song with an unpredictable melody, whimsical lyrics, and a unique, appealing female vocal could underscore a scene like that quite well.

In the Modern Pop genre in your library, under "female vocals," two titles catch your attention: "Stumbled Into Love" and "Just the One I'm Looking For." As you listen to "Stumbled Into Love," you find that the chorus refers to "Joe in San Antonio" and the song is really about a relationship that stumbled and ended. There's no Joe in San Antonio in this movie, a point that could be distracting to viewers, and the title is a clever twist that only becomes clear if you listen closely to the entire lyric—that's *not* what you want the audience to be doing. The singer's southern accent and the pedal steel guitar both suggest that this track might be closer to the Alt Country genre than Modern Pop. You move on.

The title of the other song, "Just the One I'm Looking For" underscores the content of the scene and the rest of the lyric focuses on and supports it by listing a dozen fun, fresh reasons why he's just the one she's looking for. The instrumental arrangement features the kind of off-kilter drum pattern and strummed acoustic rhythm guitars that are a feature of the Modern Pop style. The vocal is youthful and playful, another characteristic of the genre. Bingo! You found a good one.

> **Search by lyric theme and mood:**
> The film has an upbeat ending; disaster has been averted and the romantic leads end up together. You want a song with a lyric theme that reinforces that mood. Under "Lyric theme and content," there are several songs with positive, optimistic themes that might work: *The future looks bright. Good times ahead. We're gonna make it.* You'd also like a song that will put the audience in a "feel good" mood as they leave the theater. You check the songs you found under "Lyric themes" against the "Mood/Emotional feel" category and find three of them listed under "Happy/Hopeful." As you listen, you find that one starts out with an optimistic feel in the verse but turns darker in the chorus. Another has a simple, childlike quality that you feel is too one-dimensional for the end of such a complicated movie. The third one has a strong, uplifting, anthem-like sound that should give the audience exactly the emotional lift you want.

Reaching out to the music industry

At this point, you're still looking for at least a dozen or so songs to play for the director. You start making phone calls to small publishers, music libraries, and independent record labels. In order to give them an idea of what you want,

Some form of sorting is used by all music providers.

you describe a mood or feeling ("anxious, lots of adrenalin" or "lighthearted, romantic"), a theme ("hammer the enemy" or "a bright future ahead"), and artists that are similar to the sound you have in mind ("kind of like Nickelback" or "*a la* John Mayer and Jack Johnson"). It's vague and inexact, but everyone knows this is the only way to do it. Each person you call is going to search through a music database in the same way you did, with thousands of songs categorized in ways that are similar to your database.

Songwriters: Use the sorting process to your advantage

Now that you've put yourself in a music supervisor's shoes, it's time to jump back into your own. Did you notice which songs went to the top of the pile?

> 1. A song that shared some of the musical style and emotional qualities of a current hit. The hit song was too expensive but gave the music supervisor a direction in which to search (Shortcut 6).

> 2. Songs that clearly fit into a genre (Shortcuts 6, 74, 80).

> 3. Songs with titles that described their theme and lyric content (Shortcut 46).

> 4. Songs that had a universal theme, one that might support a scene or an entire film (Shortcut 45).

> 5. Songs with a well-defined emotional feel (Shortcuts 38, 39, 40).

Write a song that rises to the top!

When crafting your songs for film and TV, keep this "sorting technique" in mind as you write. You'll make it easy for music users to find your song. It may not always be the right song for the spot but you'll eliminate many factors that could disqualify it before it gets a chance to be considered seriously.

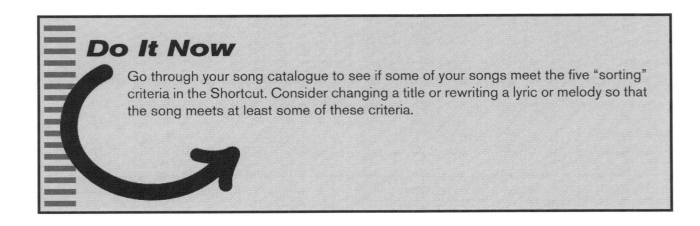

Do It Now

Go through your song catalogue to see if some of your songs meet the five "sorting" criteria in the Shortcut. Consider changing a title or rewriting a lyric or melody so that the song meets at least some of these criteria.

Shortcut #6

Use the Industry "Shorthand" to Describe Your Music

Make it easy to find your music with this important tip.

People in the music industry, including songwriters, all agree: It's hard to describe a song! Music supervisors are certainly no better at it than anyone else. You'll never hear one of them say, "Get me a song at 120 BPM with a complex rhythm, a soaring, melodic chorus in the key of E, and a poetic lyric that employs extended metaphors." Ain't gonna happen! Instead, they'll do what everyone in the music business does; they'll use a kind of musical shorthand that describes what they're looking for by comparing it to a known artist, band, or song. Music supervisors, music libraries, publishers, and record labels all use phrases like "in the style of..." or "*a la*" or "sounds like" as a means of letting people know the overall sound of the songs they're looking for. They don't mean they want a song that sounds *exactly* like that; what they want is a *similar* energy and style. Something that *feels* the same to the audience.

Why music users look for songs "in the style of..."

There are many reasons why music users look for songs with a similar feel:

➤ A producer likes the energy of a hit single but wants something audiences haven't already heard.

➤ A film director needs to replace a song in a "temp track" (a temporary music track used during the shoot) with another song that has the same feel.

➤ A music supervisor finds a song that comes close to what is needed but it isn't exactly right or it isn't affordable.

➤ A TV show attracts viewers by introducing them to new songs and artists with a certain sound.

When these people go looking for more songs, they'll search for music "in the style of..." what they already have, so they can narrow their search. If your music is in a style that's similar to the genre, group of artists, or well-known artist they're looking for, *the chances that your music will be discovered, heard, and used are vastly improved!*

Where do you fit in?

One of the questions a music library or music supervisor will ask you is: Who do you sound like? For many artists and songwriters the first impulse is to say, "I don't sound like anyone." If that's your answer, then one of three things could be happening:

- You don't know who you share similarities with.

- You're mixing musical styles and genres so your style isn't clear.

- Your songs are so unique and weird that the film and TV market will have trouble using them.

Here are some suggestions that can help you solve these problems.

➢ **If you don't know who you sound like...**
Here's my favorite way to find artists working in a similar style: If you have the name of one artist whose style you think *might* be similar to yours, visit Pandora (www.pandora.com) and create a "station" using that artist's name. When you click on "Add variety," Pandora will suggest artists with similar characteristics based on an analysis made by the Music Genome Project, a resource that categorizes songs by musical attributes.

⇐ Try this trick for finding similar artists!

Add the first two or three artist names—these will be your "seed" artists— then start listening to your station. Pandora will begin adding more artists. Notice the characteristics these artists have in common. What are the similarities in lyric and melody style? In instrumental arrangement? In vocal sound and delivery? In rhythmic feel? Do your songs share any of these characteristics? Click on "Menu" underneath a song, then "Why are you playing this song?" and Pandora will list the characteristics it shares with other songs on your station.

After listening for awhile, stop the station and play one of your own songs. Does it sound like it fits in with the others or does it feel out of place? If your song doesn't fit, try creating a new station with a different artist. Do this until you can stop the station, play one of your own songs, and feel that it fits smoothly into a mix of artists. Pandora will keep adding artists in this style so you can expand your list of similar artists.

➢ **If you'd like to write songs "in the style of..." but don't know how.**
What if you can't find any similar artists? If that's the case then your songs might be mixing several styles, lacking a clear stylistic or energy focus, or they're so unique they'll be difficult to place in this market. Consider rewriting these songs or writing new ones with a specific style and feel in mind.

Put a song under the microscope to find out how the style is created.

Choose a song by a well-known, contemporary, artist you like and spend time studying it to understand how the style and feel is created. Answer some of these questions:

- What kind of song structure and dynamics are used? (Shortcuts 23, 24, 25)

- Notice the rhythmic feel. What is it? How is it created? (Shortcut 20)

- What kinds of chords are used? (Shortcut 29)

- In the melody, what is the balance between predictable and surprising elements? (Shortcut 35).

- Are the lyrics universal? How do they develop? Is the style direct and conversational or poetic and filled with images? (Shortcuts 47, 53, 57).

- What are the characteristics of the vocal performance? (Shortcut 80).

- What instruments are playing and how are they used? (Shortcut 74).

"Sounds like" doesn't mean "sound *alike*"

Don't try to copy the song. Music supervisors and most music libraries will avoid potential legal problems by refusing to use songs that sound too close to a well-known original. (Production music libraries are the sole exception. They will sometimes request tracks that are very similar to a known hit for a specific project. Don't do this unless asked.) Instead, look for ways in which the target song creates energy, communicates emotion, and uses melody, lyrics, rhythm, and performance to evoke a response in the listener. Once you begin looking closely at how songs create an effect, you'll start to understand how you can adapt a concept or technique and use it creatively in songs of your own.

No one wants you to stop being original! In fact, the film and TV market prizes authenticity and personality. When comparing yourself with other artists, you're simply noting similarities in *energy, intensity, style,* and *overall sound.* If your song features a solo female vocal with a conversational feel, a personally revealing lyric, a melody with interesting and unexpected twists, and simple production, you might compare yourself with Ingrid Michaelson or Feist. It doesn't mean that you're any less of an original; it simply means that your song might work well in the type of scene that could be strengthened with a song by one of those artists.

Do It Now

Visit Pandora (www.pandora.com) and create a station. Look for artists with a style similar to yours. Or choose a song from the "Film & TV Song List" on page 310 and answer the questions in this Shortcut. Then try writing a song in that style.

Shortcut #7

Check Out These "Quick Start" Resources

Improve your chances for success. Get to know the market.

Today's movies and TV shows use a wide variety of songs, from high-energy Dance/Pop party songs to quirky singer-songwriter love ballads. Each one is selected and matched to the onscreen visual, with the goal of enhancing the image and creating the greatest impact on the audience. It's important to study these songs within the context of the film or television show to understand why and how they work with picture.

For example, the film and TV market likes to avoid song placements that are too obvious, like playing U2's "Vertigo" under a mountain climbing scene. Such an "on-the-nose" use can feel inauthentic, even humorous. The picture/music connection is more often one of "feel": a song that deepens the viewer's emotional experience of the scene. So, a song under a mountain climbing scene is more likely to be one that expresses feelings of exhilaration or risk-taking.

Studying how and why particular songs are used in a film or TV context will help you understand and write for this market. Just a few years ago, this was a difficult and expensive challenge but with the coming of cheap DVDs and inexpensive downloads, the films and TV shows you need are just a click away.

*<= Important!
Study film and
TV song uses
in context.*

Use the "Film & TV Song List"

On page 310, you'll find the "Film & TV Song List." It includes the names of films, TV episodes, and commercials that use the songs referred to throughout this book. For your convenience, I've included the time at which the song appears within the production in hours, minutes, and seconds. For instance, in the film *Hannah Montana: The Movie,* the song "The Climb" begins at 1:28:02 (one hour, twenty-eight minutes and two seconds). You can watch the entire film or jump to the time indicated to watch only the scene with the song.

Find good song examples on your own

For TV series that use songs, watch the first and last episodes of each season. This is where they tend to set off the big emotional fireworks and back it up with memorable songs. Many of these shows feature a closing montage—several scenes strung together—underscored with a song. You can find lists of the songs used in many hit television series, broken out by season and episode, at TuneFind.com.

Know where to
look to find good
examples of film
and TV songs.

Movie soundtrack albums are a useful resource for film songs. To find a list of the songs used in a movie, search the Internet Movie Database (www.imdb.com) using the film's title. You'll find a link to the soundtrack listing under "Fun Stuff." Look through the track listing to get an idea of the style and number of songs. If you see bands or artists that interest you, then rent or buy the film to see how the songs are used.

You never know until you see a film or TV episode how much of a song is used. It may be as little as ten seconds or it may even be an instrumental section. If there's a substantial soundtrack, there will often be one or two songs that are featured in an interesting way, making it worth your time.

Acquire films and TV shows for study

There are plenty of resources available to you for buying or renting the visual media you'll need in order to study how songs are used in film and TV. Here are just a few:

> **TV shows:**
Many successful TV series are available at Netflix.com, Blockbuster.com, and other rental outlets. You can also buy and download individual episodes of a TV series on iTunes (www.apple.com/itunes). Prices range from two to three dollars. Buy standard definition (SD) rather than HD; it's cheaper and quicker to download! If your computer isn't the latest model or you have a slow DSL line, be aware that downloading could take a while. You can pause the download and resume it later if needed. You can stream some episodes for free (with commercials) at Hulu.com. Again, you'll need a reasonably fast Internet connection.

Rent, buy, or download. It's cheap and easy!

To store downloads of TV shows, I recommend using removable flash drives. An 8-gig flash drive holds 14 to 15 one-hour TV shows.

> **Films:**
Both Netflix and Blockbuster are excellent resources for films. Blockbuster provides both in-store and rent-by-mail services. Netflix offers rent-by-mail only. While you can buy and download movies at iTunes, I don't recommend it unless you have a very fast Internet connection. Keep in mind, also, that movies require a lot of storage space on your computer. It often makes more sense to buy or rent the DVD rather than download it. Here's an idea: Amazon.com offers cheap, used DVDs. A DVD that's been played a few times is just as good as a new one. Check to see whether the seller has a good track record and buy "Used - Like New" DVDs.

> **Commercials:**
YouTube.com carries many of the top ads, however, it can sometimes be difficult to find them, so try doing a little research first. At Splendad.com you can search by the product name and see the titles of songs that are used. AdTunes.com also has useful information on songs in television commercials.

Sources for songs and music

Sometimes you'll want to study a song on its own, especially if the song is played at low volume during a scene. Purchasing the song at a legal download site like iTunes or Rhapsody.com is a great way to do this. If you don't want to buy the song, both Rhapsody and Napster.com offer unlimited streaming for a low monthly fee. Lyrics are available for free (and legally) at MetroLyrics.com. (Artists and songwriters are compensated for streams, downloads, and lyric views at all of these websites.)

Your set-up

There are times when a Shortcut will suggest that you write music and lyrics while watching a scene or test your song under a scene that you can replay as you make changes. Set up a DVD or videotape player and viewing screen where you work on your music. (I use a small television set with a built-in DVD player for watching films and TV shows as I write.) You may be able to watch the visual media on the same computer you're using to write your music. However, to do both at the same time, you'll need a lot of processing power. Try a laptop for viewing and a larger, desktop computer for songwriting.

Set up a viewing station where you write songs.

Computer speakers are notoriously bad so, to help you study songs in downloaded or streamed media, invest in an inexpensive set of speakers for your laptop or desktop computer.

Do It Now

Check out the "Film & TV Song List" on page 310. Choose a song you're interested in. Then read "Shortcut Resources" on page 307 and explore the various ways to download, rent, or buy the film, TV show, or commercial in which it is used.

PART TWO

Know Your Film & TV Opportunities

Aim your song at one of ten different uses in the field of film and television. Understand all the ways your song can add strength to a film, television scene, or commercial.

Shortcut #8

Source Music: All Styles Needed

Songs that originate in the world of the characters add realism and ambience.

Ever since Al Jolson sang "My Mammy" in *The Jazz Singer,* "source music" has played an important role in movies and, later, in television. Source music is any music that comes from a source within a scene. It could be a DJ's turntable, a jukebox, a stage performance, a car radio, a church choir, or a character singing while strumming a guitar. In some cases, the source isn't actually seen by the audience; for example, when a scene takes place backstage at a concert as the music plays onstage. As long as the music originates *in the world of the characters,* it can be considered source music.

Here are two good source music examples: In an iconic scene from the film *Say Anything,* a character hoists aloft a boombox blasting Peter Gabriel's song "In Your Eyes" to let his girlfriend know how he feels about her. The source is obviously the boombox in the character's world. In the film *27 Dresses,* the lead characters share a drink in a bar while Elton John's "Bennie and the Jets" plays in the background. We don't see the source but it's clear that the characters hear the music because they sing along with the song. The music originates in their world.

Source music exists in the world of the characters.

Source music brings the scene to life

Source music is used to add realism and ambience to a scene. If the action takes place at a high school prom or wedding reception, it will be more believable if there's a DJ or live band pumping out Top 40 songs in the background. If two characters are chatting during a yoga class, an Enya-style song floating from a CD player adds realism and conveys the atmosphere of the surroundings.

All genres of music are used as source music because there's such a wide range of scenes that use it, from the New Age yoga class to the Top 40 high school prom, from a roadhouse jukebox playing traditional Country to a hip underground bar with the latest cutting-edge tracks. Party scenes need source music in a wide range of styles depending on whether the party is taking place in a penthouse or a frat house. If you've got the greatest frat house Rock song since "Louie, Louie" you may not get major radio airplay in today's market, but you've got a shot at a placement in the next installment of *Animal House.*

If a scene takes place in a recording studio, concert hall, or late night jazz club, there's likely to be a performance in progress. Each venue needs source music in a style that suits the environment. Movies like *Walk the Line, Hustle and Flow,* and *Crazy Heart* have plenty of good examples of source music that add authenticity and energy to the concert stages, clubs, and recording studios where much of the action takes place.

Writing for source music uses

Source music may be featured for a few moments then fade into the background as dialogue takes over. It could be pouring out of speakers in a scene in a trendy retail store or playing on an elevator at a volume so low that it's barely audible. Whether your song is used for a few seconds or a few minutes, at high volume or low, *it needs to rise to the level of music that would be playing in a similar real-world situation.*

Listen for source music as you watch movies and TV.

Watch for examples of source music in film and television. Notice how the songs add realism and energy to the scene. Go through your song catalogue. Do you have a song that would sound authentic and credible if it were played in that scene? Be honest in assessing your material. If your songs are straddling styles or your recordings are not up to the level of performance or production needed, identify the areas of weakness and work on them.

The following suggestions will help you write for this film and TV use:

- Write your song in an established style (Shortcut 6).

- Target an energy level with your music (Shortcuts 38, 39, 40).

- Give your song a strong title. Support it in your lyric (Shortcuts 46 and 56).

- Make a broadcast-quality recording (Shortcuts in Part Six).

Music supervisors and music libraries like to have a stock of songs that will work well as source music for the wide range of scenes that use it. If you have a song that could add realism and energy to a scene—one that features songwriting and production values that are competitive with music that would credibly be playing from a source in a scene—check out the suggestions for pitching to music supervisors and music libraries in Part Eight of this book.

Do It Now

As you watch movies and television shows, become aware of source music. What is the source? Is it visible or implied? What style of music is being played? Why do you think they chose that style?

See the "Film & TV Song List" on page 310 for information about the song examples in this Shortcut. "Shortcut Resources" on page 307 can help you find the films and shows that include these songs.

Shortcut #9

Song-Score I: Create Mood, Energy, and Atmosphere

Songs can do the same job as instrumental music.

The great power of all music lies in its ability to create a mood or atmosphere; it can make the viewer's heart beat faster or release emotions in a flood of relief. This is one reason why the marriage of picture and music has been so successful. To give you an obvious example: the shower scene in *Psycho* depends on shrill, high-pitched violins to drive up the audience's anxiety level and generate an atmosphere of dread. Without the music, the scene loses much of its vital energy.

Now, think about this: songs share much of that same expressive power. Like instrumental music, they can be used to summon up just about any mood. While you might not want to put lyrics to the *Psycho* theme, most scenes can be just as effectively enhanced with a song as they can with instrumental music.

Underscore and song-score

Instrumental background music that does not originate in the world of the characters is referred to as "underscore." Unlike source music, there's no DJ or radio or band playing the music. The characters can't hear it but the audience can. Underscore adds richness and dimension to a scene. When a song is used in the same way, it's "song-score." Just like underscore, song-score is music that accompanies a scene, adds dimension by conveying mood, energy, or atmosphere, and does not come from a music source within the character's world.

What is song-score? <= Answer here.

Over the last decade, there has been a quiet revolution going on in the field of television music. Song-score has been taking over what was formerly the exclusive domain of instrumental underscore. Before the revolution, when onscreen lovers fell into each other's arms, it was usually accompanied by soaring violins and harps. Now, you're more likely to hear The Fray's latest single or a whimsical ballad by an unsigned artist.

There are so many uses for song-score that I'm going to split them into two groups. This Shortcut will focus on songs that create energy and mood. In the next Shortcut, you'll see how songs reveal the core of a character's emotions.

Song-score pumps up the energy

When a character walks down a city street, well, he's just walking down a street. But add a song like the Bee Gees' "Stayin' Alive" and it turns into the memorable, highly-charged opening scene of *Saturday Night Fever*. The music and lyric convey the energy of the world that surrounds this character, complete with big attitude and egos. The addition of a song turned a neutral image into one that set up a compelling story.

Similarly, the adrenalin level of an action scene can be boosted if it's accompanied by a hard-driving Rock song. The Foo Fighters' hit "The Pretender" provides an effective soundtrack to a high-speed boat chase in an episode of *CSI: Miami* and the powerful chorus lyric adds to the mood of desperation. Films and documentaries about sports, especially those featuring youth-oriented sports like snowboarding and skateboarding, use Hard Rock, Punk Rock, and Hip-Hop songs to pump up the energy and identify the sport with a tough, competitive, risk-taking attitude.

Watching a series of bad job interviews is probably not going to give any audience a thrill, but score it with a song like the uptempo, brash "Don't Give Me a Hard Time" by the Locarnos and this montage suddenly has plenty of "I'll show 'em" atmosphere. You can watch this scene in the 2009 film *Post Grad*. For song-score use that creates a sexy mood, Etta James's "At Last" has it all. It's been used in many films and TV shows. I counted 24 different uses listed on the Internet Movie Database at IMDb.com.

A little traveling music, please!

Traveling in cars is something that happens a lot in movies. After all, characters have to get from one place to another. But watching a car roll down the road isn't very exciting and doesn't tell viewers much of anything. What does the car trip signify? What are the expectations or feelings that accompany this trip? This is where a song can come in handy. In the film *Nick & Norah's Infinite Playlist* there are several scenes in which the characters get in a car and drive to a different location. Each drive is accompanied by song-score, like the upbeat, energetic "After Hours" by We Are Scientists. This song evokes a feeling of anticipation, freedom, and the endless possibilities of a teenager's night on the town.

Express the feel of the place

In order for an audience to become immersed in a storyline and its characters, it's important that they get a sense of the world in which those characters live and the environment that surrounds them. If the story is set in a fast-paced city, a song can tell the audience whether it feels exciting and stimulating or more like the frantic scrambling of a rat race. If the setting is rural, songs can evoke either the simplicity or isolation of a place.

In the film *21*, the song "I Am the Unknown" by The Aliens creates an ethereal, breathless aura of anticipation as a character experiences Las Vegas for the first time. Hardly the crass, over-the-top glitz we normally associate with Vegas. It's unique and intriguing—letting viewers know that what happens here is going to be different! On the other hand, in the film *Percy Jackson & the Olympians: The Lightning Thief,* a very different effect is created as the characters enter a Las Vegas-style casino and arcade. Lady Gaga's "Poker Face" creates a bold, strutting musical feel beneath a lyric that suggests a sinister atmosphere; the characters are unaware of the dark side of the casino's "poker face." This is a great example of a song use with a twist on the meaning of the lyric, keeping it from being too "on the nose" for the scene.

Writing songs that create atmosphere and energy

To write songs for this use, keep your lyric and music focused on a single mood and energy level. Be sure that both words and music convey the same message: if your music sets up an aggressive, hard-partying atmosphere, then use language in your lyric that's vivid and edgy, filled with the feelings and needs that drive this kind of behavior. These techniques will help you write songs that work to create atmosphere or energy:

- Think like a film composer (Shortcut 18).

- Use emotional details in your lyrics (Shortcut 52).

- Create a mood or atmosphere with your music (Shortcut 37).

- Create high energy, medium energy, slow energy (Shortcuts 38, 39, 40).

- Create an arrangement that supports the song (Shortcuts 73, 74, 75).

Try playing your own songs under scenes that feature landscapes, cityscapes, and activities like driving, walking, or playing sports. Notice whether your song enhances the atmosphere, creates energy, or suggests the potential for coming events. Listen to songs that have been used successfully in this way in film and TV. If you have songs that work as effectively as these, then consider pitching them using the suggestions in Part Eight of this book.

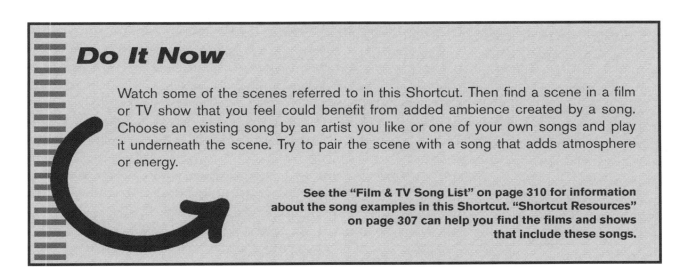

Do It Now

Watch some of the scenes referred to in this Shortcut. Then find a scene in a film or TV show that you feel could benefit from added ambience created by a song. Choose an existing song by an artist you like or one of your own songs and play it underneath the scene. Try to pair the scene with a song that adds atmosphere or energy.

See the "Film & TV Song List" on page 310 for information about the song examples in this Shortcut. "Shortcut Resources" on page 307 can help you find the films and shows that include these songs.

Shortcut #10

Song-Score II: Communicate an Emotional Message

Vocal and lyrics add information, depth, and emphasis to a scene.

In the previous Shortcut, you saw how song-score can create atmosphere and energy just as effectively as instrumental underscore. Now I want to show you something songs can do that underscore never will!

Because songs have *lyrics and vocals,* they can offer an additional layer of insight and depth, one that isn't written into the script. They can express or emphasize the emotion the character is feeling and say things that might not sound believable if a character expressed them. To give you an obvious example of this type of use, think of the classic 1952 western *High Noon.* The stoic marshal, played by Gary Cooper, isn't the type to express emotion. Instead, a theme song does it for him in a line like, "Do not forsake me, oh, my darlin'." Something this man of few words would never say.

In today's movies, song-score is never that on-the-nose. You're more likely to hear something poetic and indirect, like Frou Frou's beautiful song "Let Go" in the final scenes of the film *Garden State,* offering the audience an insight into the lead character's change of heart.

Montages and closing scenes

An excellent opportunity for this type of expressive song-score can be found in today's hour-long TV dramas. At the end of many of these shows, you'll see a closing montage, a suite of short scenes that ties together the various plot lines and emotional themes in the episode. You can see closing montages in shows like *Grey's Anatomy, Smallville, Life Unexpected, House M.D., One Tree Hill, 90210, Kyle XY,* and many more. Although there's often an underlying emotional theme that unites the scenes in the montage, it's not always obvious what that theme is. If the viewer doesn't make the connection, the sequence of scenes may feel choppy and disconnected. The right song can tie these scenes together, giving the end of the show a coherent feel and plenty of impact. This is how "Never Say Never" by The Fray was used in the closing scenes of the pilot episode (the first episode of the first season) of *The Vampire Diaries.*

A song adds strength to a montage.

Songs as a substitute for dialogue

A song can play an important role in a scene in which a character is alone or simply keeping her thoughts to herself. Here, a song can speak for the character, cluing the audience in even when there's nothing else about the scene to reveal what's going on in the character's mind. You can see this type of use in the film *27 Dresses*. Natasha Bedingfield's song "Who Knows?" communicates a character's unspoken thoughts, both what she's willing to admit to herself and what she won't.

Not only can a song tell us what a character is thinking, it can also drive the plot forward by conveying motivation and sustaining emotion, even when a character doesn't speak. In the film *Post Grad,* a young woman decides to leave home and travel to New York to be with the man she loves. From the moment she leaves for the airport until she arrives at his apartment door in New York, she says nothing. There's only a song, "Turn Back Around" by Lucy Schwartz, to tell the audience what she's feeling and what drives her on.

Song-score in dialogue-driven scenes

While there are scenes with little or no dialogue in which a song can be played at full volume, "music video" style, most often songs are used under dialogue. In those scenes, there's always the possibility of a conflict between the singer's vocal and a character's voice. If the vocal is in the same range as a character's spoken words, it could be difficult to distinguish between the two. The audience needs to clearly hear everything that's said by the characters, so the song has to get out of the way.

One solution is to play the song at a low volume level while the characters speak then raise it to a higher volume during the pauses between lines and at the end of the scene. If the characters are talking right up until the end of a scene, the song will usually rise in volume during their final lines and provide a transition into the next scene, effectively extending the scene and smoothing the transition. Another solution is to use an instrumental version of the song during the dialogue and the full vocal version when no one is speaking. (See Shortcut 86 for more information on instrumental song tracks.)

Of course, all of this means that only certain lines in a song will be heard "in the clear," without dialogue over them. The parts that are heard are likely to be the lines that resonate with the scene, summing up the situation and deepening the audience's understanding of it. A song is frequently chosen for a scene because a repeated line, such as a refrain or chorus lyric, resonates with the action. In order to get the line to fall correctly within the dialogue or at the end of the scene, the song is edited or a start time is chosen to ensure the lines will fall in the desired places. You can see and hear a great example of this in an episode of *Smallville* titled "Arctic" in which Michelle Featherstone's song "Perfect" was used. A single character speaks haltingly, emotionally; the song lyric effectively fills in the pauses, strengthens the emotion, and keeps the momentum going. It ends with a repeated line and then a final phrase, "You're perfect," which resonates strongly with the lead character. This scene is well worth watching to see the ways a song can enhance a scene.

Only portions of your song will be heard.

Writing songs with this type of song-score in mind

Song-score is all about creating and evoking a single, strong, focused emotion—something a character might feel. A chorus or repeated refrain lyric that sums up an emotional idea in a fresh, effective way is a big plus here. The melody, chords, vocal style, and production should express a unified and identifiable emotional tone that supports the lyric theme and language. If your lyric is thoughtful, vulnerable, and personally revealing, try keeping your melody in a conversational note range, the vocal performance intimate, and the production stripped down to a bare minimum.

The following ideas will help you write songs that will work as emotional song-score:

- Choose a peak emotional moment for your lyric (Shortcut 51).
- Make your title the focus of your song. (Shortcut 56).
- Write a universal lyric (Shortcut 47).
- Create a strong melodic phrase then build on it (Shortcuts 31, 32, 35).
- Record an expressive vocal performance (Shortcut 79).
- Consider a barebones arrangement (Shortcut 75).

When searching for songs for this use, music supervisors and music libraries look for material that resonates emotionally for them. They go by their own reaction to the song in judging whether it will connect with an audience. Authenticity, originality, and a strong, emotionally grounded performance, from first note to last, are very important. They'll be listening to the song as a song, not looking for a good verse here and a usable line there.

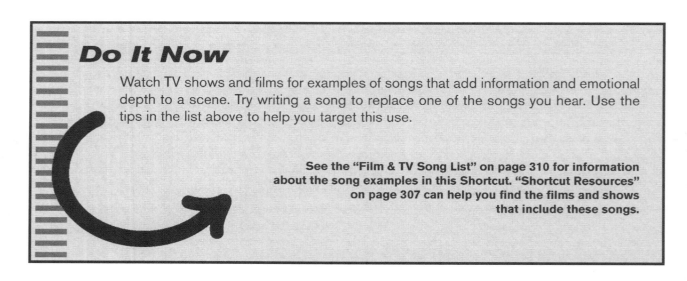

Do It Now

Watch TV shows and films for examples of songs that add information and emotional depth to a scene. Try writing a song to replace one of the songs you hear. Use the tips in the list above to help you target this use.

See the "Film & TV Song List" on page 310 for information about the song examples in this Shortcut. "Shortcut Resources" on page 307 can help you find the films and shows that include these songs.

Shortcut #11

Songs in Commercials Add a Human Touch

They're not merely selling a product; they're communicating a feeling.

From the 1950s through the 1970s, if a TV commercial featured a song, it was usually in the form of a jingle that told a story, like "Plop, plop, fizz, fizz. Oh, what a relief it is" (Alka Seltzer). That's a story: first one thing happens (plop, plop), then another (fizz, fizz), and finally the story resolves (ah, relief).

Today, TV commercials use songs in a very different way. True, you still hear the occasional story-telling song, but they seem so clumsy and obvious, like a dinosaur in a pet shop. Consumers are much more attracted to warm, fuzzy songs that give you a nice *feeling* about a product. Advertisers have learned that songs are very good at making people feel things.

Associating emotions with a product

How do you sell perfume on TV? It's almost impossible to explain what something smells like and even harder to convince the viewer that your product smells better than someone else's. So advertisers don't try. Instead, they sell the idea that a woman who wears a particular brand of perfume will be adored, self-confident, beautiful, or just plain loved. How do they do it? By using a song to evoke those feelings in the viewer as she watches the commercial. For example, a perfume called "Lovely" is accompanied by a sweet and sexy tune that tells the viewer it's "lovely just to be in love." Nobody's talking about "smell" here!

The right song can make an emotional connection.

Of course, it isn't just perfume ads. While Zale's could pitch their diamond pendants by telling you how many carats you get for your money, they never mention that. Instead you hear a song like "What Are You Doing the Rest of Your Life?" Prius could advertise their MPG and EPA ratings, but they'd rather use a whimsical, childlike version of "Let Your Love Flow," inviting you to come live in a happy, carefree world. And who wouldn't want that?

An emotional connection is far more powerful than a rational, factual one. Miles-per-gallon and carats-per-dollar are no match for feelings of love and happiness. Because a good song can make listeners feel these emotions, it makes perfect sense to use them in commercials.

Is it all just a bit manipulative? Yes, from the advertiser's point of view it is. But from a songwriter's perspective, nothing has changed; you're still writing a song first, one with an emotion at its heart. The decision to let an advertiser use your song comes later.

It's not just about hits!

The songs mentioned in the previous paragraphs all have proven track records, either as hit singles or much-recorded standards. However, right alongside the big names are plenty of examples of unknown songs and artists who gained initial exposure through national commercials. Feist's song "1234" launched her solo career when it was used in a commercial for Apple's iPod. Nick Drake, a completely unknown artist from the 1970s, was discovered by legions of fans when his song "Pink Moon" was used as the soundtrack for a Volkswagen Cabrio ad. Subaru used Sheryl Crow's "Everyday Is a Winding Road" in its Impreza ad, then turned right around and featured a totally unknown artist and song, Basia Bulat's "Before I Knew," in an Outback commercial called "Lost Sunglasses." While an established artist like Sheryl Crow can earn $500,000 or more for allowing a commercial to use her song, an independent artist with an unknown song can earn in the $60,000 to $200,000 range. Hey, I'll take that!

All styles welcome!

Ads use every style from Blues to kids' songs.

Advertisers are always looking for ways to catch the viewer's attention. A song that's in an unusual style or has a distinctive vocal or unique instrumental arrangement could just do the trick. Delta Faucets used the delightful Sesame Street song "Hands" with its catchy refrain line "So many things your hands can do," to draw the audience in. Sung by the Count, a character with a Transylvanian accent, both the unusual vocal and whimsical style made it a big hit in the advertising world. Another good example is Langhorne Slim's "Worries" used by Travelers Insurance. The message is on target and the laid-back bluesy style conveys it to the listener in an honest, believable way.

The Country, Americana, and Roots Rock genres appeal to advertisers looking to add homegrown appeal to their products. On the other hand, automakers have fallen in love with the Electronica, Rock, and even New Age genres at various times. American standards are in demand for perfume and jewelry. From Folk songs to Hip-hop, if the song has a single, focused emotion at its heart then just about any genre can find a home in the advertising market.

Keep a notebook and pencil near your TV set and start making a list of commercials with songs. Note the genre of the song, style of the vocal, and instrumentation. You can find the name of the song and the artist by doing an Internet search using some of the lyric lines.

Keep the emotion in focus

To improve your chance of getting a commercial placement, choose an emotional theme that will appeal to the audience (and advertisers). What emotions do people like to feel? Love, warmth, optimism, togetherness, happiness, hope, and confidence are all feelings that work well for commercials. Construct your lyric around one of these emotional themes and stick with it. Don't wander off.

Write a song; don't write a jingle. Even though a commercial may use only 30 seconds of your chorus, approach it as a songwriter rather than a jingle writer. Go ahead and develop the whole song. Take the time to explore the emotional theme and build dynamics into your arrangement. You could end up with a final chorus that really nails it!

Here are some tips that will help you aim your songs toward commercial and advertising uses:

- Choose a universal theme (Shortcut 45).

- Try the "Association Pyramid" using a product (Shortcut 53).

- Anchor your song with a strong melodic phrase (Shortcut 31).

- Create an arrangement in a genre. (Shortcut 74).

The ad agency's creative director is the person who looks for the right song to fit a client's needs. Like music supervisors, they have a database of songs. They also search for up-and-coming artists, bands, and songwriters via college radio outlets, local music venues, online music sites, music festivals, and by working with music libraries, pitching services, music publishers, and record labels. They're looking for songs that will resonate emotionally with consumers.

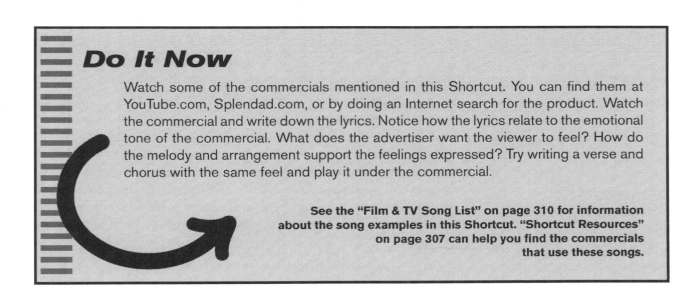

Do It Now

Watch some of the commercials mentioned in this Shortcut. You can find them at YouTube.com, Splendad.com, or by doing an Internet search for the product. Watch the commercial and write down the lyrics. Notice how the lyrics relate to the emotional tone of the commercial. What does the advertiser want the viewer to feel? How do the melody and arrangement support the feelings expressed? Try writing a verse and chorus with the same feel and play it under the commercial.

See the "Film & TV Song List" on page 310 for information about the song examples in this Shortcut. "Shortcut Resources" on page 307 can help you find the commercials that use these songs.

Shortcut #12

Songs Set a Time Period or Location

Transport the audience to a different time and place.

If you have a talent for writing or playing an instrument in a style of music that's specific to a time or place, such as Delta Blues, Zydeco, Dixieland, Celtic Folk songs, or British Invasion Pop, to name just a few, you may find that you have some excellent pitching opportunities in film and television. While there are fewer projects that use songs in niche genres like these, there's less competition in these areas than in the broader Pop, Singer-Songwriter, Rock, and R&B styles.

Songs convey time period and location

Song styles, like clothing styles, have something in common; they change over time. The clothes people wore in the 1920s are very different from our modern look. Similarly, a song written in the 1920s has a different sound from today's songs. When it comes to film and television, a song can let an audience know the time period or location in which a story takes place in much the same way that a costume designer can evoke an era by dressing the actors in the clothes of the period.

Song styles change over time and geographic location.

The same holds true for location. Over decades, rural populations developed distinct folk song styles while urban centers created their own unique sound based on a mix of the immigrant groups that settled there. Regional styles were (and still are) colorful and distinctive. Zydeco, Polka, Tejano, and Appalachian Folk songs can all conjure up a location and regional atmosphere for viewers with their unique rhythms, melodies, chords, and performance styles.

More recently, there have been cities and geographical regions that produced clusters of artists working in a style, such as the Seattle Grunge scene of the early 1990s, the Muscle Shoals sound of the 1970s, or the Jazz nightclubs of New York in the 1960s. If you were part of a scene like that and you have well-recorded songs, you've got a jumpstart on pitching to projects that need those styles to set a scene in that location and era.

Find songs to study

When working in regional or period styles, unless you're an expert, spend some time researching the musical sound. Smithsonian Folkways has an extensive catalogue of recordings from many eras and regions of American music. World Village, a division of the Harmonia Mundi record label, has a large catalogue of international artists and music styles. A search of the Internet will turn up more resources for you. Study the chords, melody, lyric, arrangement style, and instrumentation until you feel confident you can reproduce it authentically. Consider these techniques when writing in period and regional styles:

- Use music to evoke the identifiable sound of a region or era (Shortcut 41).

- Be sure your lyrics are believable for the place and time (Shortcut 63).

- Use authentic instrumentation and arrangements (Shortcut 76).

The whole point of using a period or regional song is to create a believable experience for the audience. For example, you can hear an authentic homage to the music of the early 1960s in the film *That Thing You Do!* To hear a contemporary songwriter working in a traditional Folk style, listen to Sting's "You Will Be My Ain' True Love" from the Civil War film *Cold Mountain.*

Public Domain songs

Songs that were written prior to 1922 are no longer under copyright in the United States. You can create your own musical arrangements of these songs and pitch them for period projects. "Idumea," a hymn written in the early 1800s, was used in the film *Cold Mountain.* It's just the kind of song that would have been sung in churches during the Civil War period of the movie. *Oh Brother, Where Art Thou?* includes several new arrangements of songs that are in the public domain and others that are still under copyright. Be sure the song you want to use is no longer copyrighted and that you avoid using a copyrighted *arrangement* of the song. To find out more, search the web for public domain song information; visit www.pdinfo.com or the public domain section of the Library of Congress at www.memory.loc.gov where you'll find original sheet music and even recordings available for streaming. Remember to copyright your original musical arrangement along with any lyric changes you make. Read Shortcut 95 to learn more about copyrighting your songs.

Public domain songs can give you a place to start. Rewrite or arrange to suit a project.

Music libraries are an important resource for music supervisors looking for songs for special niche uses like these. If you can create songs in a period or regional style, you can become the "go-to" person for a music library. Establish a relationship with a library. Let them know your special skills. They'll call you when they get a request for music in your style.

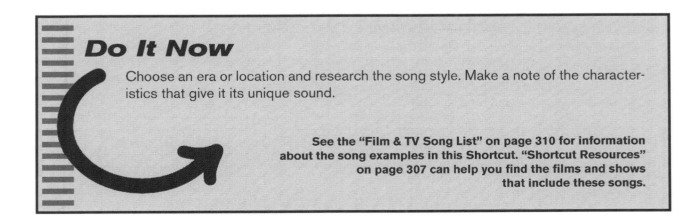

Do It Now

Choose an era or location and research the song style. Make a note of the characteristics that give it its unique sound.

See the "Film & TV Song List" on page 310 for information about the song examples in this Shortcut. "Shortcut Resources" on page 307 can help you find the films and shows that include these songs.

Shortcut #13

Theme Songs, End Credit Rolls, and Trailers

Songs reach out to viewers beyond the storyline.

There are song uses that occur *within* the storyline of a film or TV show, and others that occur *outside* the storyline. Source music and song-score are used while the story is taking place, inside the story. Theme songs and songs that play under the final credits are heard outside of the storyline. They may make a comment on or introduce the overall theme, sum up a central idea for viewers, or leave the audience with a memorable final thought or feeling.

Songs used as themes

In television, theme songs are played at the beginning of each episode in a series. There was a time when most theme songs, like commercials, told a story. They gave the audience a summary of the major characters and basic premise of the show, ensuring that new viewers weren't completely lost. A great example: the theme song from *Gilligan's Island.* Anyone who has ever heard the song knows that Gilligan and the Skipper, the Professor and Mary Ann, along with their shipmates, all went for a three-hour cruise and got stranded on a desert isle. Who could forget it after hearing the theme song even once?

Today's TV theme songs take a different approach; they're aimed at setting the emotional tone of a show, conveying only a general idea of the plot content. The theme from the TV show *Friends,* "I'll Be There for You" recorded by The Rembrandts, is a good example of this type of song, as is Remy Zero's "Save Me," the theme from the TV series *Smallville,* and the Pussycat Dolls' "Top of the World," the theme song for MTV's *The City.* All three songs get the audience in the mood for the story to follow.

Today's TV themes set the tone for a show.

While some theme songs are recorded by major label artists like The Rembrandts and The Pussycat Dolls, there's plenty of room for independent artists and songwriters. Rain Perry's "Beautiful Tree," the theme song for the TV series *Life Unexpected,* was released on her own label. The lyric theme of the song sets the tone for the show by reminding the audience of the strength of family bonds, even in a dysfunctional, highly non-traditional family like the one in this show.

As for films, some of the most successful and best-known theme songs are the ones written for the James Bond movies, like "Goldfinger" and "For Your Eyes Only." Each of these songs was specifically written for the film and, like a big billboard, they feature the movie title. Currently, very few films use stand-alone theme songs like these. Today's filmmakers want to draw the audience into the story as quickly as possible and a traditional-style theme song can delay the action.

You will, however, hear songs under the opening credits of many films. These songs create atmosphere, set a location or time period, or introduce a character. Often, they were not specifically written as themes. Watch the opening credits of the film *Juno* and you'll hear Barry Louis Polisar's "All I Want Is You." This song evokes a mood of innocence that introduces one of the major themes of the film, but the lyric never says, "Hey, Juno, you're a girl who's growing up!" That's because the song was written in the late 1970s and appeared on one of Polisar's many wonderful children's albums. It had nothing to do with the film. Both Polisar's and Rain Perry's songs were pre-existing works that suggested the right tone for the production, not theme songs specifically crafted to fit the story. That's good news for independent songwriters and artists!

Songs over end credit rolls

Do you stay in your seat after a movie is over to watch the end credits roll by? If you want to hear some great songs, you do! Packing in a couple of strong songs under the final credit roll has become standard practice in the film industry. But why bother if the audience has already left the theater? The truth is, they don't really care if you stick around to see who played Newscaster #2. In a big budget feature film, the studio may insist on including a potential hit single by a well-known artist to add weight to the soundtrack album and increase the chances of getting radio airplay, thereby promoting the film to a wider audience. It certainly worked for the film *Titanic*. The end credit roll song "My Heart Will Go On," took on a life of its own, soaring to #1 on music charts all over the world.

For low budget films and those aimed at teens and twenty-somethings, songs by independent or newly-signed artists are often used in the end credit roll. This is especially true if a song's theme sums up the message of the movie in a memorable way or leaves the audience with a strong sense of the movie's style or emotional feel. The film *(500) Days of Summer* used the catchy, insanely repetitious Indie Pop song "She's Got You High" by Mumm-Ra under the end credits. It sent the audience out with a manic-romantic, feel-good energy boost, letting them know the lead character was surely going to fall in love all over again.

Songs in promos and trailers

Movie trailers and TV promos are basically commercials for a film or TV series. Trailers for movies are aired in theaters, on TV, on the Internet, or on DVDs of other films. Promos for upcoming TV episodes are usually aired on television and the Internet. When a trailer or promo uses a song, it's frequently one that isn't in the actual film or TV episode. The song is chosen because it creates an atmosphere, energy, or mood that draws viewers in. The theatrical film trailer for the movie *21,* for example, used three songs, including "My Mathematical Mind" by Spoon. This powerful Alt Rock track with its dark, aggressive rhythm and edgy vocal set the tone of the film in viewers' minds. (Since this is a film about a bunch of math geniuses beating the odds in Las Vegas, you can see why the song title might jump out at a music supervisor!) Like movie trailers, television promos are aimed at catching the viewer's attention with a taste of the show's essential feel and energy. *Grey's Anatomy* kicked off its fourth season with a promo spot that featured Mat Kearney's "Breathe In Breathe Out" evoking the vulnerable, yearning tone that would characterize a large number of that season's plot lines. As with themes and end credit rolls, there are plenty of opportunities for songwriters and unsigned artists in this market.

What to keep in mind when writing for these uses

For themes, end credit, and trailer and promo songs, the emphasis is on creating a strong, unified mood, atmosphere, or emotional tone. Here are a few ideas that can help you add strength to your songs for this field:

- Base your lyric on a shared experience (Shortcut 48).

- Focus and develop your lyric around the title (Shortcuts 56 and 57).

- Write a memorable melody (Shortcuts 31 and 32).

- Aim for medium to high energy in your music (Shortcuts 38 and 39).

- Be sure your lyric and music are working together (Shortcut 43).

- Use a genre as an arrangement guide (Shortcut 74).

TV themes, promos, and movie trailers need to appeal to a broad range of viewers and will be heard repeatedly so the song choices tend to be a little safer than for song-score. Music supervisors will often look for a song "in the style of" a known artist or genre. These are difficult slots to fill so they'll audition hundreds of songs before making the final decision. A music supervisor will go to music libraries, publishers, and record labels as well as searching the Internet looking for bands and artists with a buzz. Make sure your music is easy to find on the Internet. Know the established artists with whom you share style, feel, and energy. Use those artist names on your website and when you pitch to music supervisors and libraries.

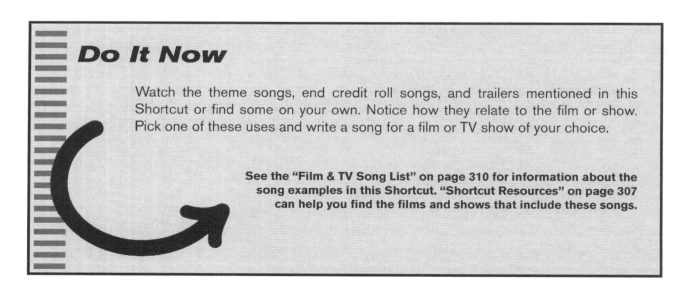

Do It Now

Watch the theme songs, end credit roll songs, and trailers mentioned in this Shortcut or find some on your own. Notice how they relate to the film or show. Pick one of these uses and write a song for a film or TV show of your choice.

See the "Film & TV Song List" on page 310 for information about the song examples in this Shortcut. "Shortcut Resources" on page 307 can help you find the films and shows that include these songs.

Shortcut #14

Instrumental Cues, Song Beds, and Transitions

Make an instrumental mix of your song and multiply the uses.

The film and television market uses millions of pieces of instrumental music each year. Although you may not be consciously aware of it, most commercials, TV shows, and film scenes are accompanied by music. Just sit down in front of your TV some evening and keep track of the number of times you hear instrumental music in the background. Then multiply that by every evening, afternoon, and morning of the year!

Your song's instrumental track, without vocals, can be pitched for these uses, multiplying your opportunities for pitching and placing your music many times over! While songs are an essential and growing segment of the film and TV music market, instrumental music can bring in a steady paycheck. It's rarely noticed and doesn't get the fans excited like songs do, but without it, TV and movies would be a lot less interesting!

How instrumental tracks are used in film and TV

➤ Instrumental music is often played under a film or TV scene to add energy and atmosphere. This is referred to as "background music" or a "background cue."

➤ As source music, an instrumental could be playing on a radio, on an elevator, or at a party. It's source music so long as the source is in the world of the characters. Read Shortcut 8 for more on source music.

➤ Short bits of instrumental music, sometimes only five to ten seconds long, are used to smooth the transition from a TV program to the commercial break and back again. To learn more about this use, read Shortcut 91.

➤ A music editor will use an instrumental mix of a song—a mix minus the vocals—to create space for dialogue, editing it into the full vocal mix as needed.

➤ Instrumental music that echoes a song used elsewhere in a program can be used to add continuity and suggest a connection between scenes or characters.

Five ways your instrumental tracks can be used in film and TV.

Writing for the instrumental market

Instrumental tracks are used to add atmosphere, mood, and energy to a scene. Since you're going to be using the tracks you created to accompany a song, you might want to edit your track, add or subtract instruments, or create more dynamics to strengthen it for these uses. Part Seven of this book will give you plenty of information on how to do this. Also, be sure to read about:

- Creating dynamic energy in your arrangement (Shortcut 73).

- How to think like a film composer (Shortcut 18).

- Expressing a mood or atmosphere in your music (Shortcut 37).

- Broadcast quality instrumental performances (Shortcut 78).

When a music library or music supervisor is interested in one of your songs, they will ask you for an instrumental version, so be sure you have one ready. And don't forget, by making several different mixes with varying combinations of instruments and track lengths, you can create many instrumental cues from that one song track. When you pitch or license your song, be sure to let the music supervisor or music library know that these are available. It could help you get added placements and increase your royalties.

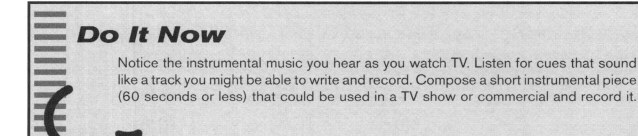

Do It Now

Notice the instrumental music you hear as you watch TV. Listen for cues that sound like a track you might be able to write and record. Compose a short instrumental piece (60 seconds or less) that could be used in a TV show or commercial and record it.

Shortcut #15

Movie and Television Musicals

From Camp Rock *to* Once, *film and TV musicals have big appeal.*

If you're interested in writing musicals for film and television, you can either write your musical for the stage first then work up to a film production—as *Dreamgirls* and *Chicago* did—or you can approach it as a songwriter, pitching songs for projects that are made specifically for the film and TV medium, such as Disney's *High School Musical* or *Camp Rock* franchises. Here's a closer look at some of the opportunities in this field.

The Classic Musical

The classic stage musical features a storyline that incorporates songs as an integral part of the plot. The songs move the story forward either by accompanying the action or by expressing a character's intentions or feelings. Masterpieces like *My Fair Lady* and *Oklahoma!* are in this style. Disney's animated musicals *The Little Mermaid, Aladdin,* and *Beauty and the Beast* are also based on this classic musical form. Because the songs are woven so tightly into the script, they're written specifically for the project. The producers will usually bring in a lyricist and composer with theatrical or hit song credentials to do the job.

But that doesn't mean that you—the independent artist or songwriter—have to miss out on the chance to write in this field! There are opportunities in "teen musicals" and independent films that could be just right for you!

The "teen musical" is alive and thriving

Disney's *High School Musical* franchise introduced the Classic musical to a 'tween audience (ages 8 to 12). It's been an enormous success, spawning three highly successful made-for-TV movies, a feature film, a concert tour, a stage musical, and the best selling music album of 2006. The songs are integrated into the plot in much the same way as in a stage musical, however, instead of using a single lyricist and composer for the songs, both the film and TV movies used a variety of songwriters.

The newest audience for musicals!

The huge success of *High School Musical* inspired imitators like Nickelodeon's *Spectacular!* Disney itself has gone on to produce more material in this style, including the enormously popular *Camp Rock* and *Camp Rock 2.* The future looks bright for this musical genre as more and more kids discover what fans of the great MGM musicals of the '40s and '50s already know: Romance, fun, and music are a great mix!

To get to know this market, watch any of the *High School Musical* or *Camp Rock* films. Dance numbers like "Now or Never" and romantic ballads a la "Right Here, Right Now" from *High School Musical 3: Senior Year* hark back to the era of classic Hollywood films. However, you can be sure that the film will feature at least one or two songs with the muscle to compete in the contemporary radio market. *Camp Rock* spun off a soundtrack album that resulted in the Billboard #1 Pop hit, "This Is Me" for Demi Lovato and Joe Jonas. The song is performed as part of a stage show but also expresses the characters' emotional growth in the storyline. So, for the best shot at a placement in one of these projects, think in terms of contemporary radio lyrics and melodies and get as much information about the storyline and characters as you can.

Musicals about fictional bands and artists

Currently the majority of successful musicals made for film and television feature fictional bands and artists. These projects combine songs that move the plot forward with others that are performed as a part of a rehearsal or concert. In films like *Once* the line is sometimes blurred. Are the characters performing a song or singing about what's happening to them? Sometimes they're doing both, as in the performance of "Falling Slowly," the Academy Award-winning song from this film. Other successful films in this style include *Music and Lyrics, Hannah Montana: The Movie, Grace of My Heart, That Thing You Do!, Paris 36,* and *Camp Rock.*

Films based on the lives of real artists, like *Walk the Line,* the story of Johnny Cash, opt to use songs originally recorded by the artist, so there won't be opportunities for you as a songwriter. But parody films like *This Is Spinal Tap* and The Rutles' *All You Need Is Cash* have achieved cult status. These projects need songs that come very close to the sound of a known artist or style. It can be a lot of fun but it requires research and the ability to suggest a song without copying it too closely.

Writing songs for film and TV musicals

Films and TV shows that are aimed at the 'tween audience, like *Hannah Montana, High School Musical,* and *Camp Rock,* look for songs that fit a character's personality, with a melody and lyric that will appeal to the show's viewing audience. If you're interested in writing for projects like these, be sure you watch the movies in the franchise or several episodes of the TV show to get a feel for the music style. Be sure your lyrics—language style and thematic content—are appropriate for the age and interests of the audience. These songs are usually solicited from established publishers or writers with whom the producers have a relationship. To break into this market, study mainstream hit songs in the Pop genre and approach a music publisher when you have a couple of strong song demos in that style.

Be sure your song fits the character's age and personality.

To write for film musicals, if you don't yet have a track record as a songwriter, consider starting with low budget independent films. The movie *Once* was shot on a miniscule budget ($160,000) and relies on the charm of its actors and the appeal of Glen Hansard's great Modern Pop songs for its success. It's a good example of what can be accomplished with talent and drive. You can start by getting in touch with the film department at a local college or university. Offer your services as a songwriter to any musical film that sounds interesting.

Record a strong demo

When pitching songs for film and television musicals, give the producers an accurate idea of what the song will sound like when it's used in the project. Convey the genre, attitude, and energy of the song in a professional way. Even though your song will eventually be performed on screen by a character, it's important that your demo convey energy and emotional feel. Don't count on them to imagine what it *could* be. If your instrumental track is good enough (and in the right key for the performer), it may be used as is. If not, the show might record a new track that sounds similar. It's not that they lack creativity, but schedules are tight and there's no time to experiment. When they hear something that works, they're not going to risk messing with it.

In Part Six you'll find suggestions for recording your songs.

Try these tips when writing songs for television and film musicals:

- Use song lyrics to say what dialogue can't (Shortcut 61).

- Know how to write lyrics that perform a classic musical function (Shortcut 62).

- Write music that's on target for the style and content of the musical (Shortcut 42).

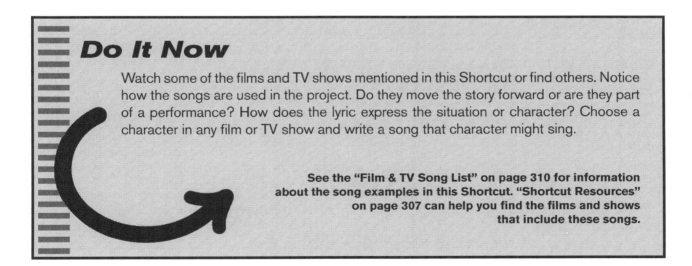

Do It Now

Watch some of the films and TV shows mentioned in this Shortcut or find others. Notice how the songs are used in the project. Do they move the story forward or are they part of a performance? How does the lyric express the situation or character? Choose a character in any film or TV show and write a song that character might sing.

See the "Film & TV Song List" on page 310 for information about the song examples in this Shortcut. "Shortcut Resources" on page 307 can help you find the films and shows that include these songs.

Shortcut #16

Children's Songs Entertain and Educate

Children's shows are big music users.
It's a market where there's room to grow!

Children love songs—they learn from them, sing along with them, dance to them, and fall asleep to them. Many children's TV shows use songs on a regular basis, some weave them into a plot line and others simply add songs to create variety. *Sesame Street, Phineas and Ferb, Dora the Explorer, Hannah Montana,* and *Jonas* are just a few of the many TV shows that incorporate songs into their storylines and sketches.

Themes and style

Songs for children's TV shows range over a wide variety of music styles and thematic content. Children's skills and abilities change rapidly and so does their taste in music. A song that's just right for a three-year-old will not impress a grown up, worldly eight-year-old!

Children's songs use a wide range of styles and themes.

TV shows aimed at very young children, from infants to four years old, tend to feature basic social themes such as sharing, relating to others, and dealing with emotions or they teach simple school-readiness skills or introduce the child to a wider world. You can use familiar themes as the basis for your songs, just be sure you approach them in an imaginative way. The music can range from nursery-rhyme style sing-alongs to catchy classic Rock and Pop with easy-to-remember chorus melodies.

Shows aimed at kids from age five and up are less obviously educational. The songs promote social skills and positive values, but in an entertaining way that avoids a preachy attitude. A song like "Nobody's Perfect" from the Disney Channel TV series *Hannah Montana* is a great example. The point-of-view and lyric language is that of a young teen, the theme is a valuable lesson for ages five and up, and the overall attitude feels completely authentic. Songs like this one rely on a contemporary melody, chord, and rhythm style. Kids as young as five are already listening to the hit songs their older siblings are playing, so make sure your melody, lyrics, and production have a current sound.

Family entertainment

Family entertainment films, like *Rugrats in Paris,* assume that both children and parents will be in the audience. A catchy, current, hit-style song with a fun or nonsensical twist works well here. "Who Let the Dogs Out?" by the Baha Men became a children's favorite after its use under the end credits of the *Rugrats in Paris* film.

Writing and pitching songs to children's shows

Songs for children's TV shows are usually pitched directly to the production company that creates the show. You can find the production company name as well as the name of the music composer or music supervisor in the end credits of the show. Look up the company's contact information on the Internet and call or send an email to ask if you can submit your songs.

Some shows only use songs written by the show's creator or music director so you really need to impress them. Be sure you're thoroughly familiar with the characters and music style of the show before you submit. If you really want to make an impression, write a song specifically for the show in the style they use. Even if a show has completed production or the producers have enough songwriters, they will remember you. You could end up getting work on their next show. When first starting out, think of your song pitches in terms of making contacts. Placements are likely to follow later on.

Record a strong demo

Send a solid, well-recorded demo of your song in the style featured on the show. If a song is to be sung by a character, the voice-over actor who plays the character will re-record the vocal. Nevertheless, most of these shows have very low budgets and they will rely on you to provide the finished instrumental tracks. The ability to produce a good sounding track in your home studio will be a big plus.

When writing for this market, try these suggestions:

- Write a catchy, memorable melody (Shortcuts 31 and 32).

- Use fresh images and ideas in your lyric (Shortcut 49).

- Read Part Six of this book for ideas on production.

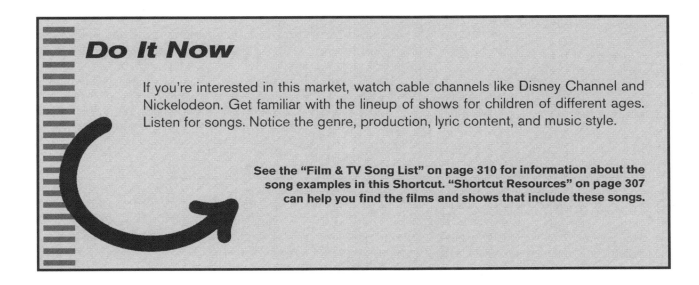

Do It Now

If you're interested in this market, watch cable channels like Disney Channel and Nickelodeon. Get familiar with the lineup of shows for children of different ages. Listen for songs. Notice the genre, production, lyric content, and music style.

See the "Film & TV Song List" on page 310 for information about the song examples in this Shortcut. "Shortcut Resources" on page 307 can help you find the films and shows that include these songs.

Shortcut #17

Niche Uses: Dance Shows, Documentaries, Sports Shows, and More

There are markets for your songs you might not have noticed.

It seems as if every day, film and television projects find more ways to use an ever-widening variety of songs. Some of these uses will be familiar to you but others might be surprising. As you watch television and films, keep your eyes and ears open for new opportunities to place your songs in the market.

Be a dancin' machine

Movies and TV shows with dance-related themes rely heavily on songs in a wide variety of genres. TV series like *Dancing with the Stars* and *So You Think You Can Dance* use songs that range from Pop/Rock to Tango, from Classic Pop to Contemporary R&B. Both shows feature songs by established artists but will drop in interesting new artists at times. Christina Perri's "Jar of Hearts" is a great example. When the track was used on *So You Think You Can Dance* the show's website was overwhelmed with viewers wanting to know the name of the song. Without a record deal, Perri suddenly found herself with a Top 20 song at iTunes and more than 100,000 downloads. If you have a song like this or one with a useful but hard-to-find dance rhythm, these shows could be a great outlet for you.

Two of the top-grossing dance films of the last decade, *Stomp the Yard* and *Step Up 2: The Streets,* feature the Hip-Hop genre. Tracks, like Robin Thicke's Latin-flavored rap "Everything I Can't Have," drive sales of soundtrack albums. The *Bring It On* movie franchise features pumping dance tracks that supply plenty of energy in competitive cheerleading scenes. This is a lucrative market for songwriter/producers with the ability to create contemporary, danceable grooves.

Exercise shows

Consider workout and exercise shows as an outlet for your music. Sports training, aerobics, yoga, and other training styles all use music to get the audience up off the couch and working out. To write and produce songs for this market, lock your track into a groove and keep it there. These music users need an energetic, upbeat feel and like to catch the consumer's attention with fresh rhythm concepts like *Zumba*. Many exercise shows and dance competition shows have websites with contact information. Send an email asking if they're looking for music and in what styles.

Sports shows

High energy, competitive sports programs are a great place to shop your songs. Hard Rock, Hip-Hop, Punk Rock, and high-energy anthems pump up the audience and add excitement. Theme songs for teams and special events are also in demand. Audiences love to stomp and clap along so put plenty of catchy hooks and rhythm in your melody! Needless to say, your lyrics should be filled with action words and vivid imagery. To pitch your songs, start with locally broadcast games and events in your area. Contact both the television station (for local sports news shows) and the owners of the team or producers of an event. For the big sports cable networks like Fox Sports and ESPN, contact the production company listed in a show's end credits.

News and documentaries: pick a theme, any theme

While the majority of mainstream radio hit songs deal with love (falling in love, out of love, discovering love, losing love), in television news shows and film documentaries, songs are used to underscore a much broader range of ideas. In fact, just about any topic you can think of has been covered sometime, somewhere, in a documentary or news show. This means that you can stretch out, explore a range of themes in your songs, and still find a commercial outlet for them.

Documentaries and news shows use a variety of themes.

Cable news shows frequently play up to 15 seconds of a song to introduce a segment that focuses on a specific issue. Pick a title that telegraphs your lyric theme, making it easy for the show's producer to determine if the song will be a good fit before even hearing it (Shortcut 46). News programs don't have a music supervisor and have little time to weigh decisions. A descriptive title can improve your chance for a placement.

Documentaries often focus on a social injustice or a situation the filmmaker feels should be brought to the attention of a wider audience. A good example of the type of song that works well in this field is Melissa Etheridge's "I Need to Wake Up" from the documentary film *An Inconvenient Truth.* This song builds energy from a conversational beginning to a big, blockbuster ending, taking the listener along for the ride. The lyrics are in the first person, "I need to wake up..." avoiding a preachy "you should do this" tone.

If there's a situation or cause you feel passionate about, consider writing a song that expresses your feelings. Avoid telling listeners what they *should* feel. Instead, put a human face on the situation, paint a picture, show the results of the problem, and imagine a solution (Shortcut 58). This is a limited market so you'll need to be creative about pitching your song. Check out student filmmakers at colleges and universities. Get in touch with organizations involved in the cause to see if they know of any films in the works.

Industrials

"Industrials" are films that are made by a company for internal or business use rather than the general public. They're shown at employee seminars or trade shows where companies get together with their wholesalers and distributors. These films introduce new products or services and convey an image of the company that is upbeat, innovative, and exciting. The goal is to create positive associations with the company's name and brands, in much the same way an ad extols the virtue of a product. Songs like Fleetwood Mac's "Don't Stop" or Will.i.am's "It's a New Day" work well here.

Business-to-business films use songs with upbeat, positive lyrics.

While large corporations can and do license hit songs to use in their industrials, smaller companies look for less expensive options that will accomplish the same goal. Many musical genres are used, from Contemporary Country to Hip-Hop to Rock. These companies look to music libraries to fill their needs.

Public Service Announcements

Television stations (and some movie theaters) air short pieces called PSAs (Public Service Announcements) that provide information intended to raise awareness about issues of public interest. A song can be a very effective way to reach an audience and get them involved in the issue. Sarah McLachlan's "Angel" raised awareness concerning animal abuse. The PSA that used this song generated millions of dollars for the SPCA. Eddie Vedder's "Rise" leant support to the Stand Up 2 Cancer PSA series.

Just as in today's ad market, songs for this use focus on an emotion—compassion, suffering, hope—rather than giving specific information. Leave that to the voice-over narration or visual material.

Get involved and use your music to help a cause.

PSAs that focus on community issues are made and broadcast locally. The content is usually contributed free of charge. If you have strong feelings about a particular issue, get involved with a local non-profit organization. If you have a song that might help to raise funds or awareness, discuss that with them to see what options are available. You won't make any money from this use, but you'll have the satisfaction of helping others while building a track record for yourself.

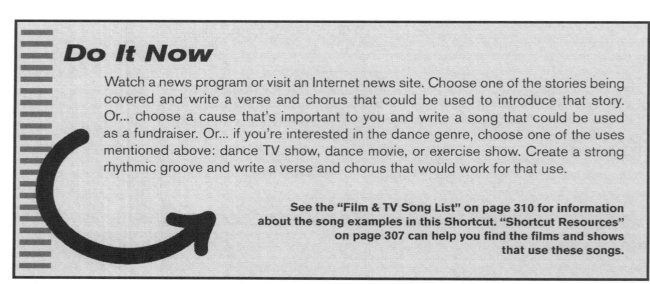

Do It Now

Watch a news program or visit an Internet news site. Choose one of the stories being covered and write a verse and chorus that could be used to introduce that story. Or... choose a cause that's important to you and write a song that could be used as a fundraiser. Or... if you're interested in the dance genre, choose one of the uses mentioned above: dance TV show, dance movie, or exercise show. Create a strong rhythmic groove and write a verse and chorus that would work for that use.

See the "Film & TV Song List" on page 310 for information about the song examples in this Shortcut. "Shortcut Resources" on page 307 can help you find the films and shows that use these songs.

PART THREE

Build Film & TV Songs on a Strong Foundation

Know where you're going when you start your song

and you'll get better results. Use the basic building blocks—

pace, rhythmic feel, and structure—to give your song

the kind of clear, focused energy that music users look for.

Shortcut #18

Think Like a Film Composer and Get Placements

Make your emotional message clear and unmistakable.

Kick back, relax for a minute, and play a little imagination game. I'm going to ask you to create a mental movie with a musical underscore. For the music, let's start with a big love ballad. An instrumental version of "My Heart Will Go On" will work well. If you're familiar with this song, you can just let it play in your mind; if not, there are several instrumental versions on sites like iTunes, Rhapsody.com, and Napster.com. You don't need to know the lyrics; all that matters is the music.

While the music plays, imagine the following scene:

Try an imagination exercise.

> A suburban street lined with trees and houses. A postman is walking along the sidewalk, stopping at mailboxes to make deliveries. A young woman emerges from one of the houses and crosses slowly to the postman. He hands her a small package. She stares at the package for a while then begins to open it, her fingers trembling...

Freeze the picture! Ask yourself what you think will be in the package. Write down your answer on a piece of paper.

Now, you're going to run the scene again and change the music. Instead of "My Heart Will Go On," use the theme music from a thriller like *Jaws* or *Psycho*. You can download both at the sites mentioned above or just play the music in your imagination as you picture the following:

> A suburban street with trees and houses. The postman makes his deliveries. A woman comes out of a house and walks slowly toward the postman. He hands her a package. She stares at it for a long moment then begins to open it with trembling hands as the music reaches a crescendo...

Now ask yourself: What do you think is in the package? Write it down then compare it with your earlier answer.

Music creates expectations

In the second version, it's likely you imagined something dangerous in the package—a threat, a bomb, maybe a body part. In the love theme version, you were probably more inclined to think the package contained a love letter or a memento of a lost love. Even though the only thing that changed was the music, your interpretation of what was happening was very different, as was your expectation about what would happen next.

Music establishes expectations and feelings.

Sometimes a visual scene is neutral, like the one I just described. It's not telling you anything about the emotional context. If there were no music, the scene would have little or no emotional content. This is why music is such an important part of films, television shows, and commercials. Music communicates mood and creates expectations. When the music changes, the viewer's experience of the scene changes right along with it.

Film composers know this; it's the foundation of every piece of music they create. Whatever the scene, it's the composer's job to tell the audience what to feel. Because songs are being used to replace instrumental underscore in today's films and TV shows, they need to perform the same function as musical score. If your song has a clear, focused emotional message in both the music and lyrics, you're more likely to get placements. So, start thinking like a film composer!

Writing songs like a film composer

Musical elements convey the emotional message.

When writing songs for film and television, begin by focusing on the emotional message you want to get across to the listener. Let's say that you want to write a song called "Your Letter" and the first line is "I've been waiting for your letter." What sort of music—melody, chords, and rhythm—will you write to that lyric? The truth is you could write just about anything, but each choice you make will convey a different emotional message. Is your song about a relationship that's in the past? The hopeful beginning of a new relationship? Or is the singer dreading the letter that says, "I don't want to see you anymore."

Each of these emotional messages will need a different kind of music in order to have the maximum impact on the listener. If the message is garbled or unclear or if the music doesn't support the lyric, listeners will be confused about what to expect and the song will be less effective.

In this section of the book and the next, you'll see how the rhythmic feel and pace of your music can affect the listener's energy level, how chords can evoke mood, and how melody can lift and lower tension and expectations. If you build your song on these concepts and tailor them to your lyric theme, your song is likely to have plenty of emotional clarity and punch. And that's exactly what music supervisors like to hear!

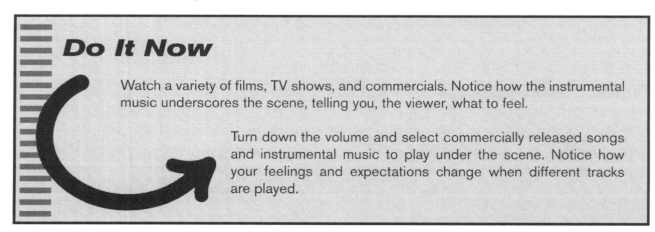

Do It Now

Watch a variety of films, TV shows, and commercials. Notice how the instrumental music underscores the scene, telling you, the viewer, what to feel.

Turn down the volume and select commercially released songs and instrumental music to play under the scene. Notice how your feelings and expectations change when different tracks are played.

Shortcut #19

Relaxing or Heart-Pounding: The Tempo Tells the Story

Set the pace of your song in beats per minute.

As far as your heartbeat is concerned, love and fear are the same thing. When you've got a crush on someone, it seems like every time they're around your heart beats faster and harder, pounding like a drum. The same thing happens when you get a sudden jolt of fear, for instance if you narrowly miss being involved in a car accident. The exhilaration of love and the shock of fear are the same; both cause your body to release adrenaline, increasing your heart and breathing rate. Both can push your heartbeat from a resting rate of 70 or 80 beats per minute (BPM) up to 100 BPM and higher.

What does this have to do with songwriting? Consider this: Like adrenaline, the pace of musical beats can affect your heart rate. Studies have shown that listening to music with a fast beat and simple rhythmic structure, like aggressive Rock songs, can increase your pulse rate, while slower music, such as ballads and lullabies, can lower it. The tempo, or underlying steady beat of a piece of music, is measured in the number of beats-per-minute (BPM), just like your heart rate. So it's easy to compare the two. A song with a tempo as slow as 60 BPM is likely to bring your pulse down to its resting state, while a song that's racing along at 160 BPM can speed it up.

Music can affect your pulse rate.

Film and TV scenes have their own tempo, or pace, depending on the situation and characters. While it won't have the obvious, regular tempo of a piece of music, a dramatic action scene will feature dialogue delivered in short bursts; the director will cut quickly from one shot to the next. An uptempo song at 120 BPM or above, could add to the effectiveness of the scene by physically pumping up the viewer's heart rate. Music supervisors will often search for music underscore (and songs) by tempo, hoping to augment the energy of a scene.

Use tempo to support your lyric theme

When writing songs for film and television, think about using BPM to give your work a competitive edge. If you've got a lyric that's likely to accompany a romantic or sensual scene, try using a relaxing tempo, like the classic romance song "At Last" by Etta James at 60 BPM. To create more of a sense of anticipation, 85 BPM might work well, as it does for Mat Kearney in "Breathe In Breathe Out."

How tempo supports a lyric.

For a lyric that's hopeful and upbeat, try 95 BPM. You can hear this tempo and lyric feel in "See the World" by Gomez. To hear a song that raises the pulse rate, listen to Emiliana Torrini's "Jungle Drum." At 118 BPM, it's used to pump up the adrenaline in a cliff-hanging conclusion to an episode of *Grey's Anatomy*.

To create the sensation of drive and momentum, try an energy-boosting 160 BPM, as in "After Hours" by We Are Scientists.

How to figure out BPM

Learn what a metronome can do for you!

To find out how fast in beats-per-minute a song is playing, you could use a stopwatch or clock with a second hand and simply count the number of beats during one minute. A metronome can make the job easier. It's designed to count beats per minute. Just set the metronome to the BPM you want for your song and begin writing. If you want to figure out the tempo of an existing song, play the song and adjust the metronome until it clicks "in sync" with the steady beat of the music. All music sequencing software comes with a metronome or "click" function. You can buy inexpensive stand-alone metronomes for around $15 and there are BPM apps for iPhone and iPod. You can find an online metronome at www.metronomeonline.com.

Take a cue from composers

Remember that songs are often used in place of instrumental underscore, so it's a good idea to listen to the instrumental cues that accompany various types of scenes: action, danger, romantic meeting or break-up, characters having fun, arguing, or being thoughtful. Although there are many cues that don't feature a steady rhythm, others can suggest tempos that might work for you.

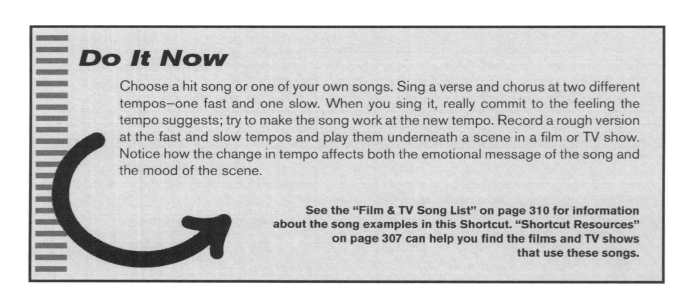

Do It Now

Choose a hit song or one of your own songs. Sing a verse and chorus at two different tempos—one fast and one slow. When you sing it, really commit to the feeling the tempo suggests; try to make the song work at the new tempo. Record a rough version at the fast and slow tempos and play them underneath a scene in a film or TV show. Notice how the change in tempo affects both the emotional message of the song and the mood of the scene.

See the "Film & TV Song List" on page 310 for information about the song examples in this Shortcut. "Shortcut Resources" on page 307 can help you find the films and TV shows that use these songs.

Shortcut #20

Use the Groove That's Right for Your Song

Choose the rhythmic feel that supports the mood you want to express.

If tempo alone could move people, then you could play a metronome under a scene and get a response from the audience. Obviously, that doesn't work. Tempo only takes into account the basic beats in a measure—the stolid, dependable 1, 2, 3, 4 of the music. No matter how fast or slow the tempo is, on its own this simple beat is predictable; it lacks character. It's the way those beats are divided up and accented that makes them interesting, giving music its rhythmic feel, or "groove."

Why groove is important in film and TV

Imagine that your song had no melody or lyric, only the underlying rhythmic feel played by an acoustic rhythm guitar and drums. Could it still be useful to a music supervisor? Yes, it could! The groove alone can communicate a message or feeling to the audience. A steady, even beat that marches along creates a feeling of determined momentum. A quirky, syncopated beat suggests a fun, playful mood or the dizzy sensation of falling in love. A simple, straight-ahead rhythmic feel can suggest sincerity and honesty.

The two grooves you should know about

Most of today's songs are built on one of two basic rhythmic grooves: a "duple feel" in which each beat is divided into two parts, or a "quadruple feel" in which each beat is divided into four parts. The best way to understand these is to hear them used in film and TV songs.

➢ **To hear a duple feel:** Listen to the following songs and count: "1 *and* 2 *and* 3 *and* 4 *and*" over and over as the music plays.

"We're Going to Be Friends" (The White Stripes) — The acoustic guitar plays a steady duple feel; just count along with it.

"Shattered (Turn the Car Around)" (O.A.R.) — The piano at the beginning and the low, pulsating guitar are playing the duple feel.

➢ **To hear a quadruple feel:** Listen to one of the following songs and count: "1 *ee and uh* 2 *ee and uh* 3 *ee and uh* 4 *ee and uh*" as the music plays.

"One" (Tina Dico) — The shaker is playing the quadruple feel.

"I'm Yours" (Jason Mraz) — The quadruple feel is played by the rhythm guitar.

"Everyday Is a Winding Road" (Sheryl Crow) — The busy bongos are playing the quadruple feel.

Which groove will work best for your song?

How do you choose which groove and tempo will work best for your song? For film and television, everything, including the groove, should support and reinforce the central message and emotion of your song. Here are a few basic rhythmic feels and the types of messages they support.

For more groove and tempo info, read Shortcuts 38, 39, and 40.

> **Fast Duple Feel (135 BPM and up):** This hyper-caffeinated groove is used in many contemporary Rock songs. It pumps up the energy under a car chase, a fight, or a wild party. It suggests motion, travel, and supports action-filled lyrics. Listen to "After Hours" by We Are Scientists to hear a fast duple feel underscoring an all-night-party lyric.

> **Mid-Tempo Duple Feel 100 – 135 BPM:** This is a versatile groove. It's perfect for a feel-good song like Colbie Caillat's "Fallin' for You" and the Black Eyed Peas "I Gotta Feeling" or the more thoughtful message of Griffin House's "Live to Be Free."

> **Slow Duple Feel (50 – 100 BPM):** A slower tempo with a very simple duple feel can work well with a folksy lyric theme and conversational language style, like the White Stripes' "We're Going to Be Friends" or a very sincere song like "Beautiful" by Christina Aguilera.

> **Fast Quadruple Feel (100 BPM and up):** An uptempo quad feel has a lot of activity in it. It can be used to pump up the energy of a party scene or night-on-the-town with a sexy side to it, as in The Pussycat Dolls' "Top of the World." It can also convey nervous energy, as it does in Beck's "Youthless" and Emiliana Torrini's "Jungle Drum." Quirky, edgy themes work well here.

> **Mid-Tempo to Slow Quadruple Feel (60 – 100 BPM):** A medium tempo with a quadruple feel can communicate a sensual, body-swaying, relaxed feel, like Damien Rice's "Cannonball" or Tina Dico's "One." A song using this groove can describe a romantic encounter or romantic yearning. A slow quad feel can be used in a sorrowful or thoughtful ballad like Augustana's "Sweet and Low" or Sarah Bettens's "Rescue Me."

Waltz feel

So far, you've been counting in groups of four beats. However, there are some songs that use groups of three beats rather than four, like a waltz. Count to three over and over, and you'll have the idea. Like a waltz, the overall feel is one of motion, of floating, and spinning. At faster speeds, this creates a breathless feel. It works beautifully in songs like "You and Me" by Lifehouse and "Turn Back Around" by Lucy Schwartz. In a twist on this idea, Ingrid Michaelson's "Keep Breathing" is written in groups of four beats but each beat is divided into three. (Count "1 *and uh* 2 *and uh* 3 *and uh* 4 *and uh*") giving it a similar floating, spinning feel.

In both Michaelson's and Schwartz's songs the title makes reference to the breathless or spinning feel of the rhythm. Getting your lyric and rhythmic feel to work together is a great idea. For instance, if you've got an aggressive, high-energy groove, write a lyric that uses plenty of action words and vivid images. Slower grooves work well with a mix of poetic and conversational lyrics. Let the groove suggest some ideas to you. Look for words that describe how the rhythm makes you feel and try using them in your lyric.

Give yourself more choices

Don't drive yourself crazy if you have trouble figuring out whether a groove is duple or quadruple, and don't limit yourself to the suggestions made in this Shortcut. Go with what feels right to you; just be aware that groove speaks to the emotion and energy of the song. There are many, many more grooves out there just waiting to be used: Shuffle, Blues, traveling grooves and funky grooves. Some of them have a contemporary feel, others are retro, still others are timeless. Each one can support or inspire a strong lyric and melody. There are too many to include them all here, but you can easily find them just by listening to the songs you like. Go ahead and explore.

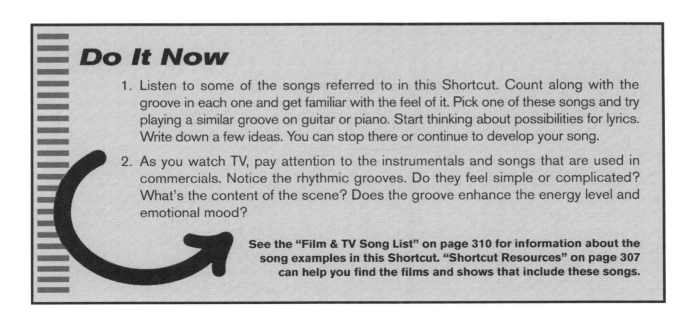

Do It Now

1. Listen to some of the songs referred to in this Shortcut. Count along with the groove in each one and get familiar with the feel of it. Pick one of these songs and try playing a similar groove on guitar or piano. Start thinking about possibilities for lyrics. Write down a few ideas. You can stop there or continue to develop your song.

2. As you watch TV, pay attention to the instrumentals and songs that are used in commercials. Notice the rhythmic grooves. Do they feel simple or complicated? What's the content of the scene? Does the groove enhance the energy level and emotional mood?

See the "Film & TV Song List" on page 310 for information about the song examples in this Shortcut. "Shortcut Resources" on page 307 can help you find the films and shows that include these songs.

Shortcut #21

Build a Film/TV Song on a Groove. Here's How!

Rhythm guitar, piano, or drum loops provide a solid foundation.

Once you become familiar with basic grooves, you can use rhythm patterns as a starting point for your film and TV songs. By choosing the rhythmic feel at the beginning of your songwriting process, you'll be setting the energy and tone of your song at the start, providing a good base on which to build melody and lyrics. As an added plus, when you get to the production phase of your song, you won't have to go searching for the right groove!

Finding and working with grooves

Don't get stuck with the same old guitar grooves.

> **On guitar:** If you play acoustic rhythm guitar, whether you fingerpick or strum, you're already playing grooves. However, you may want to update some of your rhythm patterns or add more choices. The quickest way to do that is to play existing songs that have a rhythmic feel that appeals to you. Many hit songs and successful film and TV songs use acoustic rhythm guitar to lay down the rhythmic groove. Play along until you can comfortably reproduce the rhythm guitar part. You can change the chord progression later on or damp the strings to play only the rhythm with no chord. Try learning Damien Rice's "Cannonball" or "Live to Be Free" by Griffin House, two very successful film and TV songs.

> **On keyboard:** While a piano can be used to play a steady rhythm as in The Fray's "Never Say Never" and Classic Rock tracks like "Blueberry Hill," generally keyboards don't lend themselves to the creation of grooves as easily as guitars do. As rhythm instruments, they don't have the same nuances of volume and feel. Nevertheless, you can create a rhythmic feel by repeatedly playing a piano chord on the beat or playing the individual notes of a chord one after the other in sequence (called "arpeggiation").

If you write songs on keyboard, you might want to use a rhythm loop to create the groove. This will give you more freedom on the keyboard and create a more appealing rhythmic feel.

Rhythm loops are fun, creative, and easy to work with!

> **Rhythm loops:** Rhythm loops are one-, two-, or four-bar grooves that can be "looped," played over and over for the length of a song or part of a song. A rhythm loop might be played by a live drummer with a full drum kit, or consist of ethnic percussion like congas or shaker, or it could be short percussive electronic sounds arranged in a pattern. In the Hip-hop and Rap genres, rhythm loops are called "beats." Several loops (or beats) can be synchronized to create interesting, rich-sounding rhythm tracks.

To get the most out of loops, you'll need to have some music software. Most music sequencing programs come with large libraries of percussion and drum loops. If you're already writing your songs using a computer and music software like Ableton Live, Logic, Sonar, or Cubase then you have (or can easily acquire) a huge library of rhythm patterns that can be played as you write your songs.

If you're not tech savvy and don't want to spend a lot of time crawling up the learning curve, try an entry-level program like Apple's Garageband for Mac (www.apple.com/ilife/garageband) or Music Maker Premium by Magix for PC (www.magix.com). Both come with big loop libraries that include drum and percussion loops in current styles. These programs are made for people who want to make music quickly and easily.

If you don't want to use a computer at all, you can buy song-length drum tracks recorded by professional drummers from Drum Tracks (www.drumtracks.com) and Drums On Demand (www.drumsondemand.com). The selection of styles is limited, though.

➤ **If you don't play an instrument:** Even if you don't play an instrument, you can write your song to a groove. Both of the programs just mentioned, Apple's Garageband and Music Maker Premium by Magix, provide loops that can be auditioned, played, and modified on your computer without any additional equipment, such as a music keyboard. The applications provide chords as well as drums so you can put together an entire song track, sometimes a very good one.

Build song-score on a groove

Here's a fun exercise that will get you writing with grooves.

➤ 1. **Choose a scene to work with:** Watch a film or TV show on DVD or record one so you can replay the same scene a few times. Choose a scene to underscore with a song.

➤ 2. **Create the raw material for your lyric:** Make a list of short phrases that describe the situation or characters in the scene. Try using a couple lines of dialogue. Describe the emotions being expressed.

➤ 3. **Play a groove:** Go through your rhythm loops and audition a few or play different grooves on guitar while you watch the scene. Try to capture or enhance the energy and tone of the scene in your rhythmic feel. This is an important step that will get you thinking about how rhythm conveys energy level. When you find a groove you're interested in, lower the volume level of your music and turn up the level of the scene so your rhythmic feel becomes background music. When you've got something that works, move on to the next step.

➤ 4. **Play a chord progression:** Create a simple, repeating chord progression or use one from Shortcut 28. Play it with the rhythmic feel you've chosen.

A great exercise for building a song on a groove and writing to a scene.

➤ 5. **Pick a title:** Using one of the phrases from your list, speak it out loud as you work it into the groove. This will be your title line.

➤ 6. **Start your melody:** Write a melody for your title line as you play your chord progression. Follow it with two or three more of the phrases from your list. Then repeat your title line a few times.

➤ 7. **Play the scene as you work:** Try working on the music and lyric at a low level so you can still hear the dialogue in the scene. Stay in touch with the emotion of the scene.

➤ 8. **Test what you've written:** Record what you've written and play it softly under the scene as you watch. If you like it, go ahead and develop it into a full song. If not, just treat it as a fun exercise and try writing another one!

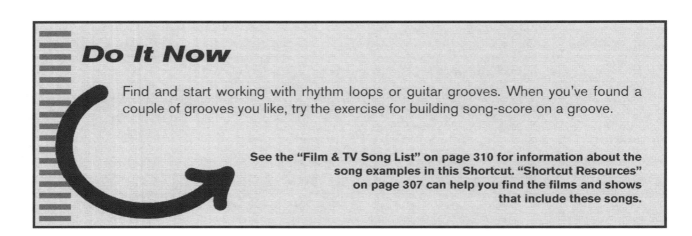

Do It Now

Find and start working with rhythm loops or guitar grooves. When you've found a couple of grooves you like, try the exercise for building song-score on a groove.

See the "Film & TV Song List" on page 310 for information about the song examples in this Shortcut. "Shortcut Resources" on page 307 can help you find the films and shows that include these songs.

Shortcut #22

A Solid Song Structure
Can Give You an Edge

*Support your song's message and increase its appeal
to music users.*

When writing songs for film and television, you have plenty of creative freedom
when it comes to song structure. In this market, song forms vary widely from a
simple series of verses to the full hit song style with a huge, memorable chorus.
There are film and TV songs with choruses that consist of a single, repeated line
and other songs with verses that flow so seamlessly into the chorus that it's hard
to tell where verse ends and the chorus begins.

So, if there's so much variety, what is the *right* song structure to use? The answer
is: the right song structure is the one that supports and enhances the emotional
message of your song.

How structure underscores an idea or emotion

In the film *Juno,* the audience gets a great introduction to the title character as
the opening credits roll. There's no dialogue in this scene; Juno simply walks along
as Barry Louis Polisar's "All I Want Is You" plays at full volume. The melody and
lyric suggest the feel of a traditional American folk song: direct, honest, earthy,
and naïve—traits that are shared by Juno herself. The song structure is typical
of American folk songs, just a simple series of verses. This no-frills song form
supports the message of the lyric and style of the melody. If the structure suddenly
veered off into a big, stand-alone chorus, it would feel artificial, destroying the
straight-forward quality of the song and giving the audience a mixed message
about the character.

*Song structure
reinforces the
message.*

In other situations, however, a song form with a strong chorus can be a big plus,
powerfully underscoring a build-up of emotional energy. In the TV series *The
Vampire Diaries,* there's a great example in Season 1, Episode 9. The song "Come
Back When You Can," by Barcelona, plays during a montage of short scenes at the
end of the show. As the scenes progress, the emotional energy intensifies. There's
no dialogue, only the song to keep the audience in touch with the characters'
feelings. As the song builds dramatically from verse to pre-chorus to chorus, it
underscores what's happening on the screen. The song's structure thus becomes
an integral part of the audience's experience.

If your song will be edited, why bother with structure?

In the film and TV market, most songs are edited to fit the scenes in which they're used; a verse might be cut in half, one line of a chorus butted up against another. Song structure is altered so that certain lines fall where they're needed and the vocal begins and ends in appropriate places. So, if it's going to be chopped to pieces why bother with song structure at all? There are a couple good reasons...

#1: As you saw in the example from *The Vampire Diaries,* a verse, pre-chorus, chorus section may be preserved whole because the dynamic build works within the context of the action.

#2: It's important to remember that music supervisors and music libraries initially hear your song *as a song*. They gauge its effectiveness for film and TV based on the strength of their own reaction. They never say, "Gee, that song was a mess but there were 30 seconds in the middle that I loved. I think I'll use that." For better or worse, you need to give them a memorable, credible, well-crafted song.

Structure gives organization, clarity, and intention to your song. It reassures the listener that this song is going somewhere and it makes your song easier to remember. While the choices of song forms in the film and TV field are not nearly as limited as they are for hit radio, it's still important to know what they are and how to use them.

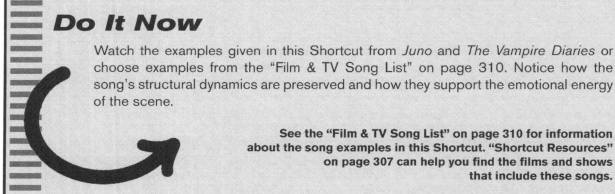

Do It Now

Watch the examples given in this Shortcut from *Juno* and *The Vampire Diaries* or choose examples from the "Film & TV Song List" on page 310. Notice how the song's structural dynamics are preserved and how they support the emotional energy of the scene.

See the "Film & TV Song List" on page 310 for information about the song examples in this Shortcut. "Shortcut Resources" on page 307 can help you find the films and shows that include these songs.

Shortcut #23

The Workhorse: Use the Song Structure That Gets the Job Done

The Verse / Chorus form delivers plenty of punch.

The most common song structure in film and television, one that's used in about 70 percent of song placements, is the Verse / Chorus form. Because this form offers plenty of dynamic motion (changes in energy), it can add impact to an onscreen scene and make it a more memorable experience for viewers. I'll be telling you more about dynamics in Shortcut 25. First, let's take a quick look at the Verse / Chorus song structure.

The building blocks of song structure

All songs consist of sections—in this case, a verse, chorus, and bridge—that work together to create an overall effect. Each section has a job to do:

- The verses convey information, deepening the listener's understanding of the situation.

- The chorus sums up the theme of the song and includes the hook.

- The bridge provides a peak moment, revelation, or twist.

In its basic form, the sections are laid out in this order:

Verse 1 / Chorus

Verse 2 / Chorus

Bridge / Chorus

In some songs, there's an additional section, a pre-chorus located between the verse and chorus whose sole function is to ramp up the emotional dynamics of a song before it dives into the chorus. When a pre-chorus is added, the song form looks like this:

Verse 1 / Pre-Chorus / Chorus

Verse 2 / Pre-Chorus / Chorus

Bridge / Chorus

You'll hear this song form (with or without a pre-chorus) in today's biggest hit songs. It works well for the radio market, catching and holding the audience's attention with its big dynamic changes and powerhouse choruses. Listen to a few current hits and see if you can identify the sections.

The Verse / Chorus form: Hit Song style

TV shows and films love to use hit songs by name artists but often can't afford them. You can take advantage of that and fill the need by writing songs in this style. Here are a few techniques that will get you headed in the right direction:

➤ **Define the song sections by using contrast.**
By clearly defining your structure, you make it easier for listeners to understand your intentions and navigate through your song. To differentiate the sections of your song (verse, pre-chorus, and chorus), try changing the note range of your melody, the pace of the notes, length of your phrases, or note rhythm patterns. If your verse lyric is poetic, try a more direct, straight-ahead approach in your chorus. Changes like these will give each of your song sections a distinct identity.

Use these three tips to add film/ TV appeal!

➤ **Write a hook that gives listeners something to remember… and music supervisors something to feature in a scene.**
The hook is the most memorable lyric and melody line in your song. It's also the line most likely to be featured in a scene or commercial. In this song form, the hook is usually the first or last line of the chorus and it includes the title. It's important that you express your theme in this line with vivid, fresh language and a catchy melody. Shortcuts 46 and 56 will help you create an effective title for film and TV songs and feature it in your chorus lyric. For suggestions on how to write a memorable hook melody, read Shortcut 31.

➤ **Change the energy level.**
One of the reasons this form is such a favorite with the film and TV market is that it has a built-in "energy elevator." Songs in this form tend to start the verses with a conversational, low-key feel, gradually increasing the energy and hitting a peak at the beginning of the chorus, then releasing the energy and returning to the verse level to start over again. Just one of these up-and-down energy trips can add life to an on-screen moment that might otherwise feel static. (For more on song dynamics, read Shortcut 25.)

The Verse / Chorus form: Variations

Just as a well-built house begins with a basic four-walls-and-a-roof plan, a proven song structure provides a good foundation for building your song. And, just as there are many variations on the basic house plan, so song structures can vary and still remain solid.

As you study the songs used in movies, TV shows, and commercials, you'll find some that fit the basic Verse / Chorus pattern perfectly, like Glass Pear's "Last Day of Your Life" or Augustana's "Sweet and Low." Others begin with two verses before going to the first chorus, like The Script's "The Man Who Can't Be Moved." Still other songs have no bridge (Jason Walker's "Down") or have an instrumental break instead of a bridge, as in Remy Zero's "Save Me."

Despite these differences, *all* of these songs use the techniques listed in this Shortcut. They all have clearly defined song sections, powerful chorus opening and closing lines, and include big trips on the "energy elevator." It's a good idea to practice these techniques using the basic song forms you learned at the beginning of this Shortcut before you start experimenting. In other words, learn to build a house with four walls before you try something that looks like a Frank Gehry architectural wonder! There's plenty of room for creativity within each song section, so you never need to feel that you're being predictable or boring.

Master the form before you get creative!

Do the music editor a favor!

The music editor will be looking for those portions of your song that can add drama or emotion to a scene. A rise in energy from verse to chorus and strong, memorable lines that sum up the heart of your song are often the very things the music editor needs in the closing montage of a TV episode when emotions are at their peak. Try using a clear, easy-to-recognize verse / chorus or verse / pre-chorus / chorus song structure to give yourself a big advantage when pitching for these important uses. These are the scenes that audiences remember, the ones that make them head over to iTunes to buy your song!

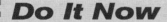

Do It Now

Listen to the song examples in this Shortcut. First, listen to the original, full-length recording. Then choose one or two and watch the way they're used in the film or TV show listed. Notice which song sections were used and how they enhanced the on-screen scene.

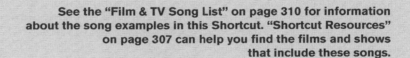

See the "Film & TV Song List" on page 310 for information about the song examples in this Shortcut. "Shortcut Resources" on page 307 can help you find the films and shows that include these songs.

Shortcut #24

Simple But Effective: Try a Streamlined Structure

Make it easy on yourself and still give them what they need.

Those big chorus-driven songs described in the previous Shortcut are exciting, but there's plenty of room in this market for simpler song structures. In fact, an ear-catching chorus can draw the viewer's attention *away* from a scene, while a song form with subtler changes in dynamics can keep the focus on the dialogue and characters.

These song forms consist of a string of verses or, more often, two verses followed by a bridge, like this:

Verse 1 / Verse 2 / Bridge / Verse 3

Each verse has a different lyric with the exception of one important line—the refrain. The refrain line consists of a lyric and melody phrase that's used in the same place in each verse, usually as the first or last line. The bridge consists of a different melody and lyric from the verses and usually does not include the refrain line.

Sometimes the third verse is followed by another bridge or an instrumental verse, returning to a final verse at the end of the song. However, you may not need to add anything at all to the basic form. To hear a good example of the basic Verse / Verse / Bridge / Verse form listen to "Can't Go Back Now" by The Weepies. This song has been used in several TV shows including *Life Unexpected, One Tree Hill,* and *Scrubs.* The refrain line begins "You and me walk on…" It appears at the end of each verse and is repeated several times at the end of the song to add more emphasis (and length).

Write a strong hook

In this song form, the refrain is the hook of your song and usually includes the title. It's the line that sums up the heart of your lyric, the one that listeners will remember, and the one that will attract a music supervisor's interest. Here are a few suggestions that will help you create a strong refrain line.

Read Shortcut 46 for more on writing strong title/hook lines.

➢ **Make it memorable.**
   Using a direct, honest, emotional statement in your refrain draws listeners into the heart of the situation: The Weepies' "You can't go back now" or "All I can do is keep breathing" from Ingrid Michaelson's "Keep Breathing" are two refrain/title lines that have worked well for songs in this form. They suggest an intense, intriguing situation, making listeners want to know more.

➢ **Keep your refrain line consistent.**
You can get away with varying a single word or two but if you change too many words, listeners may have trouble recognizing the line when it comes around. It's the familiarity of the repeated line that provides an anchor for listeners, letting them know where they are in the song.

➢ **Repeat it.**
If your refrain occurs at the end of each verse, try repeating the line an extra time at the end of your second verse and several times at the end of the song to add emphasis and memorability. For suggestions on how to do this effectively, read about "tags" in Shortcut 77.

Verse and bridge

A successful refrain line should give you a good focal point for writing the verses and bridge of your song. Use the refrain as your guide. Let the other verse lines support the refrain by offering more information, examples of what it means, or deepening the impact through the use of emotional language. The bridge frequently provides a peak moment. It may state something that was only hinted at in the verses, express the singer's hopes for the future, or dig deeper into the real cause of the situation.

For more on developing your lyric, read Shortcut 57.

Adapt as needed

To hear variations on the Verse / Verse / Bridge / Verse song structure, listen to "Rescue Me" by Sarah Bettens, used in the TV series *90210*. The refrain begins with "Will you rescue me? Will you soften every blow?" It continues on for two more lines. That's a long refrain! Because the melody flows smoothly from the first three lines of the verse into these lines without a big emotional release, it feels like a refrain rather than a chorus. Try something like this in a song of your own. It's subtle and effective.

"Violet Hill" by Coldplay, used in the TV series *One Tree Hill*, consists of a string of verses with no real bridge at all, just an instrumental verse. The refrain is "If you love me, won't you let me know." It occurs at the end of each verse and is varied after the third verse. In this song, the title is not included in the refrain, a risky move if you want listeners to be able to find your song at iTunes.

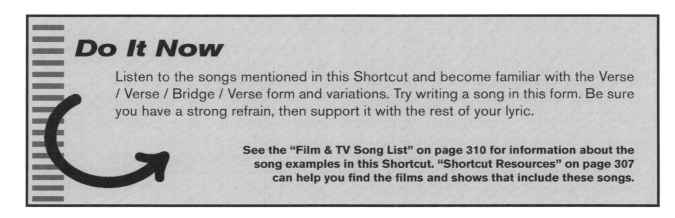

Do It Now

Listen to the songs mentioned in this Shortcut and become familiar with the Verse / Verse / Bridge / Verse form and variations. Try writing a song in this form. Be sure you have a strong refrain, then support it with the rest of your lyric.

See the "Film & TV Song List" on page 310 for information about the song examples in this Shortcut. "Shortcut Resources" on page 307 can help you find the films and shows that include these songs.

Shortcut #25

Use Dynamics to Create Drama and Energy

Build and release tension in your song's structure.

Film and TV scriptwriters know that an audience will lose interest if the characters in a scene interact for too long at the same emotional level. Viewers want to feel the tension rising to a confrontation or the release of energy in an onscreen kiss. The same holds true for action scenes. Even a high-energy chase scene can become boring without a few ups and downs in the thrill level.

A song can emphasize the changing energy levels of a scene or even add energy when the action itself doesn't provide enough. By embedding dynamic changes into your song—building energy then releasing it—you offer the director a surefire way to increase the impact of a scene.

What are song dynamics?

Change dynamic levels to keep your song interesting.

In music, the word "dynamics" specifically refers to changing levels of loudness and softness. Your verse might be at a relatively low volume level and the chorus louder. But in a song, the notion of "dynamics" encompasses more than that: it refers to the building up and releasing of emotional energy. For instance, a song might begin with a conversational, matter-of-fact tone then escalate to a more intense level of feeling just before the chorus, reaching a peak on the first few lines of the chorus. Just as it does on screen, a change in dynamic levels keeps the song interesting and creates a sense of drama and momentum.

Build dynamic changes into your song structure.

Dynamic changes work with each section of a song—verse, chorus, and bridge—to help it do its job. The emotional energy in the verse, for example, tends to start out lower than in the chorus because you want to make sure the listener has a chance to hear and understand information. You can use the last line or two of the verse or a separate pre-chorus section to increase the tension as you move into the chorus. Then let the first few lines of the chorus generate plenty of emotional sparks because that's where the heart and soul of the song lies. You want listeners to really get into their feelings at that point, and then release those feelings as the song moves to the end of the chorus and into the next verse.

Here are two ways to build and release tension in a song. The amount of tension and release, the time you take to create it, and the tools you use are all up to you. Try playing with these ideas:

➤ 1. **Change the note range.** When people become emotional, their voices tend to rise. Use that to your advantage; as you increase the emotional energy from verse to chorus, raise the overall note range of your melody. Save the highest notes for the point of greatest emotional impact. Then gradually lower the note range to get back to your verse. You can hear this technique in Griffin House's song "Live to Be Free," and Jason Walker's "Down."

In "The Climb," recorded by Miley Cyrus, the melody keeps on climbing right to the end of the chorus, building energy steadily. The listener goes right along for the ride, experiencing the song's theme in a very immediate way.

In Augustana's song "Sweet and Low," a rising melody line in the bridge underscores a powerful peak emotional moment in a scene in the *Kyle XY* episode "The Tell-Tale Heart." This scene is worth watching to see how song dynamics can be very effectively used to underscore an emotional onscreen moment.

➤ 2. **Try a change of pace.** Someone who is growing excited or more emotional will tend to speak more rapidly and in shorter phrases than someone who is feeling relaxed. You can pick up the pace of words and notes to increase urgency and tension and release it in long, smooth lines. The Fray's "Never Say Never" is a good example of building and releasing tension using pace. The pre-chorus builds tension ("You can never say never...") then releases into a big chorus with a smoother feel on the repeated line "Don't let me go." Demi Lovato and Joe Jonas's "This Is Me" keeps the energy and tension building right up to the peak moment of the chorus ("...shine on me") and the payoff (final) chorus line.

Try a change of note range or pace.

Experiment with tension and release

Within a single section, a song can mix both tension and release. It's not all black or all white. But if you look at the *overall* dynamics of each section you'll see that it's generally building or releasing energy. Try mixing changes in notes range and pace to vary the dynamic levels between song sections. When you create your instrumental arrangement, *add support* for the dynamics that are written into the song (Shortcut 73). As always, let the emotions of the song be your guide.

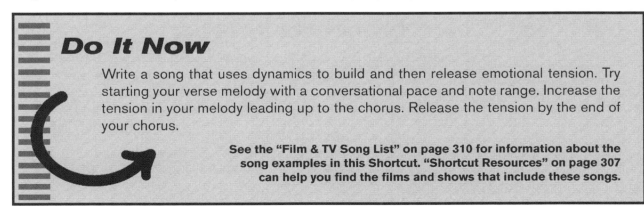

Do It Now

Write a song that uses dynamics to build and then release emotional tension. Try starting your verse melody with a conversational pace and note range. Increase the tension in your melody leading up to the chorus. Release the tension by the end of your chorus.

See the "Film & TV Song List" on page 310 for information about the song examples in this Shortcut. "Shortcut Resources" on page 307 can help you find the films and shows that include these songs.

Shortcut #26

Add Edit Points to Your Song Structure

Give music editors a break by clearly defining your song.

Music editors perform an indispensable job in today's movies and TV shows. When a film director or TV producer decides to use a pre-existing song in a scene—a song that was not written or recorded with that scene in mind—the music editor must seamlessly cut and rearrange the song until it sounds like it was created for that moment in that production.

What a music editor does

Understand the importance of editing in film, TV, and commercials.

In movies and TV shows that use songs, the music editor's job is to ensure that the song supports the scene by making the desired lyric lines or song sections fall in the right places. To do that, he may need to edit from the middle of one verse to the middle of another or from the end of the first pre-chorus to the final chorus. TV commercials are a little different. A 30-second commercial hasn't got time for anything extraneous and must make the lyric work with the picture. A music editor might need to make several edits within a single song section and all of them must sound natural.

It's not an easy job. It may take an editor an hour or more to find an edit point in the track that will work. An edit point is the place at which a line or whole section of a song is cut or length is added by repeating a section or line. Edit points need to join together so smoothly that they go unnoticed by the audience. Using today's digital audio technology, an editor can search for good places to get in and out at an almost microscopic level.

But that may not be enough. The challenges of editing a completed track with vocal can be enormous. What happens when the vocalist is singing where an edit is needed? What if every chorus is melodically and lyrically different? How can a section be repeated if it begins at a slower tempo and ends at a faster one? Solving these problems can take hours, if they can be solved at all.

Give the music editor a little help

Whether your song is used for 20 seconds or two minutes, by defining your song structure clearly a music editor has a better chance of finding edit points that will work. A song use of 45 seconds or more will often consist of a partial verse and a repeated chorus or refrain line. The chorus or refrain, after all, sums up the heart of your song and is probably the reason the director or producer decided to use it in the first place.

> ➤ *Record to a click track.* All sequencing software and recording studios provide a click or metronome for recording. Playing to the steady beat of the click on headphones while recording, keeps the tempo consistent throughout the

song. A good musician knows how to play with feeling while staying locked to the click track. Use a click even if you're recording a solo guitar and vocal track. Without it, editing can be a nightmare because the tempo of the song could change from one section to another. Cutting from one verse to another or a verse to a chorus at a different tempo may be impossible.

➤ *Edit points don't always occur at the beginning of a section.* The editor may need to cut from the middle of a first chorus to the middle of a final chorus that has a definitive ending, for example. If you keep your song structure clear and consistent a good editor will be able to find a workable solution.

➤ *Be sure to make an instrumental mix* (with no vocal) and a mix of your vocal (with no instruments). If needed, these can be edited separately and then remarried.

Help the music editor. Keep your song form clear and consistent.

To hear some effective examples of song editing and how it affects the song's use in a scene, check out the following. (Use the "Film & TV Song List" on page 310 to locate the show and scene location.)

"The Pretender" (Foo Fighters) in *CSI: Miami*

"Sweet and Low" (Augustana) in *Kyle XY*

"Songbird" (Fleetwood Mac) in *Alias*

"Keep Breathing" (Ingrid Michaelson) in *Grey's Anatomy*

Can a happy music editor help you get placements?

Songs are pitched to directors and producers from many sources. One very important source is the music editor. In fact, in some cases, the music editor will replace the music supervisor as the primary source of songs for a project. Of course, in the end, it will always come down to the quality and appropriateness of your song but it never hurts to have a music editor on your side!

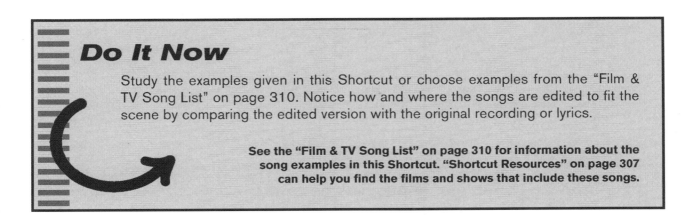

Do It Now

Study the examples given in this Shortcut or choose examples from the "Film & TV Song List" on page 310. Notice how and where the songs are edited to fit the scene by comparing the edited version with the original recording or lyrics.

See the "Film & TV Song List" on page 310 for information about the song examples in this Shortcut. "Shortcut Resources" on page 307 can help you find the films and shows that include these songs.

Shortcut #27

How Long Does Your Song Need to Be?

*Even if they're only going to use a little bit of it,
write a whole song.*

If you've been listening to songs in films and TV shows, you've noticed that frequently only a single chorus or verse is used, sometimes less. Does that mean you can write a single verse and chorus, then call it quits? Here are a few things to think about that might help you answer that question.

Make an impression

Over and over, music supervisors and music library owners tell me they look for a song that resonates for them, one that gives them an emotional buzz or creates a "ping." However they describe it, they want a song that strikes them personally before they will consider placing it in a project. A partial song, one that clocks in between 45 seconds and one minute, may be too short to build dynamics effectively, failing to reach a peak or develop fully enough to make a lasting impression on a producer, music supervisor, or music library owner. These are the first people you have to reach. If you don't make it past this round, your song will never have a chance to reach viewers.

How short is too short?

Aim for two minutes or longer.

The Verse / Verse / Bridge / Verse song form can result in a song that's under two minutes in length. Some music libraries will accept songs that are under two minutes; others won't. To be safe, aim for the two-minute mark at least. It's easy to add or lengthen a tag section at the end of your song, repeat the bridge, or add one more verse, so go ahead and do it. Get an exact time on your song by making a good rough demo *before* you spend money and time recording a final version. Read Shortcut 68 to learn more about rough demos.

If your song is on the short side, remember this: You can use more repetition in songs for the film and television market than in those aimed at radio airplay. However, be sure you make your repetitions compelling by building the instrumental arrangement underneath and varying the lyric and melody just enough to prevent it from becoming monotonous. You can find out more about using repetition in the section on "tags" in Shortcut 77.

When length can be a plus

A song with a full Verse / Pre-Chorus / Chorus structure offers the music user plenty of material to choose from. While a song use is almost guaranteed to include your chorus or refrain line, the music editor will have to determine which verse will work best, whether the bridge will add dynamics that could be useful, and where the song will end. By giving him plenty to work with, you make the job easier and might even increase the length of the use. This could mean more money for you and more time for the audience to notice your song.

Make your entire song usable

Your goal is to make sure that *all* of your song is usable. Music users won't go through your song listening for the good bits. Give them what they need: an expressive song that moves them emotionally, one that gives them an experience they'll remember. So go ahead and write a complete song, one that's fully developed and expressive. That's the best way to ensure you have a chance of hitting a home run with the people who can get your songs placed.

Do It Now

Go through your song catalogue and note the length of each song. If you have any songs that run less than two minutes, consider adding some extra length. If you have songs with sections that are weak, think about rewriting these to make your entire song strong.

PART FOUR

Shortcuts to Music for Film & TV Songs

Learn to build a strong film and TV song

on a chord progression, create an anchor melody line,

and write a melody that supports the emotion in your lyric.

Ready? Then let's get started…

Shortcut #28

Keep Your Chord Progressions Simple

*Seven easy chord progressions you can use
for film and TV songs.*

Many songs that are successful in the film and TV field are built on simple chord progressions. For example, Meiko's "Reasons to Love You," used in more than a half-dozen TV shows, features a familiar, basic four-chord progression, repeated throughout the entire song. In this market, it's *feel* they're looking for, not an impressive chord chart. If you find yourself using more than five different chords in a song or if you're changing chords on every beat in a measure, you may be overwriting for the majority of uses.

In this Shortcut, I'll show you a variety of chord progressions you can use, from simple, repetitive progressions of two or four measures (2-bar or 4-bar progressions) to complete song progressions. This is a small but representative sample of the chords that are used in the Pop, Rock, and Singer-Songwriter music styles that dominate the film and TV market.

On their own, contemporary chord progressions don't sound very interesting; they really come to life when melody, lyrics, and instrumental arrangements are added. As you play through these progressions, try adding a drum loop to give them a little flavor and keep the beat steady (Shortcut 21). If you're using a synthesizer, explore different sounds to add some color. On guitar, experiment with different strum and picking patterns.

Chord progressions provide a backdrop for your song.

If you don't know how to play the chords in these examples, you can search the Internet for a "Chord Finder" for guitar or piano. Select the chord you're looking for and the Chord Finder will show you how to play it. You can also purchase Chord Finders online and in music stores.

Each box in the following chord progressions represents one measure of four beats. Each slash represents a beat. You can play the chord on every beat or hold the chord through the beats marked with the slash.

Do It Now

Learn some of the chord progressions on the following pages. Play them on acoustic guitar or keyboard using a rhythm loop to provide the groove. Create a rough recording on your audio software or record your progression on a cassette or digital recorder while the groove plays in the background. This is a great way to start writing a film and TV song.

Progression #1: Easy repeated 2-bar chord progression

Verse and chorus

F / / /	G / C /

This simple chord progression (IV-V-I) has been used in hundreds (if not thousands) of songs. Just repeat these two measures. You can hear a great example of this repeated progression in "Live to Be Free" by Griffin House. It's played through the entire song. If you want to play along with the recording, move the chords one whole step lower: Eb, F, Bb.

Progression #2: Easy repeated 4-bar chord progression

Verse and chorus

Em / / /	C / / /	G / / /	D / / /

Here's a beautiful, easy-to-play chord progression that was used in the hit song "Apologize" by OneRepublic. Both verse and chorus are based on this progression. To play along with the recording, move the chords two whole steps down to Cm, Ab, Eb, Bb.

Progression #3: Another easy 4-bar chord progression

Verse

C / / /	Em / / /	F / / /	F / / /

Chorus

C / / /	Em / / /	F / / /	Dm / / /

The change in the fourth chord from F to Dm gives this simple, repeated progression enough variety to consider splitting it into a verse and chorus. You can hear this progression in the verse and chorus of The Script's "The Man Who Can't Be Moved." To play along with the recording, move the chords one whole step lower to Bb, Dm, Eb, Eb and Bb, Dm, Eb, Cm.

Progression #4: Verse /Verse / Bridge / Verse form (Shortcut 24)

You can hear this familiar verse chord pattern in "Can't Go Back Now" by The Weepies. To fill out your song structure, play the verse progression twice then go to a bridge progression like the one included here. After that, return to the verse.

Verse

C / / /	F / / /	C / / /	F / / /
C / / /	F / / /	C / / /	F / / /
Am / / /	G / / /	Am / / /	F / / /
C / / /	F / / /	C / / /	F / / /

Bridge

Dm / / /	F / / /	C / / /	G / / /
Dm / / /	F / / /	F / / /	G / / /

Progression #5: Verse / Chorus form (Shortcut 23)

Play through the entire progression then repeat it. You can then use the bridge from Progression #4 followed by this chorus to complete your song structure. Try a metronome setting of 126 BPM (Shortcut 19) to pick up the pace and energy.

Verse

Am / / /	F / / /	C / / /	G / / /
Am / / /	F / / /	C / / /	G / / /
Am / / /	F / / /	C / / /	G / / /
F / / /	Am / / /	Am / / /	G / / /

Bridge

F / / /	C / / /	G / / /	Am / / /
F / / /	C / / /	G / / /	G / / /
Am / / /	F / / /	C / / /	G / / /
Dm / / /	Dm / / /	F / / /	G / / /

Progression #6: Verse / Pre-chorus / Chorus form (Shortcut 23)

At this point, you can combine what you've learned in previous Shortcuts to really launch your song. For this longer song form, pick up the pace. Try a tempo of 140 BPM and use a guitar strum or rhythm loop with a strong Duple Feel (Shortcut 20). Play through the entire progression then repeat it. After that, you can use the bridge from Progression #4 followed by this chorus to complete your song structure.

Verse

C / / /	C / / /	Am / / /	Am / / /
F / / /	F / / /	C / / /	C / / /
C / / /	C / / /	Am / / /	Am / / /
F / / /	F / / /	C / / /	C / / /

Pre-chorus

F / / /	G / / /	Am / / /	F / / /

Chorus

C / / /	C / / /	Am / / /	Am / / /
F / / /	F / / /	G / / /	G / / /
C / / /	C / / /	Am / / /	Am / / /
F / / /	F / / /	G / / /	G / / /

Progression #7: Minor feel

Up to this point, the progressions have featured a blend of major and minor chords. Here's a progression that has a strong minor feel. See Shortcut 30 for more on how you can use a progression like this to convey an emotional message. Repeat the verse and chorus sections up to four times (more if you like). Listen to "99 Times" by Kate Voegele to hear this progression starting on Em rather than Am.

Verse

Am / / /	Em / / /	F / / /	G / / /

Pre-Chorus

Dm / / /	Em / / /	F / / /	G / / /

Chorus

Am / / /	Dm / / /	F / / /	G / / /

Shortcut #29

Add Color and Life to Your Chords

*Adding, subtracting, or moving a single note
can change the feel of a chord progression.*

You can add more emotional tone and color to your songs by simply altering one
or two notes in your chord progression. Changing a single note in a chord can
shift the feel from sweet to bittersweet, from airy to dark, from simple to subtle.
The best way to explore this idea is to play a simple chord progression and begin
making small changes. If you like what you hear, keep it; if you don't, throw it out
and try something else!

Fun with Chord Finders

In the previous Shortcut, I suggested using a Chord Finder to learn how to
play the basic three-note chords that were used in the progressions. But Chord
Finders can do more than that. Besides the basic major and minor chords, they
can lead you to a wealth of altered three-note and four-note chords you'll love
using. (Remember, you can locate Chord Finders for piano and guitar on the
Internet or buy one at any music store.)

Chord Finders include a lot of chords you won't use — chords that are harmonically
challenging and draw a lot of attention to themselves. You'll find yourself zeroing
in on just a few useful chords, like these:

Chord type:	Chord Finder name
Major chords	maj
Minor chords	min
Minor 7th chord	m7 or min7
Suspended chords	sus4 and sus2
6th chords	6

To hear how these chords can add richness and depth to a chord progression,
play the verse in Progression #3 with these changes:

| C / / / | Emin7 / / / | F / / / | F6 / / / |

*Simple changes
can make a big
difference!*

One of my favorite chords is found in only a few Chord Finders. It's called
"add2." It's very popular in the singer-songwriter genre because it creates a warm,
complex sound. To play an "add2" chord, just play a major chord and add the note
that's a whole step up from the root (the root is the note that's the same as the
name of the chord). If you're playing a C chord, for instance, add the D note in
between C and E. Play all the notes of the C chord and the D. (This is easy on
keyboard, a little harder to work out on guitar.)

Bass motion

One of the most effective changes you can make is to use a "slash chord." They're called "slash chords" because they're written using a slash, like this: F/A. This chord is referred to as "F over A." Play an F chord with an A note on the bottom. For keyboard players, the easiest way to do this is to play an F chord with the right hand and an A in a lower octave, like a bass part. For guitar players, make sure the A on the low strings is the lowest note and listeners can hear it clearly. Sometimes it's easier to just play the F chord and record a bass part separately. Try this progression to see how it sounds:

C / / /	Em/B / / /	F/A / / /	F6 / / /

Arpeggiate it

Playing the notes of a chord separately, *one after the other rather than all at once,* can create a pleasing effect. It reveals the chord over the space of a few beats instead of all at once. Breaking up a chord in this way also allows you to play more complex chords without being too obvious about it, especially if the chords share some of the same notes. In this progression, all of the chords share a D note. Try playing this progression in an arpeggio style.

C add2 / / /	Em7/B / / /	F6/A / / /	F6 / / /

De-tune your guitar

Guitar players have one wonderful option that keyboard players don't. By changing the tuning on the guitar from standard tuning (EADGBE) to, for example, a D chord (DADF#AD), you have at your fingertips a world of gorgeous, evocative chords that are easy to play and will inspire your songwriting. There are many tunings that will suggest interesting chords to you. You can find them in guitar books or on the Internet. (Search for "alternate" or "open" guitar tunings.) I recommend checking out some of the tunings used by singer-songwriter Nick Drake. You can find tunings and tablature for his songs online.

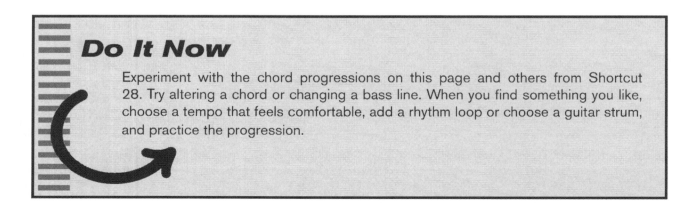

Do It Now

Experiment with the chord progressions on this page and others from Shortcut 28. Try altering a chord or changing a bass line. When you find something you like, choose a tempo that feels comfortable, add a rhythm loop or choose a guitar strum, and practice the progression.

Shortcut #30

Major and Minor Chords: Speak the Language of Feelings

Use a chord progression to enhance the emotional message of your lyric.

Today's mainstream music genres rely on three- and four-note chords. These chords are basically of two types: *major* and *minor*. Major chords are the candy factories of the music world. They pump out sweet, feel-good emotions like happiness and satisfaction, creating a sense of optimism and hope in the listener. Minor chords elicit a range of emotions centered on sadness and yearning; they can evoke a sense of uncertainty or loss.

An E major chord and an E minor chord are very similar—only one note is different and only by a small amount—but the difference in the emotional tone is unmistakable. Studies have shown that your brain reacts differently to major and minor chords, but you don't need a scientific study to prove it; you can test it for yourself.

Play an E major chord on keyboard or guitar. As you play, hum each of the three notes of the chord—E, G# and B—in any order you like. Now, using those notes, sing the phrase, "When I look in your eyes…" As you sing it, imagine what the next lyric line might be. Perhaps it's something like, "When I look in your eyes / I see the sunrise." This is an upbeat image that agrees with the major chord feel.

*Major chords =
Upbeat
Hopeful
Happy*

Now, play an E minor chord. Sing the same phrase, "When I look in your eyes…" on the notes of the E minor chord—E, G, and B. If you follow that with the phrase "I see the sunrise," it seems less optimistic than when it was sung with the major chord. Maybe this sunrise is obscured by clouds. This is a very different emotional message from the same phrase sung to a major chord. You can feel it and listeners can, too. You could either change the lyric so it's supported by the minor chord—"When I look in your eyes / I see the tears you cry"—or go on to tell the listener more about an unusually sad sunrise.

*Minor chords =
Sadness
Yearning
Uncertainty*

Use a mix of major and minor chords

Of course you can't always match a major chord with a happy, upbeat lyric phrase or a minor chord with a sad one. If you tried to do that, you'd have a mess on your hands. Instead, think in terms of groups of chords—chord progressions—that have an overall major or minor feel. If you emphasize minor chords, if you linger on them, start phrases on them, and use more of them in your progression, the overall emotional tone of your song will lean toward a sorrowful, introspective, or yearning tone. The same holds true when you emphasize major chords; the overall feeling will tend to be more optimistic. Ask yourself what you want the audience to feel as they listen to your song.

To hear the difference in emotional tone between songs that feature either major or minor chords, listen to Coldplay's "Violet Hill" which circles around minor chords throughout the song, underscoring the dark tone of the lyrics. Compare this with a song like Colbie Caillat's "Fallin' for You" with its sweet, hopeful major chord feel and lyrics. Kate Voegele's "99 Times" is an angry song full of accusations and has an appropriately minor chord feel while "We're Going to Be Friends" by The White Stripes is upbeat and friendly and uses major chords to underscore that message.

Many film and TV songs fall in between these emotional extremes, using chord progressions that feature a mix of major and minor chords. However, think about adding a few songs to your catalogue that are clearly in one camp or the other—angry and devastated or totally in love and walking on air. For a scene with a strong emotional situation, it could be just what the music supervisor is looking for!

Do It Now

Watch for scenes in films and TV shows in which characters express strong emotions. Play a chord progression while watching the scene. You can use the chord progressions in Shortcut 28 or create progressions of your own. Or you can play the chord progressions to some of the songs referred to in this Shortcut. You'll find them in song books and online.

Once you have a chord progression, choose a tempo and groove that seem to be the best fit for the scene. Record your chord progression and groove and listen as it plays under the scene. Try changing the chord progression to see what effect it has on your reaction to the scene.

See the "Film & TV Song List" on page 310 for information about the song examples in this Shortcut. "Shortcut Resources" on page 307 can help you find the films and shows that include these songs.

Shortcut #31

Anchor Your Song with a Fresh Melodic Phrase

Use these tools to write hundreds of strong, appealing hook melodies.

While songs for film and television don't need to be as attention grabbing as hit singles, you still need to give the audience (and music supervisors) at least one phrase that will stay in their memory. A good lyric and melody hook is essential. In the Verse / Chorus song form, it's often the first line of the chorus. In the Verse / Verse / Bridge / Verse form it will be the refrain line—the first or last line of each verse. Hooks consist of both lyrics and melody. You can write your hook lyric first or lyric and melody at the same time. For just a moment, though, let's look at melody alone. Specifically, creating a hook melody.

A good hook melody acts as an anchor in your song. If it's written well, it holds the rest of the melody together, preventing it from wandering, giving it a central, memorable focus. As you'll see in the following Shortcuts, by building your melody around an anchor, you keep it organized and compelling. This is especially helpful when writing film and TV songs that lack the big contrast of a hit-style chorus; melodies can tend to meander and lose shape, losing listeners along the way. So let's refer to your hook melody as an "anchor" line.

Tools for writing a memorable anchor melody line.

Here are four suggestions you can use to build a melody line that will provide a solid anchor for your chorus melody.

> **Mix note lengths:**
> Sing a phrase or five or more notes, mixing up the rhythm of the notes, short notes with longer ones. You can hear this style in Colbie Caillat's "Fallin' for You." The first line of the chorus ("I've been spendin' all my...") starts with a long note followed by several short ones. It sets up an easy-to-remember, catchy rhythm pattern in the melody. Damien Rice's "Cannonball" features a chorus anchor melody consisting of the melodic rhythm pattern: long, short, short, short, long ("Stones taught me to fly...").

> **Choose a starting point for your phrase:**
> Listen again to the two hit songs I just mentioned by Damien Rice and Colbie Caillat. Try counting along with the chorus. Count a steady 1 *and* 2 *and* 3 *and* 4 *and*. Notice that the anchor line of the Damien Rice song begins on Beat 1. Then count along with the other song and you'll find that the anchor line ("I've been spendin' all my...") starts on the "and" *after* Beat 1. This melody has a lot more rhythmic interest and bounce than

For more on counting beats, see Shortcut 20.

the Damien Rice song because it emphasizes the weak "and" between beats. It's also, fittingly, a more lighthearted, flirtatious song. Neither choice is better or worse. Both songs were hit singles and both have been used in film and TV. Just be aware that you can change the feel of your hook depending on your starting point.

➤ **Mix interval leaps with note-to-note motion:**
Melodies consist of note-to-note motion, like musical scales, mixed with jumps from one note to another that may be several notes away. Once more, "Fallin' For You" provides a good example. The chorus starts on a high note ("I've...") then jumps down in an interval leap, followed by a melody line that has more of a scale-like sound ("been spendin' all my..."). To hear melodies that feature a lot of interval jumps, listen to Jem's "Flying High" and Jason Walker's "Down." The verse melodies in both have some small jumps but when the choruses kick in, the melodies suddenly take some huge leaps!

Create a memorable anchor melody line now

To practice writing melodic anchor phrases, use a metronome, click track, or drum loop to help you keep a steady beat. You can strum a rhythmic feel on guitar if you prefer but damp the strings on the neck so you don't have to think about playing chords. You're going to focus on melody *only*. Use a metronome or choose a loop that has a steady underlying beat in groups of four and emphasizes Beat 1. (This is 4/4 time.) As the rhythm plays, improvise melody ideas by singing whatever syllables feel comfortable to you: "la la" or "da da" will both work just fine.

➤ **Work with a pattern of long and short notes.** Sing or play one of the three melody patterns shown below. Use any note pitches you like. Choose any starting beat. Repeat the pattern until you feel comfortable.

#1 Short Short Long Long Long

#2 Long Short Short Short Long

#3 Long Long Short Short Short

A great exercise for melody ideas!

There are hundreds of great hooks in these three simple patterns. You might not hear something you like right away but that's okay, you're just getting started.

➤ **Play with scale melodies and interval jumps.** Using the rhythm pattern you selected, try singing or playing a simple upward or downward scale. Do that a few times then add an interval leap between the first and second notes and continue with a scale. Try a couple of interval jumps, a big one and a small one. Mix up the pitches any way you like but try to keep the interval and scale idea going. If you sing something you like, record it for later.

➤ **Experiment with phrase start points:** Try starting your pattern on different beats. You've probably been starting on Beat 1, which is what most of us do from habit. Make an effort to start your phrase on Beat 2. It might take a few tries. Once you can start on Beat 2, try Beat 3 and then Beat 4. After that, try starting on the "and" between some of these beats. In each case, the feel of your melodic phrase will be different even though the pattern itself and the pitches remain the same. This is where a drum loop can be helpful. It will keep emphasizing Beat 1 and help you hear the difference each time you move the phrase. For most people, this takes some practice but it will pay off by giving you many more choices when writing melodies.

➤ **Change up the melodic rhythm pattern:** You don't have to stick to the three patterns included in this Shortcut. Feel free to extend a phrase by adding more notes. Or try removing a note, repeating short or long notes, or adding a pause in the middle. When you find something you like, record it and continue on to the next Shortcut or keep working. You can create dozens of hook ideas for later use.

You may already be using some of these ideas in your melodies. If not, play with them until they start to come easily to you. You'll find that you have more freedom and wider choices when writing and rewriting melodies.

Do It Now

Listen to the song examples in this Shortcut then do the exercise at the end of the Shortcut for creating a memorable anchor melody.

See the "Film & TV Song List" on page 310 for information about the song examples in this Shortcut. "Shortcut Resources" on page 307 can help you find the films and shows that include these songs.

Shortcut #32

Expand an Anchor Phrase Into a Memorable Melody

Explore the five melody patterns that listeners love.

Which of these two series of numbers is easier to remember? Look quickly, then look away and see how many numbers in each series you can recall.

123123123123   or   746394518372

It's obvious: you can recall more numbers in the first series. It's organized into a simple repeating pattern that your brain can quickly recognize and store. Something similar happens with melodies. A melody with a pattern that includes a certain amount of repetition is easier to remember (and has greater appeal) than a melody with no pattern of repetition. All melody patterns are built on one basic rule: the repeated line must sound similar enough to the original line that listeners recognize it as a repeat.

Repetition patterns in melodies

Here are five patterns that can help you write a well-organized chorus (or verse) that listeners will remember easily. The best way to understand these patterns is to hear them in successful songs so I've included examples of each one.

You can develop the anchor melody line you created in the previous Shortcut into a full chorus using any of these melodic repetition techniques.

Expand your anchor melody line with one of these ideas.

> **Pattern #1: Simple repetition**
> Simply repeating an entire line will set it in the listener's memory. Just be sure your line is interesting enough to keep the listener involved during a repeat.
>
> "Apologize" (OneRepublic) — The chorus ("It's too late to apologize...") is a simple two-line repeat with an interesting interval jump.
>
> "Never Say Never" (The Fray) — The memorable hook of this song ("Don't let me go") is repeated over and over with only a slight variation at the end of the third line. Chord changes underneath the repeated lines help to add interest and momentum.

> **Pattern #2: Repetition at the beginning of lines**
> Start each line with the same melody. Try keeping three or more notes the same then use a different ending.

"Reasons to Love You" (Meiko) — Each line of the chorus begins with the same three notes under "I wanna…" but ends differently.

Here's another example of this type of repetition using a longer repeated phrase. Altering the lyrics while repeating the melody line can keep repetition interesting.

"The Climb" (Miley Cyrus) — The first six lines of the chorus begin with the same long melodic phrase. The lyrics vary with each repeat.

➢ **Pattern #3: Repetition followed by a "payoff line"**
Repetition builds tension that can then be resolved with a payoff line, a line that creates a sense of release and completion. (Read Shortcut 25 for more on *tension* and *release.*)

"Shattered" (O.A.R.) — In the chorus, a pair of lines with strong repetition ("How many times… / Over the line…") is followed by a line that releases the tension and wraps up the melodic thought. Then the whole pattern is repeated.

"The Man Who Can't Be Moved" (The Script) – The long, sinuous melody lines of the chorus are repeated (with different lyrics) until the payoff beginning with "And you'll see me waiting for you…" Very effective!

➢ **Pattern #4: Repetition with variation**
Even if some of the note pitches are changed, listeners will perceive a similar line as a repeat.

"Cannonball" (Damien Rice) — In both the verse and chorus, the repeated lines are followed by a third repeat that varies the note pitches but preserves the note rhythm pattern. This is followed by a payoff line. This beautiful hit song was used in several television shows.

➢ **Pattern #5: Alternating repetitions**
Instead of a series of repeated lines, some patterns alternate between two phrases, repeating a melody on the first and third lines and a different melody on the second and fourth lines.

"Breathe In Breathe Out" (Mat Kearney) — You can hear a strong example of this pattern in the verse section. It opens with a long line that begins with the title ("Breathe in, breathe out…") then moves on to a different melody line ("Everybody bleeds…"). Afterwards, the pair of melody lines repeats to create an alternating pattern.

Verse melody patterns

Verse melodies also use a lot of repetition, often one of the same patterns listed in this Shortcut. However, it's a good idea to avoid using the *same* pattern in both your verse and chorus. For instance, if you use an alternating pattern in your verse, try a pattern that features a series of repeated lines in your chorus. If you do decide, for some reason, to use the same pattern in both sections, then consider adding a pre-chorus between them to create contrast and give listeners a break.

Use a pattern to build a melody on your anchor line

Just as the title of your song provides a focal point from which you can develop the rest of your lyric, so a single melodic phrase, like the one you created in Shortcut 31 can be used as the beginning of a pattern, a foundation on which to build a strong, focused melody. As you listen to songs you like, notice how often melodies are built on the note pattern of the first line, repeating and varying it before moving on to something new.

Do It Now

Listen to the song examples given in this Shortcut and learn to recognize patterns of repetition. Listen to some of the other songs in the "Film & TV Song List" on page 310 to practice finding and recognizing patterns. Write down the patterns you find.

See the "Film & TV Song List" on page 310 for information about the song examples in this Shortcut. "Shortcut Resources" on page 307 can help you find the films and shows that include these songs.

Shortcut #33

Write a Melody to a Chord Progression. Do It Now!

Take what you've learned and begin writing your film/TV song.

You can put together the melody and chord techniques from the previous Shortcuts and use them to begin creating the music for a strong film and TV song. Start by creating a single song section, either a verse or chorus. You can add on to it later.

1. **Decide on a groove and tempo.**
   Use a drum loop or guitar strum to create a rhythmic feel and keep a steady beat at a tempo that conveys the energy you want for your song. Remember, rhythmic feel and tempo can make a big difference in the type of scene your song will enhance and the effect it will have on the audience (Shortcuts 19 and 20).

2. **Choose a chord progression.**
   Use one of the progressions in Shortcut 28, vary it by adding or changing notes (Shortcut 29), or write a progression of your own.

3. **Make a rough recording.**
   Record your chord progression and rhythmic feel so you don't have to think about them while you work on your melody. You can use music sequencing software or just record it directly onto a cassette or digital recorder. The quality isn't important at this stage.

   Put it all together and see what happens!

4. **Write an anchor melody line.**
   Create a melody line to use as the first line of your song section. Use the suggestions for creating an anchor melody line in Shortcut 31.

5. **Develop your anchor line into a full song section.**
   Build on your anchor melody line using the suggestions for melodic patterns in Shortcut 32.

If you like where your melody is headed, then consider using it as the raw material for this song section. Make a rough recording and keep it as a reference while you move ahead.

Moving forward

At this point, you have a choice: You can either write a melody for another section of your song (a verse or bridge) or begin writing lyrics to the melody you have.

➤ **Add another song section:** Go through steps 2 through 5 to create a new section for your song. If you wrote a chorus the first time through, then write a verse. If you're writing in the Verse / Verse / Bridge / Verse form, then write a bridge.

➤ **Begin writing lyrics:** Add a lyric to your anchor melody line. If you're working on a chorus, consider writing a lyric that includes a song title in the first line. Use Shortcut 46 to help you choose a strong title for film and television. Look for a phrase that works with the feel and rhythm of your melody. It may take a little searching but you'll find it. If you want to try a different approach, you can create an anchor melody line with a built-in lyric. Read Shortcut 34 to find out how.

Rewriting your melody

Don't stop with your first draft. Rewrite!

In the next few Shortcuts, you'll find tips for rewriting your melody. Feel free to play around with it, shape it, mold it into something that you like better. If you find that you're drifting too far away from your original idea or you don't like a change you've made, just undo it. Go back to an earlier version and pick up from there.

Keep a fun, playful attitude as you work. Don't be critical at this stage. This is just an exercise, a way to explore song ideas. Give yourself permission to write something that doesn't sound good the very minute it pops out. Rewriting can turn a mediocre melody into a powerhouse but you've got to give it a chance.

Know when to walk away

It's important to stay fresh and keep some perspective on your song. Overworking a song can cause you to make changes just because you're bored. Remember, listeners will never play your song over and over for hours, thinking about tiny changes. Come back after a 30-minute break and listen with fresh ears. Make notes of anything you'd like to change, work for a while then take another break. You'll be glad you did!

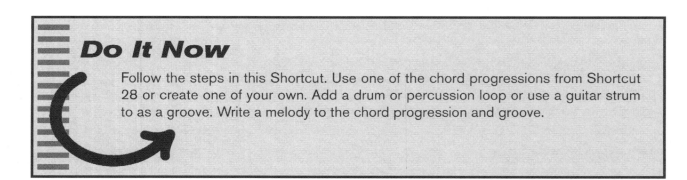

Do It Now

Follow the steps in this Shortcut. Use one of the chord progressions from Shortcut 28 or create one of your own. Add a drum or percussion loop or use a guitar strum to as a groove. Write a melody to the chord progression and groove.

Shortcut #34

Create a Melody
That Expresses Emotion

Try the techniques that actors use to communicate feelings.

Good actors know how to deliver emotional dialogue in a compelling, convincing way. They know that emotions change the way we speak. Excitement makes the voice rise in pitch; disappointment and resignation make the pitch fall. Anxiety and fear increase the pace of speech; relaxation and a sense of security slow the pace. An actor can vocalize strong emotion by using:

- Pitch . . . . high or low voice

- Emphasis . . . . . loud or soft voice

- Rhythm . . . . patterns of emphasis

- Pace . . . . fast or slow speech

Now, think about this: When your song is used in film and TV, it becomes another actor in the scene, delivering lines before, after, and between the dialogue lines. Your song makes an important statement and, like an actor, you want to be certain that the pitch, rhythm, and pace of your melody support it and add believability to it.

Add emotional expression to your melody

Here's a great songwriting game that will help you practice writing melodies that support the emotion in a lyric.

1. **Watch a TV show or movie.** Look for scenes with plenty of emotion, maybe a relationship that's breaking up, a happy reunion, or a verbal confrontation.

2. **Choose one or two emotional lines of dialogue to work with.** Replay the scene a couple times and listen to the way the lines are delivered. Now say the lines yourself; try to copy the way the actor said them. Repeat them a few times.

3. **Notice the pitches of the words.** Some words will be pitched a little higher, some lower. Start your melody by exaggerating these pitches. Raise the high ones higher and drop the low ones lower. Keeping the overall high and low pattern, try singing a rough melody line using the words.

4. **Preserve the rhythm and pace.** If there's a pause during the phrase, keep that pause in your melody. If the lines were delivered in a choppy or smooth manner, at a fast or slow pace, keep that feel in your melody, too.

Exaggerate the actor's delivery to create a melody that supports emotion.

5. **Increase the emphasis.** Notice the words in the phrase that were emphasized by the actor. See if you can increase this emphasis in your melody by accenting those words.

Use this exercise as a starting point for a song melody.

The melody you end up with at the end of the exercise might not sound like something you want to use. However, if you spend a little more time massaging the pitches and rhythm, it could turn into the start of a good film and TV song. You'll have a melody line with a lyric already attached to it, a lyric that's supported by the melody. You can develop a strong lyric from these lines using the Shortcuts in Part Five of this book. You can also treat the melody you created based on character dialogue as an anchor line and expand it with repetition as I showed you in Shortcut 32.

Variations on the melody game

You can mine other sources for expressive dialogue lines. Here are a few:

➤ **News shows:** Many news programs feature interviews with people who have been through a difficult experience. The emotions are real and so is the subject matter. You may find both strong, emotional lines and powerful themes for your songs here.

➤ **Talk and reality shows:** Aggressive tabloid talk shows and conflict-driven reality TV series are filled with emotion-laden dialogue.

➤ **Daytime Dramas:** These characters are constantly going through crises that result in strong, emotional dialogue lines. Look for the peak moments when events reach a turning point. Unfortunately, given the pace of these shows, it may take a while to get to one of those.

➤ **DIY:** If you find that using existing dialogue is too limiting, look for a line that interests you and then say it yourself with plenty of feeling. Pump up the emotion as you repeat the line until you can begin to hear the pitch and rhythm in the phrase.

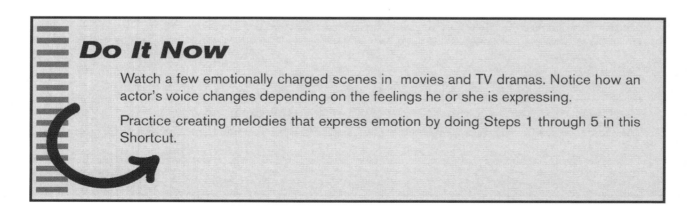

Do It Now

Watch a few emotionally charged scenes in movies and TV dramas. Notice how an actor's voice changes depending on the feelings he or she is expressing.

Practice creating melodies that express emotion by doing Steps 1 through 5 in this Shortcut.

Shortcut #35

Take Your Melody to the Next Level

*Use a mix of predictable and surprising elements
to captivate listeners.*

Up to this point, I've been suggesting ways to create a melody that's memorable, one that sticks with the listener after a film or TV show is over. But wait a minute! Songs like "Twinkle, Twinkle, Little Star" and "Pop Goes the Weasel" are memorable. Is that the kind of melody you should be writing? I was going to answer that by saying, "Of course not!" but I had second thoughts. The answer is actually, "Yes and no." If you take the first seven notes of "Twinkle, Twinkle, Little Star," start the phrase on an unexpected beat, then repeat that seven-note phrase, and play an interesting groove under it—suddenly it could work! It still needs a new lyric, but the music would be fine underneath a wide range of scenes.

➤ A mix of *predictable* and *surprising* elements works well for film and TV. The familiar, predictable aspects of a melody make it memorable while unexpected, surprising twists keep it interesting.

Create a mix of predictable and surprising elements

Predictable List:
1. Melodic phrases that start on the first beat of the measure, Beat 1.
2. A phrase that consists of notes that are all the same length.
3. A series of phrases that are the same length.
4. Pauses that occur regularly, for instance at the end of every line.
5. High notes or long notes that fall on the strong beats (Beat 1 or Beat 3).
6. Repetition of melody lines.

For a memorable, interesting melody, mix items from these two lists.

Surprise List:
1. Melodic phrases that start on Beat 2, 3, 4 or the "and" between beats.
2. A phrase that includes both long and short notes.
3. A variety of phrase lengths.
4. Pauses that occur in the middle of lines.
5. Lines that run together without a pause.
6. High or long notes that fall on weak beats (Beat 2, Beat 4, or the "and" between beats).

The "Twinkle Test"

Although "Twinkle, Twinkle, Little Star" is memorable, it includes too many of the features on the Predictable List to capture the interest of today's listeners.

However, if you start the first phrase of the song on the "and" after Beat 1 and shift the rest of the phrase accordingly, you then get rid of #1 and #5 on the Predictable List and add #1 and #6 on the Surprise List.

Try the Twinkle Test for yourself. Sing nonsense syllables like "la la" instead of the words. Tap or clap a steady four-beat rhythm. Count "1 *and* 2 *and* 3 *and* 4 *and*. Start singing on the "and" after Beat 1. Sing the first seven notes then repeat them. It will feel odd at first but as you continue to sing and get comfortable with it, it will begin to sound like a new melody. Try playing a C chord under the first phrase, then an A minor under the repeat.

Bring it on home

You can have fun mixing items from the two lists (Predictable and Surprise) in melodies of your own. Use a drum loop or guitar strum that emphasizes Beat 1 to help you keep track of where you are. Then you can...

> **Shift a melody phrase earlier or later:** You can move a phrase that starts on Beat 1 to the "and" just before or after it. In fact you can start it on any beat you like. Try starting your phrases on a variety of different beats.

> **Change the lengths of your notes:** If you have a series of notes that are all the same length and your melody sounds predictable, try lengthening some and shortening others.

> **Extend or shorten your phrases:** Add a few extra notes to one of your phrases. Run it right up to the phrase that follows to create one long phrase. Or drop a couple notes from the middle to create two short phrases.

> **Sing a high note or start a long note on a weak beat:** Add unpredictability by raising a note pitch so that a high note lands on an "and" or on Beat 2 or 4. Starting a long note on an "and" or on Beat 2 or 4 also creates a feeling of surprise.

Go ahead and try reworking a melody of your own using elements from the Surprise List. If you feel your melody is getting too complicated, add more items from the Predictable List. Change the mix to suit your taste.

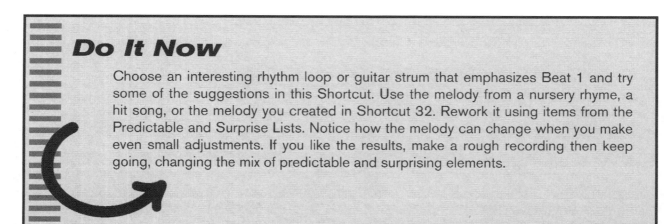

Do It Now

Choose an interesting rhythm loop or guitar strum that emphasizes Beat 1 and try some of the suggestions in this Shortcut. Use the melody from a nursery rhyme, a hit song, or the melody you created in Shortcut 32. Rework it using items from the Predictable and Surprise Lists. Notice how the melody can change when you make even small adjustments. If you like the results, make a rough recording then keep going, changing the mix of predictable and surprising elements.

Shortcut #36

Give Your Melody and Chords a Fresh Relationship

Move emphasized melody notes away from your chord changes.

Melody and chords are so closely woven together it's hard to think about popular song melodies without hearing the chords that accompany them. However, as in most relationships, melody and chords can fall into a rut—doing things by habit, recycling the same tired ideas. When that happens, it's time to stir things up and get the excitement back again.

When chords and melody get too close

Songwriters who write a song while playing a chord progression often fall into the habit of starting a new melody and lyric phrase when they make a chord change, usually on Beat 1, the strongest beat in a measure. It's only natural: your hands move, you think "new chord" and it gives the signal to your brain that now's the time to start a new melody and lyric thought. Everything changes at once and it's all emphasized. This is what listeners expect to hear so it feels predictable, too predictable for today's melodies.

You could keep the emphasis on Beat 1 in your melody and change your *chord* on a different beat but that's not very popular with listeners right now. They like to hear hypnotic, repetitive chord progressions that emphasize Beat 1. Instead, try changing your *melody* so that the important notes, like the first note of a phrase, don't parallel your chord changes. Here are some tips that will help you freshen up what could become a dull relationship.

Emphasized notes

In a melody, all notes are *not* created equal. Some notes are emphasized by virtue of their pitch, length, or the beat on which they land. Listeners notice these emphasized notes more than they notice other notes in your melody; they have more importance for listeners.

All notes in a melody are not equal! Emphasized notes have greater importance.

Some of the emphasized notes in a melody are:
- The note that falls on Beat 1 of a measure
- The longest or highest notes in a phrase
- The notes that are in the basic three-note chord you're playing
- The note that accompanies the first *important* word in a phrase

When a lyric phrase begins with pick-up words like "then," "and," or "Oh, baby," these notes are not emphasized even though they may be the first in a phrase. The lyric and melody will often work just fine without them.

Change the emphasis

To create an interesting relationship between your melody and chords, think about moving emphasized notes so they don't fall on a chord change.

Four ways to change the relationship of melody to chord progression.

➤ **Start your phrase after a chord change on Beat 1.**
Play the chord, then start singing your melody a beat or two later. Even a half beat later can make a big difference. Listen to "The Climb" by Miley Cyrus. All of the verse lines, beginning with the first line of the song, start on the "and" after Beat 1 and they emphasize Beat 2.

➤ **Start your phrase before a chord change on Beat 1.**
You can anticipate a chord change by starting your melody one or two beats earlier and lead up to the chord change. The chorus of Sheryl Crow's "Everyday Is a Winding Road" is a great example. It begins on Beat 4 with the word "every" which is naturally emphasized because it is the first important word of the phrase. However, the words "day" and "road" are also emphasized because both words land on Beat 1 so there's a lot of interesting emphasis going on in this simple, catchy line.

➤ **Shift your phrase so the highest or longest note lands on a chord change on Beat 1.**
Here's an idea to play with: Write a phrase in which the highest or longest note is *not* the first note of the phrase. Then figure out where to start singing your phrase so that high or long note lands on Beat 1. It may take a little juggling to work out where to start singing but the effect is worth it. "Everyday Is a Winding Road" again provides a good example. "Day" and "road" are the longest notes of the phrase and "day" is also the highest note. Both land on Beat 1.

➤ **Emphasize a note on Beat 1 that's not in the chord.**
If a melody line relies heavily on notes that are in the basic three-note chord you're playing, it will have a predictable sound. Folk songs and traditional hymns like "Amazing Grace" have melodies that rely heavily on the notes in the accompanying chord. If that's the style in which you're writing, by all means emphasize notes like that—a song in that style would sound strange if you didn't.

However, if you want something that sounds more contemporary, consider emphasizing notes that are *not* in the chord, like the ones *between* the notes of the chord or just above or just below it. Use one of these notes on Beat 1 as the first note of your phrase or as the longest or highest note in the melody line. Sarah Bettens's song "Rescue Me" has many wonderful examples in the refrain that begins "Will you rescue me...." The emphasized note (the first syllable of "rescue") is a C# sung over a D chord. This song seems simple and repetitive at first hearing but the surprising, emphasized notes in the melody and harmony parts add plenty of interest.

Put the melody in charge

If you let the chord progression lead the way when composing a melody, you're likely to end up with a song that sounds predictable.

➤ **Record your chord progression.**
Try breaking free of the habit of starting every melody line when you change chords by recording your chord progression so you're not physically playing it while you compose the melody. You'll have more freedom to explore different ideas like shifting the beginnings of phrases and singing notes outside the chord.

Try this idea for freeing up your melody.

➤ **Sing through a chord change.**
Keep your melody and lyric thought going as you change chords. To hear this technique, listen to the verse and chorus of "The Man Who Can't Be Moved" by The Script. Both sections feature long lyric and melody phrases that weave through several chord changes. In general, long phrases put more weight and attention on the melody and less on the chords.

When you change the relationship of a melody line to an underlying chord progression, you're moving your song away from what listeners expect to hear and toward something that surprises them. This is a good thing but be careful not to overdo it. If you add too many unexpected twists, listeners could feel overwhelmed. Consider repeating lines that have a surprising melody and chord relationship before moving on to something new. Use the patterns of line repetition in Shortcut 32 to help you keep your melody well organized and keep your listener by your side.

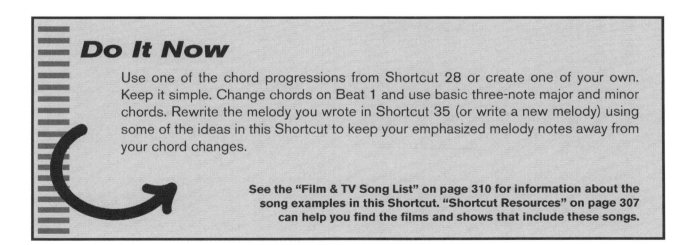

Do It Now

Use one of the chord progressions from Shortcut 28 or create one of your own. Keep it simple. Change chords on Beat 1 and use basic three-note major and minor chords. Rewrite the melody you wrote in Shortcut 35 (or write a new melody) using some of the ideas in this Shortcut to keep your emphasized melody notes away from your chord changes.

See the "Film & TV Song List" on page 310 for information about the song examples in this Shortcut. "Shortcut Resources" on page 307 can help you find the films and shows that include these songs.

Shortcut #37

Communicate a Mood or Atmosphere with Your Music

The best exercise for learning how chords, rhythm, and melody support a scene.

Tip: Don't wait around for inspiration. Go out and find it!

A camera panning across a city street is just a view of buildings and cars, but if you play Frank Sinatra's "Theme from New York, New York" as you watch it, suddenly the scene springs vividly to life, full of energy and possibilities—it has an emotional atmosphere. Creating an atmosphere or mood to underscore a scene and enhance the viewer's experience is one of the most useful jobs your song can perform! It can set the tone for a wild party or a walk down a spooky back alley, evoke an atmosphere of romance and adventure, or put viewers in the mood for a high-energy car chase.

While lyrics play an important role in creating this effect, the heavy lifting is done by the music—chords, melody, and rhythmic feel. After all, if you watched that same city street scene and *read* the lyrics to the "Theme from New York, New York" you wouldn't have the same reaction at all! Lyrics are useful for focusing and directing attention but it's the music that establishes and amplifies atmosphere, mood, and energy.

Use your ears to get ideas

Here's a great exercise for quickly tuning your ear to the kinds of songs that will work for various types of onscreen scenes. TV shows, films, and commercials all make frequent, effective use of instrumental music. As you watch a scene or commercial, notice the type of music that's used and the mood it creates. For instance, a high-energy action scene that's pumped up with a fast paced, repetitive music cue will get your pulse racing and draw you into the action. *A song that has those same qualities is likely to work just as well in a similar scene.*

Listen to background instrumental music and write down the aspects of the melody, chords, and rhythmic feel that are most obvious to you. Use the following questions as a guide.

Study background instrumental music.

- What is the predominant mood of the scene? For instance, is it sad, upbeat, romantic, angry, yearning, or anxious?

- Does the pace of the music feel fast or slow or somewhere in-between to you?

- Is there a rhythmic feel or groove? How is it being created (drum kit, guitar strum, piano, orchestra, other)?

- Does the music have an overall major or minor feel?

👂 Is there a melody line? Does the melody have a lot of repetition or a little? Are the melodic phrases short or long?

👂 If you close your eyes and listen to the music, what kind of atmosphere or energy does it convey? Does it support the scene?

It's not an exact science

No one can tell you *exactly* what type of music will work best with a scene. Directors, producers, and music supervisors are always looking for the music or song with the right feel; it's a decision that's often made on instinct or gut reaction. However, in the following three Shortcuts, you'll find suggestions for grooves, chords, and melody in three different ranges of mood and atmosphere that cover the majority of scenes in film and TV.

Follow your feelings!

You may hear different emotions in some of the songs listed as examples in the following Shortcuts. You might label a mood differently than I do. That's perfectly all right. Study the ways in which other songwriters and composers handle emotion but, ultimately, follow your own feelings. This is merely a starting point.

Remember this: If you keep a mood or atmosphere clearly in mind while you write, you're *much* more likely to get placements in film and TV than if you just take a stab in the dark and hope your song will work for something somewhere!

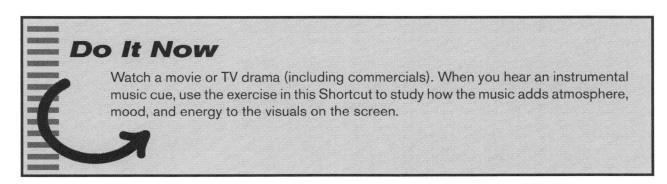

Do It Now

Watch a movie or TV drama (including commercials). When you hear an instrumental music cue, use the exercise in this Shortcut to study how the music adds atmosphere, mood, and energy to the visuals on the screen.

Shortcut #38

Create Music for a Song in a "High Energy" Scene

Use rhythm, chords, and melody to convey action and excitement.

High-energy scenes are generally easy to spot. They often feature a lot of physical activity: a chase, a fight, or a wild, out-of-control party. In some high-energy scenes, the emotion takes place in the character's thoughts, as in the case of fear or anticipation. In all of these cases, a high-energy song can be a very effective tool for communicating mood and atmosphere to the audience.

As you work through this Shortcut, focus on the music—rhythmic feel, chords, and melody—and don't worry about lyrics for now. Practice creating energy and mood with music alone. You can use nonsense syllables like "da da" as you write your melody, or, if you prefer to work with a lyric, use a rough lyric idea that gets the concept across. Rewrite and polish it later.

Mood or Atmosphere:

Excitement, Aggression, Momentum, Anxiety, Fear.

➤ **Groove:** To create a sense of motion or excitement, try a fast-paced duple rhythm at 140 BPM or faster. Or you can use a quadruple rhythm between 114 and 125 BPM. Remember that quad rhythms have many more accents and beat divisions than duple rhythms, so a slower tempo with a quad rhythm feels just as energetic as a faster duple feel.

See Shortcut 20 for info on duple and quad grooves.

You can use a guitar strum or drum loop to create the feel. For excitement, aggression, or a feeling of momentum, avoid cluttering up the groove; keep it straight ahead and steady as the Foo Fighters do in "The Pretender." To create anxious or nervous energy, try a more complex quad feel like Beck uses in "Youthless." Listen to the High Energy song examples at the end of this Shortcut for rhythm ideas.

➤ **Chord progression:** Keep it simple. Change chords once every two measures or once per measure at most. Changing chords more frequently than that could make your track sound too busy and detract from the rhythmic feel. Basic three-note major and minor chords work well here (Shortcut 30). Feature minor chords for a more aggressive, darker sound. If you feel you must use chords with added notes like min7 and add2, try holding them for more than one measure to give listeners a chance to really hear them (Shortcut 29).

➤ **Melody:** To create a sense of aggression, use short melodic phrases with plenty of repetition. You can hear this type of melody (with a minor feel in the chord progression) in "The Pretender" by the Foo Fighters. To underscore a feeling of motion and travel, hold some of your melody notes over several beats, as Sheryl Crow does in the chorus of "Everyday Is a Winding Road."

Also, in this type of uptempo song, you might want to aim for a linear melody, one that doesn't feature a lot of big interval jumps. In a fast-paced song, large jumps in the melody create a choppy feel and slow the sense of momentum. Save a big interval leap for the beginning of your chorus or verse where it will grab attention.

Use your melody to clearly define the structure of your song—chorus, verse, and bridge. At fast speeds, a verse and chorus can blend into each other, giving your song a monotonous feel. Try changing the note range or note pace of your melody between your chorus and verse to distinguish one from the other as Sheryl Crow does in "Everyday Is a Winding Road."

High Energy examples:

Duple groove: "The Pretender" (Foo Fighters), "After Hours" (We Are Scientists), "Don't Give Me a Hard Time" (The Locarnos)

Quad groove: "Top of the World" (Pussycat Dolls), "Everyday Is a Winding Road" (Sheryl Crow), "Youthless" (Beck), "Jungle Drum" (Emilana Torrini)

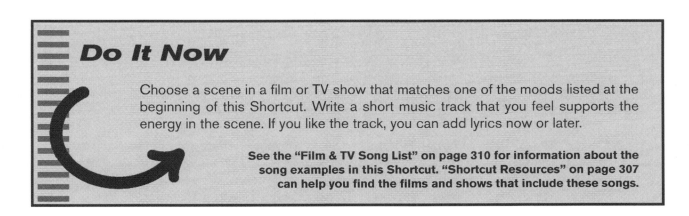

Do It Now

Choose a scene in a film or TV show that matches one of the moods listed at the beginning of this Shortcut. Write a short music track that you feel supports the energy in the scene. If you like the track, you can add lyrics now or later.

See the "Film & TV Song List" on page 310 for information about the song examples in this Shortcut. "Shortcut Resources" on page 307 can help you find the films and shows that include these songs.

Shortcut #39

Create Music for a Song in a "Medium Energy" Scene

Use rhythm, chords, and melody to express desire, determination, and more.

The majority of placements in film and TV are in the Medium Energy category. It covers a wide range of moods and atmospheres so it's appropriate for many scenes. These songs can be played at a low volume level to enhance a mood without distracting the audience, or at a high volume level to cap off an emotional scene. Overall, this type of song has a more deliberate, controlled feel than the High Energy group, but more momentum than the Slow Energy songs.

As in the previous Shortcut, keep your focus on the music and don't worry about lyrics for now. If you feel you need to work with a lyric, a rough idea of the final lyric will be fine. Rework it later.

Mood or Atmosphere:

Desire, Happiness, Determination, Concern, Romantic love, Anticipation, Frustration.

> **Groove:** For a Medium Energy feel, consider using a duple rhythm from 100 and 135 BPM or a quadruple rhythm in the range of 80 to 100 BPM. Both guitar strums and rhythm loops work well. In the quad rhythms, the strums and loops can range from body-swaying, sinuous styles like Tina Dico's "One" to basic guitar strums like Gavin Rossdale's "Love Remains the Same." Listen to the Medium Energy examples listed at the end of this Shortcut to hear a variety of different rhythmic feels in this category.

> **Chord progression:** The current sound in this style uses familiar, repetitive chord progressions, like the ones in Shortcut 28. You can create color and interest with added notes like min7 and add2, as well as bass motion with slash chords. At the faster tempos (120 BPM and above) be cautious about changing chords more than once per measure. In this category, you'll hear examples of progressions that lean on both major chords and minor chords depending on the mood the song expresses.

Read Shortcut 29 to learn more about slash chords and added notes.

> **Melody:** Melody is also a reflection of the emotion expressed in the song. For happy, upbeat themes try a chorus melody with rising lines that emphasize the notes in the basic chord accompanying the line, like the chorus of Colbie Caillat's "Fallin' for You." For a song that expresses desire or concern lean more on descending lines. Compare the chorus melody of "Save Me" by Remy Zero with "Fallin' for You" to hear the difference.

In the tempo range of this category, the audience has time to absorb interesting melody lines. Give your melody and chord progression a fresh relationship by using notes that complement but are not in the accompanying chord. If you change chords on Beat 1, try starting your melodic phrases on a different beat (Shortcut 36).

Medium Energy examples:

Duple groove: "I Gotta Feeling" (Black Eyed Peas), "Fallin' for You" (Colbie Caillat), "99 Times" (Kate Voegele), "Shattered" (O.A.R.), "Poker Face" (Lady Gaga)

Quad groove: "Save Me" (Remy Zero), "This Is Me" (Demi Lovato), "One" (Tina Dico), "Waiting On the World to Change" (John Mayer), "Rescue Me" (Sarah Bettens), "Sun Comes Up" (John Legend), "Love Remains the Same" (Gavin Rossdale)

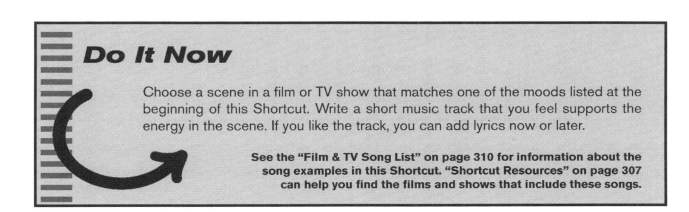

Do It Now

Choose a scene in a film or TV show that matches one of the moods listed at the beginning of this Shortcut. Write a short music track that you feel supports the energy in the scene. If you like the track, you can add lyrics now or later.

See the "Film & TV Song List" on page 310 for information about the song examples in this Shortcut. "Shortcut Resources" on page 307 can help you find the films and shows that include these songs.

Shortcut #40

Create Music for a Song in a "Slow Energy" Scene

Use rhythm, chords, and melody to support introspective or sad scenes.

"Slow" doesn't mean "no" or "low" energy. A slow song can express plenty of energy, emotion, and atmosphere. "My Heart Will Go On" from the film *Titanic* is an excellent example of a very slow song that sustains interest, creates a haunting, ethereal atmosphere, and inspires emotion. Rap songs create tremendous energy at slow tempos by piling up rhythmical words between the beats.

As in the previous Shortcuts, make the music your focal point for now. Don't worry about writing a final, polished lyric. If you feel you need to work with a lyric, a rough version of your idea will be fine. You can always rewrite it later.

Mood or Atmosphere:

Resignation, Sorrow, Uncertainty, Sensuality.
(Some Rap styles use slow energy to express anger.).

➢ **Groove:** Quadruple rhythms work well at these slower tempos. They create energy by dividing each beat into four parts and using accents to add interest. Try a quad feel in the slow range of 60 to 80 BPM for this style. Hip-hop beat loops often utilize a slow quad feel. If you play keyboard, try using one of these grooves. You can lay a singer-songwriter style melody and lyric on it for an interesting, fresh sound.

Guitar strums work well at this slow pace. A strum with a quadruple feel can accent a variety of beats, drop out beats, or move from a sparse to a steady beat to create changes in dynamics. For instance, a verse could feature a light strum, or even fingerpicking, then develop into a steadier, fuller strumming pattern in the chorus. Listen to the dynamic build from the duple verse to the quadruple feel of the chorus of "Falling Slowly" by Glen Hansard to hear how this is handled.

A duple feel in the 50 to 80 BPM range can work for a big ballad like "My Heart Will Go On" but could be risky otherwise. If you're using a duple feel, consider playing on every beat, as well as the "and" between each beat to add energy as The Fray does on "Never Say Never."

A triplet feel is a good alternative at this slow pace. Just subdivide each beat into three parts. Listen to Etta James's "At Last" to hear this groove.

➤ **Chord progression:** At slow tempos, you can draw attention to your chord progression without worrying about whether it will compete with groove and melody. There's plenty of room for everything! Consider changing chords more frequently than once per measure during one of the sections of your song, perhaps on the measures leading up to the chorus or during your verse. Full, rich chords work well here; the audience has enough time to savor an interesting four-note chord. Try a mix of basic three-note chords with others that have more color and complexity (Shortcut 29).

➤ **Melody:** It's very easy for listeners to lose focus at slow speeds if the melody sounds like it might be wandering. It's a good idea to use a clear pattern of repetition and variation in your melody. One popular pattern features a repeat of your opening melody line, then a move to a different line, then back to your first melody again. Listen to the examples in the list at the end of this Shortcut to hear how repetitive melody patterns are used at slow speeds.

You'll find melody patterns you can use in your songs in Shortcut 32.

Keep your melody moving. At slow speeds, long pauses will try the patience of your listener. If your melody lines are followed by two- or three-beat pauses, consider filling those in by adding a couple of notes and words to the end of a line. Soaring melodies with a wide note range give listeners a sense of motion and change that can compensate for a slow tempo.

Slow Energy examples:

Duple groove: "Beautiful" (Christina Aguilera) "Never Say Never" (The Fray), "My Heart Will Go On" (Celine Dion)

Triplet groove (each beat is divided into three): "At Last" (Etta James)

Quad groove: "Sweet and Low" (Augustana), "I'm Yours" (Jason Mraz), "Cannonball" (Damien Rice)

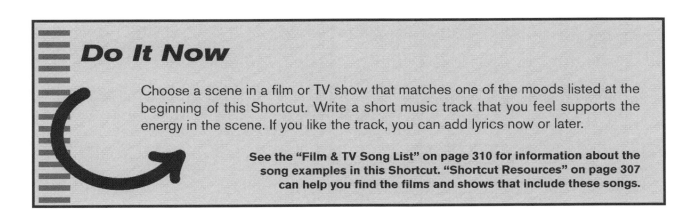

Do It Now

Choose a scene in a film or TV show that matches one of the moods listed at the beginning of this Shortcut. Write a short music track that you feel supports the energy in the scene. If you like the track, you can add lyrics now or later.

See the "Film & TV Song List" on page 310 for information about the song examples in this Shortcut. "Shortcut Resources" on page 307 can help you find the films and shows that include these songs.

Shortcut #41

Transport the Audience to a Location or Past Era

Summon up a time or place with an authentic music style.

Films and TV shows sometimes use songs and instrumental music as a quick and effective way to tell the audience when and where a scene takes place. A few seconds of a Rockabilly song, the rhythm of a Charleston, an Appalachian Folk tune, or a Beach Boys-style Surf song can evoke a whole world for the viewer. To be effective, though, the music must sound authentic. Whether you're writing songs for a period musical, like the British Invasion-style of *That Thing You Do!,* or evoking a locale with a regional style like the songs in *The Big Easy* or *Paris 36,* the music and lyrics of your song need to be credible in order to believably summon up the time or place.

Write authentic sounding music

Every historical and regional music style has a recognizable sound that is the result of a unique mix of musical elements—chords, melody, and rhythmic feel, as well as instrumentation and performance. To be authentic, every aspect needs to be true to the style you want to evoke.

Research the songs of a specific era or locale.

To recreate one of these styles in a song of your own, start by focusing on the music itself. Listen to authentic recordings whenever possible. There are specialty record labels, like Smithsonian Folkways, that offer hard-to-find genres. You can find re-releases of classic recordings from labels like Chess Records and Stax Records. If the style you're interested in is from an era before recorded music, look for sheet music. Check the large collections available for free through the Library of Congress at www.memory.loc.gov. For ethnic music styles, search YouTube for video of performances by authentic musicians and explore some of the labels that specialize in regional styles, like Arhoolie Records, Putumayo, and Harmonia Mundi.

Choose songs that are characteristic of the style, ones that you feel have *many* of the qualities that are associated with the era or regional sound. Don't pick something on the fringes, that one unique song that could have been written anytime, anywhere! Use this list of questions to explore the rhythm, chords, and melody characteristics of the style in which you want to write.

Rhythmic Feel
- What is the tempo (BPM) of the song?
- What kind of rhythmic feel is played? Try playing along to see how it feels.

🦻 Chords

- What chords are used? Are they basic three-note chords? If there are four-note chords, which ones are they?
- How often do the chords change, once per measure, more than once?
- Do the chords follow the melody closely or stick to a steady, regular chord progression?
- What chords are used to transition from one song section to another? To resolve at the ends of sections?

🦻 Structure

- What is the song structure?
- Is there a dynamic build and release in the song? Where?
- How long is the intro?
- Does the ending fade out or is there a definitive ending?

🦻 Melody

- Does the melody use a variety of phrase lengths?
- On which beats do the phrases begin?
- What is the pattern of repeated melody lines? Where do the lines vary?
- Does the melody use syncopation (emphasis on Beat 2, Beat 4 and the "and" between beats)?

Once you can answer these questions, you should be able to write a melody, chord progression, and rhythmic feel in a regional or period style. Read Shortcut 63 for suggestions on writing lyrics for songs in these styles.

Do It Now

Choose a regional or historical style that interests you. Listen to songs in the style and answer the questions in this Shortcut. Try writing a verse and chorus in your chosen style.

Shortcut #42

Write Music for Film and TV Musicals

Is it Classic, Contemporary, or a tale of another time or place?

When it comes to writing music, there are three broad categories of film and TV musicals. Each one takes a somewhat different approach to chord progressions, melody style, and rhythmic feel. If you're pitching songs to a specific project, you'll want to find out as early as possible which style the project is using so you can tailor your songs to fit. If you're developing a complete musical from scratch and hope to pitch it to the film and TV market, knowing which style currently appeals to audiences can help you find a financial backer.

The Classic musical style

Songs in this musical genre often feature the music and chord style of standards from the big Broadway musicals of the 1950s. Many of the songs from Disney's popular animated musicals, *The Little Mermaid, Aladdin,* and *Beauty and the Beast,* are in this style. A catchy song like "That's How You Know" from Disney's *Enchanted* is a good example of the Classic musical sound.

Study some of the great songs from Classic musicals of the 1950s to learn this style.

> **Chords:** Chord progressions in these songs are more complex than a contemporary Pop or Rock song. They follow the melody more closely, and use diminished, augmented, and four-note chords to add richness and color. There are abrupt key changes in these songs, sometimes in unexpected places, and single chords are used that are outside of the basic seven chords within the key.

> **Melody:** The Classic musical melody features plenty of motion and emotion. Big ballads rely on soaring chorus melodies to create peak moments. Interval jumps, a wide note range, and interesting melodic rhythm patterns work well here. Melody is one of the featured elements in this style so you can add complexity without losing your audience.

> **Rhythm:** The emphasis in these songs is clearly on melody and lyrics. The rhythmic accompaniment is de-emphasized except when needed to create a specific feel, as in Caribbean, African, or Latin songs. Even then, the rhythm is generally familiar and comfortable. This ensures that it won't grab too much attention, allowing melody and lyrics to remain in the spotlight.

> **Song types:** The Adult Contemporary radio singles from Disney's animated musicals, songs like "Beauty and the Beast" and "A Whole New World," are written in the classic Pop ballad style favored by artists like Celine Dion. The wide note ranges of these songs and changes in dynamics show off the vocal skills of the singer. Musically, they mix the chords and melody style

of Broadway standards with some of the more repetitive, simpler chord progressions of today's Pop and Rock hits.

The Classic musical also includes humorous songs called "patter songs." These are songs with fast-paced lyrics that surprise and entertain the listener with rhymes and wordplay. "Mine, Mine, Mine" from Disney's *Pocahontas* is a great example. The music takes a back seat, supporting the lyrics, never getting in the way. Short phrases and repetitive note patterns at a lively tempo work well here. (See Shortcut 62 for suggestions on writing lyrics for these songs.)

The Contemporary Musical style

Examples of film and TV musicals with a contemporary Pop, Rock, and Hip-hop sound include *Hannah Montana: The Movie,* Disney's *High School Musical* and *Camp Rock* franchises, *Hustle and Flow,* and *Once.* The songs in these projects use the chord, melody, and rhythmic styles that are heard on contemporary radio. In fact, some of the songs crossover to radio and become hit singles in their own right.

These musicals need a current sound.

➢ **Chords and Melody:** The chords and melody Shortcuts in this book and in my book, *Shortcuts to Hit Songwriting: 126 Proven Techniques for Writing Songs That Sell,* can help you craft your music for this style. Use current hit songs as guides, especially if you're writing for a teen audience. A song like "This Is Me" from *Camp Rock* is a good example of the Teen Pop hit song style that will interest record labels and music publishers. Making a deal for the soundtrack album can help raise your credibility and financial backing.

➢ **Rhythmic feel:** Rhythm is a much more important element in the Contemporary musical style than in the Classic musical. A solid rhythmic groove creates energy and drives the momentum of songs like "Now or Never" (*High School Musical 3: Senior Year)* and "This Is Me" (*Camp Rock*). A cutting-edge rhythm track is essential for a Hip-hop song like "It's Hard Out Here for a Pimp" (*Hustle and Flow*). Strong, well-crafted rhythm tracks help to give these songs the current, commercial flavor audiences expect to hear. When you record your demos, be sure to spend time crafting the rhythmic feel to give it a fresh sound.

Check out Shortcut 20 for more on rhythmic feels and grooves.

➢ **Song types:** Contemporary musicals often feature fictional artists or bands or real artists playing that role. The songs are a mix of featured performances (in concert, in rehearsal, in a recording studio) alongside songs that express the character's emotions. Keep the music appropriate for the artist's fictional music style. For emotional ballads with a contemporary sound use a mid-tempo feel, create a memorable anchor melody line, and use a pattern of phrase repetition (Shortcut 32). Adding plenty of dynamic build from verse to chorus will intensify the overall emotional energy as it does in "The Climb" (*Hannah Montana: The Movie*).

Contemporary musicals also include humorous songs, dance numbers, and character songs by the bad guys and sidekicks. Good examples of these songs: "I Want It All" (*High School Musical 3: Senior Year*) and "Hoedown Throwdown" (*Hannah Montana: The Movie*). Here, too, the music style is current, with a strong emphasis on rhythm. The lyrics need room to shine so avoid drawing too much attention to the melody and chords.

Musicals that feature an era or locale

Many film and stage musicals are set in time periods and locations that have their own particular sound; *Music and Lyrics, Grace of My Heart, That Thing You Do!, Paris 36, Dreamgirls,* and *Chicago* feature songs that spring from an era and locale, as well as the characters' emotions.

> **Chords, melody, and rhythmic feel:** To write music for this style, study the songs of the time or place in which the musical is set. Use the list of questions in Shortcut 41 to help you identify the characteristics of the musical style then incorporate those into your songs.

> Sometimes a song is meant to suggest rather than authentically represent a time or place, especially if the producers are looking for a radio single. *Dreamgirls* features several songs with an authentic Motown sound while other songs, especially the blockbuster "And I Am Telling You I'm Not Going," blend R&B and Gospel with elements of the Classic musical style.

> **Song types:** The songs in this style are generally the same as in the Classic musical style with extra emphasis on music that sets the scene and atmosphere. Big ballads, patter songs, dance songs, and character songs are all part of the mix.

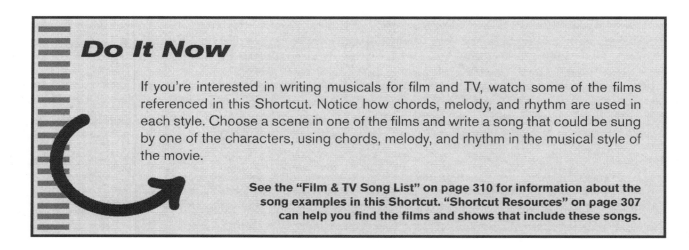

Do It Now

If you're interested in writing musicals for film and TV, watch some of the films referenced in this Shortcut. Notice how chords, melody, and rhythm are used in each style. Choose a scene in one of the films and write a song that could be sung by one of the characters, using chords, melody, and rhythm in the musical style of the movie.

See the "Film & TV Song List" on page 310 for information about the song examples in this Shortcut. "Shortcut Resources" on page 307 can help you find the films and shows that include these songs.

Shortcut #43

Make Your Music and Lyric Work Together

Match the mood of your music to the emotion in your lyric.

Like good friends, lyrics and music bring out the best in each other. But even good friends don't always get along. When words and music disagree, the effectiveness of both can be diminished. Is your music flying along so fast that a thoughtful lyric is getting lost? Is your melody rising, creating optimism, when your lyric is telling listeners that the singer is sinking into despair? While the music doesn't need to (and shouldn't) underline each and every word, overall it should add to the impact of the lyric by supporting the emotional content.

What is the mood of the music?

Tempo, groove, chords, and melody can all convey emotional feel and atmosphere. So what mood is your music conveying? If you wrote a music track using the Shortcuts in Part Three and Part Four of this book then you should have a pretty good idea of the mood of your track. But if you're still not sure or if you want to figure out the mood of an existing song, compare your song's tempo, groove, chord progression, and melody with the information and song examples in these Shortcuts:

➢ **Shortcut 38: Create Music for a Song in a "High Energy" Scene**
Find out if your music conveys excitement, aggression, momentum, anxiety, or fear.

➢ **Shortcut 39: Create Music for a Song in a "Medium Energy" Scene**
Find out if your music conveys desire, happiness, determination, concern, romantic love, anticipation, or frustration.

Identify the overall feel of your music.

➢ **Shortcut 40: Create Music for a Song in a "Slow Energy" Scene**
Find out if your music conveys resignation, sorrow, uncertainty, or sensuality.

Remember that music is not specific; it suggests and evokes an emotional direction. Once you identify an emotion or range of emotions in your music track, use your lyric to zero in on the feeling.

What is the emotion in the lyric?

If you're working with a song or lyric you've already written, try this: Read through the lyric, underlining the phrases and words that most effectively express the emotion in the song. You're likely to find them at the beginning or end of each section—chorus, verses, and bridge. Make a list of these words and phrases. This should be a summary of the emotional message in your song. Ask yourself what feeling is being described. If the emotion isn't clear to you, rewrite your lyric using Shortcuts 56 and 57.

Once you've identified a single emotion in your lyric, decide whether the overall mood of your music will complement or work against this feeling. If your music and lyrics aren't a good match, consider reworking the rhythmic feel, tempo, chords, or melody to support your lyric.

To write a lyric to a music track, build on the mood created by the music.

If you haven't yet written a lyric to your music track, this is a great opportunity to build on the mood you've created with your music. Use the overall feel of the music to suggest a lyric theme (Shortcut 18). Pick out the anchor melody line (Shortcut 31) and hum it a few times then begin writing lyric phrases suggested by the melody and your overall lyric theme. You don't have to limit yourself to just one or two ideas; make a whole list of lyric lines that are suggested by the melody and relate to your theme. Try singing your phrases to the melody. Which one feels like the best emotional fit to you? Develop that lyric phrase using the Shortcuts in the lyric section of this book. Use the rest of the lines somewhere else in your lyric.

Revising your song

There are many ways to match a lyric with music. We've all heard recordings of the same song that were very different in tempo and rhythmic feel. Each version interpreted the match between music and lyric in a new way. For your own song, choose the interpretation that feels right to you. There's no right or wrong way and nothing is final. You may decide to re-record your song later with a different tempo and feel. Anything can happen!

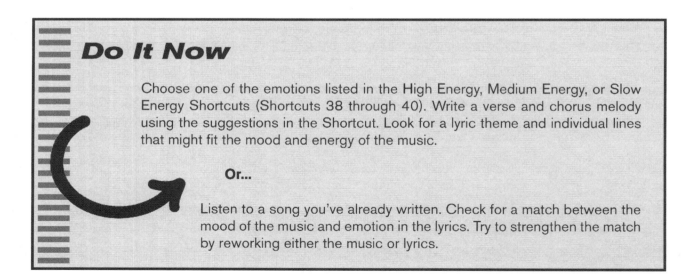

Do It Now

Choose one of the emotions listed in the High Energy, Medium Energy, or Slow Energy Shortcuts (Shortcuts 38 through 40). Write a verse and chorus melody using the suggestions in the Shortcut. Look for a lyric theme and individual lines that might fit the mood and energy of the music.

Or...

Listen to a song you've already written. Check for a match between the mood of the music and emotion in the lyrics. Try to strengthen the match by reworking either the music or lyrics.

Shortcut #44

The Film & TV Music Checklist

Strengthen and target your music for potential placements.

If you use the Shortcuts in this section of the book and Part Three, "Build Film & TV Songs on a Strong Foundation," you'll be able to create music that has emotional focus, a memorable melody, and solid structure. But, chances are, it will need some rewriting and polishing to really make it shine. Use this checklist to go over your structure, rhythmic feel, chords, and melody to ensure you've got the strongest film and TV pitch possible.

THE MUSIC CHECKLIST

1. **Do the rhythmic feel and tempo support your message?**
   The speed (in beats per minute) and rhythmic feel of your song affect the viewer's energy level. Be sure you've chosen a BPM and groove that support the message and mood you want to communicate to the audience. Take a look at the list of grooves and tempos in Shortcut 20 to see where your music fits.

2. **Is your song structure well defined?**
   Be sure your song structure is recognizable. A music supervisor will be looking for a strong, repeated refrain line or chorus section to punctuate a scene. Read Shortcuts 23 and 24 for suggestions on song structures that work well for the film and TV market.

3. **Did you build dynamics into your song structure?**
   To keep audiences interested, film and TV scenes must build and release intensity. Creating and releasing tension in your melody can help your song reinforce a scene's effectiveness in this important area. Shortcut 25 has several specific suggestions for creating dynamic changes like these in your music.

4. **Have you checked your song's length?**
   Is your song too short or underdeveloped? Consider fine-tuning your structure with the ideas in Shortcut 27.

5. **Are the chords appropriate for your song style?**
   Choosing whether to use three- or four-note chords can depend on what song style and message you want to convey. For more information on choosing the right chords for your song's energy and style, take a look at Shortcuts 38 through 40.

Give your music a final inspection. Tune up any weak areas.

✍ 6. **Did you write a solid anchor melody line?**
This is the melody line that listeners will remember. Try using a mix of note lengths and note motion. Read Shortcut 31 to find out more.

✍ 7. **Did you use a pattern of melodic phrases?**
Make your verse and chorus melodies easy to remember. Organize each section into patterns of phrases that include repetition and variation. Try one of the five patterns in Shortcut 32.

✍ 8. **Does your melody mix predictable with surprising elements?**
If your melody feels too familiar or predictable, try varying the phrase lengths, emphasizing weak beats, or eliminating a pause where one is expected. If your melody is too unpredictable for listeners to follow, add more familiar elements. Select from the lists in Shortcut 35.

✍ 9. **Is your song aimed at high, medium, or slow energy scenes?**
Fine-tune your song pitches by targeting a type of scene. Shortcuts 38 through 40 offer suggestions for creating a mood or atmosphere with your melody, chords, and grooves.

Target potential pitches while you're writing. Don't wait until your track is finished.

✍ 10. **Give your song the "film composer" test!**
Play your song (with or without lyrics) underneath a variety of scenes. Does it work better with some scenes than it does with others? Write down a brief description of the types of scenes your music supports effectively. If you haven't written your lyric yet, the description may help you choose a theme and language style.

Do It Now

Use the Shortcuts in Part Three and Part Four of this book to create a music track (with or without lyrics). Use the "Music Checklist" in this Shortcut to make sure your track is targeted at the film and TV market.

PART FIVE

Shortcuts to Lyrics for Film & TV Songs

Write lyrics that draw viewers deeper into a scene,

add depth to characters by revealing inner thoughts,

and pump up the energy with vivid language.

Shortcut #45

Choose a Theme That Will Get Your Song Noticed

The scriptwriter can be a songwriter's best friend.

The theme you choose for your song can make the difference between having a lot of opportunities for film and TV placements versus a mere handful. So it's worth taking the time to explore the kinds of themes that are featured frequently in film and television and learn how those same themes can be used in your song lyrics.

What is a theme anyway?

A theme is a unifying idea that runs through an entire story or song. It's often as simple as "Love hurts," or "Revenge is sweet." Think of it as the thread that ties everything together.

It's easy to confuse "theme" with "story." A story is a collection of events that illustrates a theme. For example, here's a story idea—"I'm moving to L.A. so I can become a famous Rock star and show those creeps in my high school that I'm not a loser." That sentence is a storyline illustrating the theme "Revenge is sweet." The theme itself is not stated; it's implied through the story line.

Find song themes that grab audiences

Ever since people began creating songs, plays, and stories, they've been looking for ideas that intrigue audiences and draw them in. Because television programming is driven by ratings and film success is measured in box office receipts, scriptwriters, now more than ever, must look for themes and storylines that attract a large number of viewers. They look for a central idea that audiences can understand and identify with; then they dress it up with characters and events to give it a fresh feel.

When a song is used with an onscreen scene, the lyric frequently echoes the theme that's being illustrated in the scene. By studying the themes that are used in TV dramas, films, and commercials, you can uncover ideas that will provide the basis for strong songs that will work well in this market.

A song lyric will often echo the theme of a scene.

Try this exercise for identifying themes: After watching a scene, write a one-line summary of the events. Imagine you're telling a friend what you saw and you only have five seconds to do it. Then look through the themes included in this Shortcut to see if one of them comes close to your summary, even if the wording is somewhat different.

Use a theme with proven appeal

Some basic themes have proven so consistently popular with audiences that they have become staples of every entertainment genre. These familiar themes have universal appeal; they connect with a wide audience. They're an important resource for you as a songwriter.

A strong theme can usually be stated in three to five words. If it takes more than that, it's probably starting to turn into a storyline. Here's a list of themes that are proven winners:

*List of =>
Universal Themes.*

> Life/Love is wonderful.
> Love hurts.
> Love conquers all.
> Revenge is sweet.
> Strength triumphs over adversity.
> Growing up is difficult/exciting.
> Hope lives on.
> Good defeats evil.
> Life is full of surprises.
> Success can change a person.
> Family/friends are important.
> Challenges lead to self-discovery.

By using these themes and adding more of your own, you'll be tapping into the well from which all writers draw inspiration and ideas. More specifically, you'll be working with the same basic material on which film and TV scriptwriters build their scenes, creating songs that complement and support those scenes.

In the Shortcuts that follow, you'll find plenty of ideas for fleshing out your theme, building on it, and bringing it to life.

Do It Now

Watch a scene in a TV drama or film and see if you can identify the theme. Use the list in this Shortcut to help you. If you don't see the theme listed there, add it to the list. Then, write down, in short phrases, the events and dialogue in the scene that illustrated the theme. These could provide ideas for a lyric based on the theme.

Shortcut #46

Make Your Title a Natural for Film & TV

Suggest a character, situation, or action in your title.

Have you ever strolled past a rack of books in the airport or supermarket and picked up one that "just looked interesting." Among all the books on the shelf, why did you choose that one? It was probably a combination of the artwork and a strong title that promised the kind of experience you were looking for.

When a music supervisor or ad agency creative director is looking for songs, they may scan hundreds of titles, just the way you scanned those rows of books. But in this case there's no cool artwork to grab their attention. The song title has to do *all* the work.

What's in a title?

A title can tell a music supervisor whether or not a song is a fit for her current needs. Here are a few examples of titles that got the job done.

A title can suggest ways your song can be used.

"Make Me Believe": This is a great example of a title that suggests the song might have good scene potential. It practically begs to be used under an onscreen moment in which a character desperately wants to believe that something is true even if it isn't! That's exactly how this song, recorded by Angel Taylor, was used in an episode of *90210*.

"Full Moon": Here's a title that might suggest a haunted atmosphere, a dark and mystical mood. It works beautifully as the opening song in the first film in the *Twilight* series.

"Technicolor": Tim Myers's title reached out to the ad agency looking for a song to use in a commercial for Tide laundry detergent, telling consumers just how bright their clothes could be.

"Save Me": This title from the song by Remy Zero suggested right away that the song might be a good fit for the TV series *Smallville*. Every week the superheroes in this show are saving folks and often in need of saving themselves.

Evoke a character, situation, or action in a short phrase

A phrase of one to five words that captures the essence of a character or situation can make a very effective title, as in the examples above. Here are some ideas that will help you write good film and TV song titles.

> **Look for character titles:** A good "character title" focuses on human traits that are universal. "Always a Lover" or "Never Satisfied" are titles that describe someone you might know (and will certainly find in film and TV scripts). A title like "Wild-Eyed and Reckless" immediately suggests a character who takes too many chances, a personality that's out of control. This type of character turns up in many dramatic situations because he or she can kick-start the action.

Try a short, expressive phrase.

> **Emotional situations provide strong, usable "situation" titles:** "You Never Told Me," "I Don't Know You Anymore," "Why Are We Fighting?" Any one of these direct, conversational phrases can kick off a strong song that will work well under an onscreen situation with that content.

> **Action phrases suggest potential scene uses:** Active, physical phrases and commands like "Stop Running," "Take Your Time," "Falling, Floating" and "Can't Keep from Smiling" can be used in a wide variety of scenes.

Your title is the very first thing music supervisors and libraries are likely to see, and certainly the line they will remember when the song is over. By giving them a title that works with the characters and situations they deal with in many projects, you'll make them say, "Hey, I can use that song!"

Titles now!

Watch TV dramas or films and study the various characters in the story. Write five short phrases that convey five different characters and five short phrases that sum up five different situations. Try using one as the basis for a lyric using the Shortcuts that follow.

CHARACTER TITLES

_____

_____

_____

_____

SITUATION TITLES

_____

_____

_____

_____

Do It Now

Watch TV shows or films and fill in the list of character titles and situation titles in this Shortcut.

See the "Film & TV Song List" on page 310 for information about the song examples in this Shortcut. "Shortcut Resources" on page 307 can help you find the films and shows that include these songs.

Shortcut #47

Write Universal Lyrics for the Best Chance of Success

Lyrics that reach a large audience and work with many scenes are a plus.

The word "universal" gets tossed around a lot when talking about song lyrics for film and television. Music users in the film and TV market often say they're looking for songs with "universal lyrics." But just what does that mean?

A universal lyric is …

A lyric that a large number of people can identify with or relate to.

A lyric that will not conflict with the specific content of a scene.

<= What is a universal lyric?

Be a good communicator

Some songwriters buy into the mistaken notion that in order to create a lyric that reaches a large number of people you have to "dumb down" your writing. Not only is this untrue, it will prevent you from doing your best work. A lyric that moves a lot of people is one that is original, vivid, and believable. Most importantly, it *communicates* with listeners.

Think of it this way: Imagine you've invited a group of friends over to watch the movies you took on a recent vacation trip. As the images go by, you start out by describing the feeling of freedom and fun and the surprising discoveries you made. Everyone is engrossed, identifying with your experience and enjoying it vicariously. Then, suddenly, you begin obsessing about your failure to get the cheapest tour package, you start talking in clichés; you toss off the names of people no one knows. Your rant is unrelated to the images and means nothing to the viewers. One by one, they excuse themselves and exit the building. By getting caught up in your own concerns and forgetting your audience and the images on the screen, you stopped communicating effectively.

A good film and TV lyric is one that evokes an experience for the audience. While the onscreen action takes care of the physical details—the who, what, when, where—your job is to fill in the emotional details, making the audience feel or understand the experience on a deeper level, identify with or sense what it would be like to *be there*.

In the following Shortcuts, you'll learn how to write a universal lyric you can be proud of, one that will work well for the film and TV market.

Shortcut #48

Universal Lyrics: Use a Shared Experience

Connect with your audience by identifying common ground.

Writing a universal lyric means, first and foremost, being *human*. The simple fact that we're all human beings guarantees a certain amount of shared experiences, attitudes, and emotions. By writing about those, you create something your audience can identify with and relate to. People are *always* interested in something that has relevance to themselves.

Sometimes, especially when writing about a personal experience, songwriters lose sight of the common ground that underlies their feelings, shutting out the broader audience. Opening the song up, getting the audience to identify with it, can often be a matter of an easy rewrite.

For example, if your song lyric describes a meeting between two climatologists in Antarctica, you won't have a situation that many listeners can identify with. So, here's the trick: Leave out the physical details of "climatologist" and "Antarctica" and focus on the broader human experience that lies behind it: *Finding love where you least expect it.* This is a much more universal lyric.

Now, just think about all the movies and TV shows that have used the "love in unexpected places" story idea. A song lyric featuring that shared experience, expressed in a lyric that evokes the feeling for the audience, could be used in any of them, increasing the potential for placements.

Build a lyric on a common, shared experience.

Writing about shared experiences

As you can see from the example I just gave you, using the specific physical details of a situation may limit the audience that can identify with your song. Here are three ways to avoid that problem.

- Keep your lyric focused on emotional details and let the script deal with the specific physical details. Read Shortcut 52 to learn more about using emotional details.

- Focus your song tightly on a single feeling at a peak moment when emotions are at their highest. Shortcut 51 can help you find and write about peak moments.

- Keep in mind that the viewer is most likely to identify with the singer. A first person point of view ("I" "me") is a good way to encourage that. Reveal how the situation looks and feels through the singer's eyes. If the singer is commenting on someone else ("you"), try a direct, conversational approach in which the singer shares his or her thoughts and feelings with the person. Keep things in the present; avoid referring to events and people in the past. It's all about *being there.*

Five groups of shared experiences

➤ **Love relationships:** A lyric that reveals the emotions driving a relationship or explores the reasons why people fall in or out of love is something that listeners never grow tired of; it's the ultimate human experience. Finding love, losing love, and keeping love alive provide an endless source of inspiration for both songwriters and scriptwriters. Many film and TV scripts are built on these ideas because viewers find them irresistible.

To hear a variety of love songs and lost-love songs that have been used in film and TV, listen to "Songbird" by Fleetwood Mac, "Sun Comes Up" by John Legend, Jem's "Flying High," and "Gravity" by John Mayer. There are many more songs like these in the "Film & TV Song List" on page 310.

➤ **Family relationships:** Everyone, simply by virtue of being human, has been through the ups and downs of family relationships. As with love songs, rather than writing about the specifics of your family or someone else's, leave that to the script and focus on the emotions between and around family members: dealing with a family member's weaknesses or strengths, sibling rivalries and bonds, a parent's feelings watching a child grow up.

Avoid being too specific about personal stories.

Take a look at the lyrics to "Can't Go Back Now" by The Weepies or Rain Perry's song "Beautiful Tree" to see two different but universal lyric approaches to family relationship songs.

➤ **Becoming an individual:** Life is full of challenges. Work, school, or just plain growing up (at any age) is something everyone goes through. We never stop learning and life is always throwing curveballs our way. Discovering who we are and what we want from life often puts us in situations where we don't or won't do what others expect. These are common situations with the potential for a powerful lyric.

Try keeping your lyric centered on the feelings at the heart of this situation: the fear of taking chances, the exhilaration of freedom, and the uncertainty in the first steps. You can start before the process begins ("I want to find myself") or after it's completed ("Now I know who I am").

"Unwritten" by Natasha Bedingfield is a great example of a song that describes the beginnings of self-discovery. Self-awareness happens at the other end of the journey; you can hear a lyric with this theme in "The Climb" sung by Miley Cyrus near the end of the film *Hannah Montana: The Movie.* "Let Go" by Frou Frou, from the movie *Garden State,* is a song about the lessons we learn from life as adults.

➤ **Conflict:** Confrontation and violent conflict form the core of action and crime dramas of all kinds. While the specific situations in a film like *The Matrix* or the unusual murder scenarios in television's *CSI* series are not common experiences, viewers do share feelings of anger, fear, and frustration. Audiences can live vicariously through the action in the film, experiencing these emotions.

Conflict songs: Keep the lyric in the present. Give it a human face!

A lyric filled with strong, direct statements that convey the intensity of the singer's own thoughts and feelings works well here. Use plenty of action words and vivid language. Keep it in the present. You don't need to tell viewers what specific event led to the singer's feelings; leave that to the script and just give them his or her reaction to it.

"The Pretender" by the Foo Fighters is an excellent example of a high energy, confrontation song. It provides powerful support for an action scene in *CSI: Miami,* evoking a sense of recklessness and danger as well as letting the audience inside the character's own self image as a rebel.

➤ **Good times and celebrations:** The human desire to party hearty is truly universal. There are many types of shared situations that bring people together in joy and friendship: weddings, birthdays, anniversaries, holidays, or just a Saturday night out with friends. A large number of TV shows and films feature a party or celebration scene at some point and they need upbeat songs with a feel-good message. Several music users I spoke with mentioned The Black Eyed Peas' "I Gotta Feeling" as the type of universal, good-times song they can always use.

Keep your lyrics focused on the feel-good emotion. Use action words and vivid language that describe the physical expressions of happiness, anticipation, friendship, and exuberance. Don't just tell listeners about the experience; make them feel it!

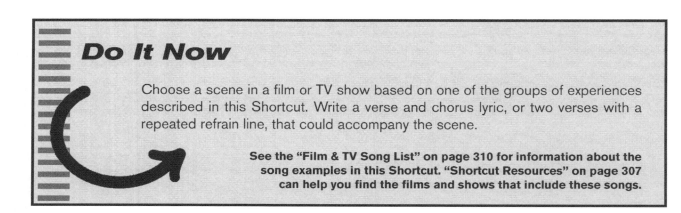

Do It Now

Choose a scene in a film or TV show based on one of the groups of experiences described in this Shortcut. Write a verse and chorus lyric, or two verses with a repeated refrain line, that could accompany the scene.

See the "Film & TV Song List" on page 310 for information about the song examples in this Shortcut. "Shortcut Resources" on page 307 can help you find the films and shows that include these songs.

Shortcut #49

Write Universal Lyrics Without Writing Clichés

Four ways to turn a predictable line into one that's fresh and memorable.

Have you ever noticed how some people can describe a simple, everyday occurrence and make it sound hilarious or tragic, while another person can tell the same story and have you snoring with boredom in an instant? If the language is vivid and fresh, even a familiar event or idea can come to life. However, if the language is trite, overused, and predictable—in other words, if it's filled with clichés—even the most exciting story can be deadly dull.

People often speak in clichés. It's an easy form of shorthand that doesn't require much thought and ensures that everyone knows what you mean. For example, here's a simple description of a common experience that's filled with clichés (underlined).

> "I guess <u>I got up on the wrong side of the bed</u> this morning; I just <u>couldn't seem to get in gear.</u> I took the bus to work. It was so crowded <u>people were packed in like sardines.</u> I was late getting to the office and the boss was <u>hopping mad.</u> The day <u>seemed to drag on and on.</u> I thought five o'clock would never come!"

While this paragraph gives you an idea of what the speaker's day was like, it doesn't make you *feel* the boredom and frustration. Cliché phrases such as "packed in like sardines," "hopping mad," and "seemed to drag on and on" have been so overused that they've lost their emotional impact. Listeners no longer picture the images or notice the comparisons.

Avoid clichés and still be universal

Because clichés are so widespread and so well understood, songwriters sometimes think that writing a universal lyric means they should use a lot of clichés. However, because listeners don't really hear the clichés, what you end up with is a lot of wasted lyric lines that could be put to much better use. So here are four ways you can get rid of the clichés!

Overused phrases are wasted space in your lyric.

1. **Use an unexpected comparison:** Comparisons are a great way to add energy to a description. "People were packed in like sardines" is a comparison phrase—people being compared to sardines. When someone first thought of this comparison, it was vivid and funny; in fact, so many people liked it and used it, it eventually became stale. (That's how a cliché is born.) Try creating new comparisons that associate one thing with another in ways listeners

haven't heard before. For instance, you could express exhaustion by saying, "I felt like a balloon that was losing air. Floating an inch off the ground, being kicked around." Or describe a crowded bus: "People were wedged together like pieces in a jigsaw puzzle."

2. **Give it a character:** When you give human characteristics to an inanimate object, it literally brings it to life for listeners. Try personifying an object in your story: "Some days are criminal. They ought to be locked up." Of course days are not criminals and no one can literally "lock up" a day but listeners are able to understand that this is what the day *felt* like.

Four ways to turn a cliché into a killer line.

3. **Twist a cliché:** You can use a cliché if you surprise the listener by creating a different payoff or explain it in a way that offers a new insight. Instead of "the day dragged on and on," you might try, "the day dragged on and dragged me down." You can hear some excellent (and subtle) examples of cliché twists in Jack Savoretti's "One Day." Check out the lyrics online.

4. **Change the order of events:** Keeping to the logical progression of events is what listeners expect; it's a cliché story structure. While you don't want to alter things so much that the story becomes unclear, you could start with the end of the day, with the feeling of exhaustion, then work backwards, showing listeners what led up to it.

To hear good examples of lyrics that express universal ideas while avoiding or reworking clichés, listen to "Cannonball" by Damien Rice, Sarah McLachlan's "World on Fire," and John Mayer's "Gravity."

The Cliché Game

Choose a cliché and rewrite it using any of the four techniques listed above.

- I depend on you; you're my ace in the hole.
- You think you've got it made, but soon you'll change your tune.
- We fight like cats and dogs, but we're friends to the end.
- I've got to get my feelings out; it's now or never.

To keep playing, find more clichés online, in books and magazines, and on TV. They're everywhere! Practice rewriting them to get in the habit and exercise your creative muscle. Keep a list of your rewritten lines and refer to it next time you're looking for a song title or lyric idea.

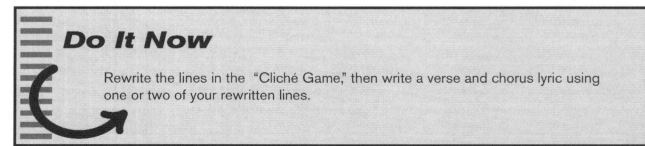

Do It Now

Rewrite the lines in the "Cliché Game," then write a verse and chorus lyric using one or two of your rewritten lines.

Shortcut #50

Avoid Proper Names, Place Names, and Dates

Increase your opportunities for placements with this simple tip.

It's the end of a TV season. Everyone is watching the final episode of a hugely successful TV drama. The two most popular characters are finally getting married after nearly losing each other to jealous ex-lovers, life-threatening diseases, and the usual dramatic twists. For the wedding scene, the music supervisor has chosen a romantic Pop ballad, "Sheila, I Love You." The bride walks down the aisle, the groom stares lovingly at her as the song fades in and swells to full volume and the audience wonders, "Who the heck is Sheila?" The bride and groom are Ben and Britney!

Make sure your lyric doesn't conflict with the script

Character names, locations, and dates are the kinds of specific physical details determined by the scriptwriter. Since songs come into the picture very late in the process, often after the script is written and shooting completed, you can give your song a better chance of being placed by avoiding these kinds of details.

Be sure your song doesn't conflict with script details!

Yes, you will occasionally hear songs used in the film and TV market that include a place name or a person's name. Sometimes a song like this makes the cut because it's by the director's favorite band. Maybe someday *you'll* be her favorite band, but right now, you're not. This type of song can be used as source music. It doesn't matter if a radio in the background is playing a song called "Sheila." But why limit your placement opportunities to source music? Give yourself the best shot you can by pitching songs that avoid specific names.

Replace specific names with descriptive phrases

There's an easy way to avoid this problem. You could change the song title "Sheila" to the less specific "She Is." Or you could rewrite your lyric to sum up the essence of Sheila instead of using her name. For example, she could become "the girl who moves like a dream." Then the song can be used in any scene that features a graceful, beautiful girl. Or you could replace a name with something about the person that's particularly noticeable. If a song is about a boy named Taylor, try calling him "green eyes" instead.

Replace names with descriptions.

You can do the same thing with place names. Chicago could be "the city of wind and steel." Los Angeles might be replaced with "palm trees and paparazzi." While a song that includes a specific place name may eventually find a home in a movie or TV show that features the specific location, the opportunities are limited. So, try recording two versions, one with the place name and one without.

Specific dates

If you refer to a specific date in your song, as The Four Seasons did in "December 1963 (Oh, What a Night)" you could have the same type of conflict with script details as you would with a proper name or place name. However, while specific dates are a problem, general time periods are acceptable. You could use the line "It was a cold December" because this phrase evokes a feeling as well as a time period. Coldplay's "Violet Hill" is a good example of this use. In the Coldplay lyric, the month of December evokes a dark, threatening atmosphere and it's accompanied by a family of images that includes "cold," "froze," "fog," and "silent still." In this context, the month is less likely to create confusion for the viewer. Naming a day of the week is not likely to present a problem either, since you could be referring to *any* Tuesday or Sunday.

Explicit lyrics and slang

If your lyric includes explicit language, record a clean version.

While explicit lyrics can prevent a song from being placed in many TV series, films are more open to it. R-rated (and even some PG-13 rated) films that feature urban violence, gang life, or aggressive confrontation can use hardcore Rap songs without censoring the lyrics. If you're writing in this style, consider recording two versions, one explicit and a clean version of the lyrics that could be used for television. Music libraries will be more likely to accept a song they can pitch either way.

Slang is often specific to a place and time and could limit your opportunities for placements. If you use slang in your lyrics, you may also find that your song becomes dated. A Teen Pop lyric that uses the word "rad" might have worked for TV a few years ago, but won't sound credible now. Avoid slang if you can. If not, then be prepared to update your lyric and recording every couple years.

Do It Now

Look through the songs you've written and see if you can make your lyrics more universal by replacing any proper names, place names, or dates.

Shortcut #51

Tabloid Technique #1:
Focus on a Peak Moment

Choose the most dramatic moment for your lyric.

Could there possibly be any reason for recommending that someone spend time actually *studying* a tabloid newspaper like *The National Enquirer*? Well, in fact, I think there is. Tabloids sell millions of copies every day. They know how to appeal to readers, how to write a headline that draws people in and holds their interest for the length of an article. They do it by hitting the peak moments! It's the train wreck of extreme highs and lows that drives those big tabloid sales. They strip away everything but the high drama.

To give you an idea of what I mean by a peak moment, just imagine a typical tabloid headline about a celebrity going through a tough time. Is it more likely to be "He Hasn't Been Feeling Too Happy Lately" or will it be "He's Devastated!!!"? The first title suggests that, whatever it is, he might get over it in an hour or two and it's no big deal. The second title implies something much bigger and more interesting to us. We pick up the scent of vulnerability. We have questions: "What's the problem? What will he do? How bad is it?" And there's a little bit of "I'm glad it's not me."

The Peak Moment technique.

Of course, I'm not suggesting that you write songs about lonely celebrities or politicians caught in love nests. You're still going to reach into your own feelings and experiences to create your song lyrics. However, you could use the "peak moment" technique to add drama and interest to your songs: Choose the moment when feelings are running the highest, the moment of greatest emotional risk, joy, or sorrow and build your lyric around it.

Choose a single slice of time

Every emotional situation has a peak moment. Falling in love, learning that a lover is cheating, moving to a new town, growing up and leaving home: each of these is a powerful story. Trying to tell the *entire* story, though, will not have as much impact as choosing a single slice of time as your focus. What are the feelings at the exact moment of discovering love? What happens the very second that someone realizes a lover is cheating? Choose *that* moment for your song. Put yourself into the situation and feel it, then use what you find. If you're writing about something that happened to you personally, go back through the events and look for a moment of realization, final confrontation, or discovery. What did it feel like? Stay focused on that. Describe it so listeners can feel it, too.

Here are two songs that have been used successfully in film and TV. Each describes an emotional peak moment of a different kind. Listen to the songs and read the lyrics. Notice how tightly the lyrics focus on what's happening right here, right now, how important the present moment is.

"Save Me" (Remy Zero) — The lyric describes the realization of vulnerability and need. While using poetic imagery, the message is very clear and urgent. Everything in the singer's world is centered on this plea.

"Top of the World" (Pussycat Dolls) — The song places the singer on the threshold of a new experience. Is it just a night on the town or a whole new life? Whatever it is, it holds the promise of big changes and the singer realizes she's ready for it.

"Down" (Jason Walker) — Right from the opening lines this song lyric focuses tightly on a peak moment of realization. The singer "shot for the sky" but has now fallen to the depths.

Why Peak Moment songs work for film and TV

In film and television, the scriptwriter will create all the events, from the big dramatic moments to the smaller ones that lead up to it. Often there will be little peaks throughout the story, building up to a big climax near the end. The climax and smaller peaks are exactly the points at which your song can be useful. Music and lyrics can increase the emotional energy at those important points, creating a more memorable experience for the audience. That's what a director wants to accomplish and music supervisors look for in the songs they audition.

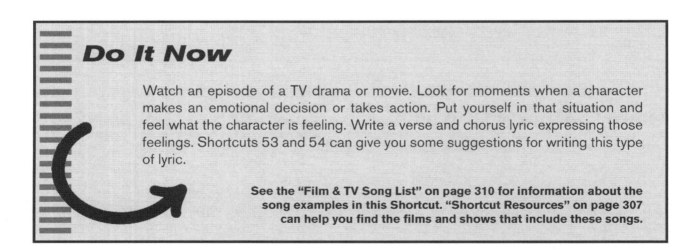

Do It Now

Watch an episode of a TV drama or movie. Look for moments when a character makes an emotional decision or takes action. Put yourself in that situation and feel what the character is feeling. Write a verse and chorus lyric expressing those feelings. Shortcuts 53 and 54 can give you some suggestions for writing this type of lyric.

See the "Film & TV Song List" on page 310 for information about the song examples in this Shortcut. "Shortcut Resources" on page 307 can help you find the films and shows that include these songs.

Shortcut #52

Tabloid Technique #2:
Use Emotional Details

Write a universal lyric with plenty of details.

Even though we know that stories in tabloid newspapers like *The National Enquirer, The Globe,* and *The Star* may have only the flimsiest connection to the truth, the more we read, the more we find ourselves inclined to believe them until finally, by the time we're finished reading, we may accept them as true. How does that happen? How do they do that? The secret is in the details!

If a tabloid story claims that an improbable couple is dating, it will tell us exactly where they were seen, what they were wearing, what they were overheard saying, and what the ex-girlfriend or boyfriend's feelings are. The more details there are in the story, the more likely we are to be convinced that it's true. Details create a plausible, convincing reality, painting a picture of the situation that *feels* real. The more complete that world is, the more we believe in it.

Details create a sense of reality and believability.

Whatever your opinion of these papers might be, the technique certainly works. So how about adapting it to songwriting? You, the songwriter, also want your audience to be drawn into your story and believe in the truth of what you're saying. Details can work just as hard for you as they do for the tabloids!

Different kinds of details

There are two kinds of details: physical and emotional. Physical details of a situation include things like the time of day, a description of a place, a person's name, specific objects, or brand names. Emotional details consist of images and statements that express what someone is feeling. For instance, "I met you at a diner on the south side of town" is a physical detail. If you go on to say, "You looked like you could use a friend," that's an emotional detail.

Here are a few examples of physical details:

> ➤ Sitting on a park bench on a hot summer night

> ➤ I bought my bus ticket and my bag is packed

> ➤ You asked me to meet you at the club at eight o'clock

> ➤ Let's go for a ride in my Chevy

> ➤ You were wearing a faded green dress

These phrases give listeners an idea of where the singer is or what's happening, but they're all emotionally neutral. They might suggest a feeling, but the song could really go in any direction.

Now, here are a few examples of emotional details:

> Your words are as sharp as nails

> I get high on your smile

> You turned your angry face to me

> I simply melt in your arms

> You look like a girl with a broken heart

> You were wearing a ragged smile

These phrases give listeners insight into what the singer and others are *feeling*. They open up the song emotionally and let listeners inside.

By packing your song with details of both kinds—physical and emotional—you create a credible, authentic world for the listener. The more detail there is, the more believable the singer is and the more listeners become involved in what the singer is telling them.

For universal lyrics, emphasize emotional details

Emphasize emotional details for film and TV.

While it's a good idea to include physical details in your lyric, if these details are too numerous and too specific they may conflict with the content of a film or television scene. For this reason, universal lyrics, the ones that work best for film and TV, tend to lean more on emotional details that immerse the audience in a vivid world of feelings while still allowing the lyric to support a broad range of scenes. Three good examples of song lyrics built on emotional details are Griffin House's "Live to Be Free," Tina Dico's "One," and "Rescue Me" by Sarah Bettens.

This doesn't mean you shouldn't use physical details at all when writing for film and television. They can help to ground your lyric in the real world and give it substance. If you use too many, though, if your lyric becomes too specific, it may limit your pitching opportunities. Songs in the Country genre are often filled with physical details, like Jason Aldean's "Big Green Tractor" or Dierks Bentley's "What Was I Thinkin'." The large number of very specific, descriptive details gives these songs a lot of appeal, both were Country radio hits, but it can make them hard to place in the film and TV market.

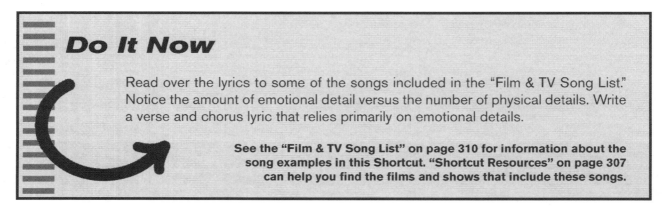

Do It Now

Read over the lyrics to some of the songs included in the "Film & TV Song List." Notice the amount of emotional detail versus the number of physical details. Write a verse and chorus lyric that relies primarily on emotional details.

See the "Film & TV Song List" on page 310 for information about the song examples in this Shortcut. "Shortcut Resources" on page 307 can help you find the films and shows that include these songs.

Shortcut #53

Express Emotions with Vivid, Physical Language

Use the "Association Pyramid" to give your lyrics substance and energy.

As I was researching songs to use as examples in this book—songs that have been successfully used in film, TV shows, and commercials—I noticed over and over how the lyrics in these songs communicated strong emotions while avoiding the specific events or stories that surrounded them. But emotions are so vague, so hard to describe! "I love you" may be a true statement but, no matter how true it is for you, it doesn't make your listener feel very much. The same holds true for other emotions: How can you make someone feel what anger feels like to you? How can you describe the emotions of final, irreversible loss or heart-soaring happiness? The answer is: You can't, not with factual, logical, rational language. But you *can* if you jump into the irrational, non-linear, always surprising world of *associations*.

Convey emotions with images, sensations, and associations

Comparing love to a "kiss from a rose," as Seal does in the song by that title, may not make rational sense but listeners get a jolt of feeling that catches their attention in a good way. Why is a phrase like "a kiss from a rose" so much more expressive than simply saying, "I love you"? First, it's fresh and original and therefore people notice it; but more importantly, it associates the abstract notion of love with the physical objects: "kiss" and "rose." Listeners can visualize both, and both appeal to the senses. Even if they aren't conscious of it, listeners see and feel those rose petals and kisses and, on a deep level, they experience the sensual, healing power of love the song is describing.

Make listeners feel the emotion. Don't just tell them!

In Alan Parson's song "Eye in the Sky," recorded by Jonatha Brooke, she sings this line: "Don't let the fire rush to your head." This is a much more compelling phrase than "Don't get mad." The image evokes the heat and intensity of both anger and fire, making listeners *feel* what's happening instead of merely being told that it's happening. Similarly, Josh Radin uses the phrase "your name is the splinter inside me," in his song "Winter," an effective association of an emotion (the pain of lost love) with something listeners can physically experience (the pain of a splinter). Listeners become more involved as an emotion becomes less abstract and more physical.

Making an association

Here's a technique that will help you make associations between an emotion and a physical object, sensation, or experience. Because we so often associate emotions with colors ("green with envy" "red hot anger") I'm going to give you the version that's based on colors, but you can associate feelings with seasons, weather, modes of travel, times of day, and more. Here's how it works...

Emotions are often associated with colors.

Take a look at the two lists of words below. Begin by connecting any emotion in the first column with any color in the second. Is there an "optimistic" color? Is there a color you associate with "falling in love"? If not, then just choose a color at random to go with the emotion and see what happens. You only need one emotion/color association to get started.

Anger	White
Suspicion	Red,
Jealousy	Dark Blue
Falling in love	Dark Green
Longing, yearning	Yellow
Happiness	Black
Contentment	Gray
Pride	Blue-Green
Optimism	Sky Blue
Sadness	Orange
Sympathy	Violet
Fear	Purple
Anxiety	Dark Brown
Frustration	Neon Pink
Surprise	Light Green
Regret	Tan

The "Association Pyramid"

Making an association between a color and an emotion is a good beginning. Now, let's take it further. On a separate sheet of paper, write down the emotion and the color you associated with it. Like this...

ANGER
RED

Below that, write down any objects, physical sensations, actions, ideas, or phrases that the color suggests to you. For example, below "red" you might write "fire, hot, blaze."

ANGER
RED
fire, hot, blaze

Red also suggests fast cars to me, so I would write that down, as well as other associations, like roses, rubies, and blood. Then I can use those words to suggest more associations. "Hot," for example, suggests stolen goods. Blood brings up more associations. Beginning with your emotion/color association, try laying out these new words in the form of a pyramid with ANGER and RED at the top of the pyramid.

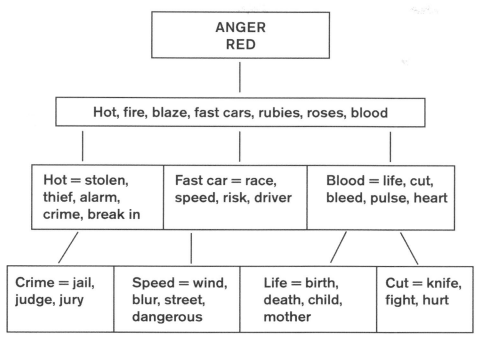

ANGER
RED

Hot, fire, blaze, fast cars, rubies, roses, blood

| Hot = stolen, thief, alarm, crime, break in | Fast car = race, speed, risk, driver | Blood = life, cut, bleed, pulse, heart |

| Crime = jail, judge, jury | Speed = wind, blur, street, dangerous | Life = birth, death, child, mother | Cut = knife, fight, hurt |

Once you've built a pyramid, you can begin describing the emotion of anger using the words in the pyramid blocks. You could try phases like "blood-red anger" or "anger blazes" or "reckless anger like a speeding car." Or you might eliminate the word "anger" altogether, describing the feeling as "a hundred cuts with a burning knife." These phrases can provide the basis for vivid lines to drop into a lyric, lines that will get listeners feeling the heat, the speed, the heedlessness and threat of anger.

One word of caution: If you use a lot of vivid associations in your song, the lyric can begin to sound contrived. Try mixing them with conversational lines that use simple, direct language. To hear songs that use associations effectively, listen to OneRepublic's "Apologize," "Breathe In Breathe Out" by Mat Kearney, and "World on Fire" by Sarah McLachlan.

<= Important! Use sparingly.

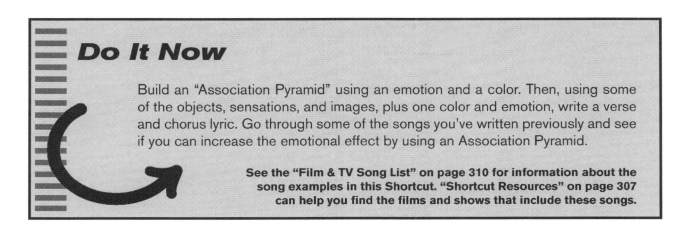

Do It Now

Build an "Association Pyramid" using an emotion and a color. Then, using some of the objects, sensations, and images, plus one color and emotion, write a verse and chorus lyric. Go through some of the songs you've written previously and see if you can increase the emotional effect by using an Association Pyramid.

See the "Film & TV Song List" on page 310 for information about the song examples in this Shortcut. "Shortcut Resources" on page 307 can help you find the films and shows that include these songs.

Shortcut #54

Upgrade Your Action Words

Add intensity and energy to your lyric with this simple technique.

Most song lyrics are about internal experiences, the things that go on inside our heads and hearts: emotions, thoughts, decisions, and realizations. Let's face it, it's hard to reach out and grab someone with an idea or get attention by flaunting an internal experience. But there is a way to do it. Loading up your lyrics with plenty of action words gives your idea or emotion a *physical* dimension, adding energy, life, and fire.

Action words engage mind and body

Action words evoke a physical response in listeners.

When you hear someone shout the word "Stop!" your body automatically reacts. Your muscles tense up and you prepare to make a change in whatever you're doing. Whether you actually stop or not depends on who said the word and how urgent it sounded. Nevertheless, until you're sure there's no danger, your body is still in "prepare to change" mode. Although this is an obvious example, in fact, your body reacts in subtle ways to all action words, words like "run," "shout," "laugh," "fall," and "whisper." When you hear those words, not only do you picture the action, your muscles involuntarily respond. It's rarely as obvious as the example I gave with "Stop!" Often, it's below you're conscious awareness, but it *is* there.

By expressing a passive mental thought as a physical action, you bring it to life for listeners on both the mind and body level. Here are a couple of examples from songs that have been used successfully in film and television:

> **Thought:** I don't know what to do next.
> **Action version:** "running from questions," "uncertainty controls you"
> ("One" — Tina Dico)

> **Thought:** I have to get through this.
> **Action version:** "All I can do is keep breathing."
> ("Keep Breathing" — Ingrid Michaelson)

Using words like "running" and "breathing" gives these lines a physicality that isn't present in the thought alone. Listeners can get a mental picture of the idea, as well as physically experiencing, in a subtle way, the exertion of running and breathing.

Be more active

An action phrase can be as simple as "I look at you." This direct, conversational phrase can work if you follow it with an interesting description or reaction to what you see. However, if you want to use this phrase on its own, you could make it more compelling by replacing "look" with a word that's more active. "I watch you." "I stare at you." Or you might exchange "look" for the less familiar word "glance," and then add more action: "I glance at you a hundred times an hour." Just by replacing a passive word with a more active word or phrase, you add energy and emotion to your line.

Upgrade your action words

Not all action words are created equal. Often, a great action word is one that comes with its own associations. Words like "sneak," "rage," or "snuggle" suggest an attitude or motivation that colors the action. Choosing words that come with extra baggage can add layers of meaning to your line. Think of it as a "language upgrade." Here are a couple of examples:

Add energy and richness to your lyric.

Action: We're staying out late.
Upgrade: "We're soaking up the hours that everyone else throws away."
("After Hours" — We Are Scientists)

Action: I don't think I can take any more.
Upgrade: "How many times can I break till I shatter?"
("Shattered" — O.A.R.)

Words like "soaking up" and "shatter" are vivid action words that draw attention because they're out of the ordinary and rich with associations. "Shatter," for instance, is associated with fragility, finality, and loss. Something shattered is impossible to repair. Language like this engages listeners beyond what is said on the surface.

So give your lyric more punch per word with these four techniques:

*   Use physical action words to describe passive ideas.
*   Replace a passive or less active word with a more active one.
*   Pump up an action by adding a description.
*   Exaggerate the action and add associations.

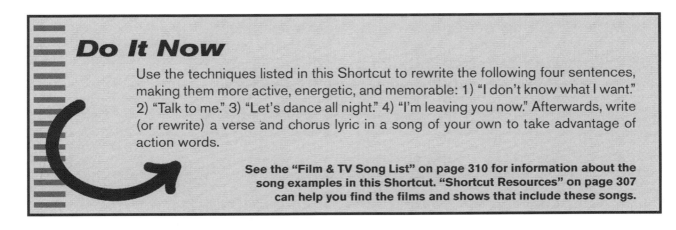

Do It Now

Use the techniques listed in this Shortcut to rewrite the following four sentences, making them more active, energetic, and memorable: 1) "I don't know what I want." 2) "Talk to me." 3) "Let's dance all night." 4) "I'm leaving you now." Afterwards, write (or rewrite) a verse and chorus lyric in a song of your own to take advantage of action words.

See the "Film & TV Song List" on page 310 for information about the song examples in this Shortcut. "Shortcut Resources" on page 307 can help you find the films and shows that include these songs.

Shortcut #55

Don't Be Afraid to Go "Over the Top"

No need for restraint. Go ahead and let it out!

Have you ever noticed that in TV dramas nobody ever has a dull, uninteresting day? Life is a never-ending parade of conflicts, joys, failed romances, new romances, problems, and betrayals. One thing you can say about TV characters: they don't lead boring lives!

And you can say the same about the song lyrics that accompany these characters. They're filled with lines that tell us "walls are caving in," "there's always gonna be an uphill battle," "all we can do is keep breathing" and then "dream of ways to throw it all away" (from "Break Me Out," "The Climb," "Keep Breathing," and "Gravity" respectively). Phew!

Take it to the limit

Because songs are often used during onscreen moments when feelings or events are at their most intense, a lyric that is not afraid to be revealing, even excessively so, can be just what a director or producer needs to give a scene an added emotional kick.

Many film and TV songs push the emotions to the limit!

Many of the songs used in film and television express emotional extremes. This is as true for songs about happiness as it is for songs about sorrow and loss. Whatever it is, it's either the best thing or the worst thing that has ever happened! So don't be shy about pushing your lyric themes, imagery, and language to the limit.

- Focus on a peak moment (Shortcut 51).

- Use strong, vibrant associations (Shortcut 53).

- Upgrade the action words in your lyric (Shortcut 54).

- Avoid clichés. Make every line count (Shortcut 49).

- Raise the stakes as your lyric develops (Shortcut 57).

Keep the emotion interesting!

There are some emotions that just don't seem to lend themselves to over-the-top treatment. For example, if you want to write a song about how bored you are with love or with life, whatever you do, don't write a *boring lyric* in order to express that! The audience won't feel the ennui and frustration, they'll just *be* bored and they'll stop listening.

To solve this problem, write a lyric that expresses the feelings of hopelessness, helplessness, disappointment, and dissatisfaction that accompany boredom by using images of, for example, being caught or imprisoned, living in grey or colorless surroundings. To pump up the feeling, compare it with its opposite, using vibrant, rich colors and motion-filled imagery to create contrast. Reminding the listener of what's missing increases the impact of the feeling.

The emotion comes from you

The most important thing to remember is that the emotion has to come from you. While song craft can show you how to pump up your action words and avoid clichés, it can't tell you what to feel or which emotions to write about. Song craft is there to give you support for expressing your feelings but it can never take the place of them.

The emotions are yours. Song craft helps you express them to listeners.

Spend some time exploring your feelings. Many emotions that we think of as simple are, in fact, quite complex, made up of many different feelings. What we call "love" is really a whole group of emotions that may include compassion, attachment, passion, yearning, surprise, joy, empathy, and affection. Reading about emotions in psychology books doesn't take the place of feeling them yourself. Watch your own emotional reactions. Recall emotional situations from the past. What did you feel? How did you react? What happened to you physically and mentally when you felt those emotions?

If you only scratch the surface of an emotion and look no further, if you accept the clichés that are commonly used to describe emotions, then your songs are not likely to move your listeners.

- Respect your feelings and give them importance. Be honest.
- Examine emotions to see what they're made of.
- Use song craft to make sure you express those emotions effectively.

What if it's hard for you to express emotion?

First, I want to point out that it's hard for just about everyone! You're not alone. Even if it were easy to express big emotions, you can't go around living like a character in a disaster movie just so you can write songs. There will be plenty of times when you need to write a song and nothing in particular is sparking your emotions.

➤ **Use a memory:** Go back to a strong emotional situation from your past. Experience the feelings. Say something about them that you haven't said before. There's no limit to the number of songs you're allowed to write about an experience and as you grow you're sure to gain new insights. Remember, focus on the emotions, not the specific details of what happened.

➤ **Use a character:** If you're uncomfortable expressing personal emotions in your lyrics or you feel you don't have anything to write about, try this:

1. Watch a scene in a film of TV show in which a character is expressing strong feelings.

2. After watching, run the scene in your mind and write your own dialogue lines for the character. Make them honest, expressive, and emotional.

3. Choose one or two lines from your dialogue and use them in a chorus or verse.

4. You can continue to write dialogue or go deeper by imagining what the character is thinking and feeling, using those lines to build up your verse and chorus.

5. Then use the lyric Shortcuts in this book to add associations, pump up the action words, and avoid clichés.

Do It Now

Write a verse and chorus lyric that expresses a heightened emotional state, something that the singer feels very strongly about. Mix associations, images, and action words with direct, honest statements. You may write it from the point of view of a character in a TV show or film, as described in this Shortcut.

See the "Film & TV Song List" on page 310 for information about the song examples in this Shortcut. "Shortcut Resources" on page 307 can help you find the films and shows that include these songs.

Shortcut #56

Make Your Title the Focus of Your Song

Feature your title and use it to provide the raw material for your lyric.

In Shortcut 46, your learned several ways to create a title that will work well for film and television. Once you have that title, keep it in focus as you develop your lyric. Many music supervisors and music libraries express frustration at finding a song with a title that seems to suggest a useful theme or emotion, only to find that most of the lyric is about something else!

To give music users the best chance of using your song, make your title the centerpiece: feature it, frame it, explain it, emphasize it, and repeat it. By doing this, your title will...

Put your title in the spotlight!

- Act as a guide, keeping your lyric focused and on track.
- Remind viewers of the message at the heart of the song.
- Give a music supervisor a strong payoff line for a scene and a lyric to support it.

Turn it into a complete thought

Consider using a title that's a complete phrase or stand-alone thought to give music users a clear idea of what your song is about. A title like "Every Day" doesn't say much, but Sheryl Crow's title—"Everyday is a Winding Road"—completes a thought and conveys a strong thematic idea.

If you do decide to use a compelling one- or two-word title, like OneRepublic's "Apologize" or Ingrid Michaelson's "Keep Breathing," try expanding it into a complete phrase before you write the rest of your lyric. You'll have a better picture of what the title means and *you'll be less likely to interpret it in different ways as the song develops*. A song called "Apologize" could be developed in many ways. The complete title line, "It's too late to apologize" conveys a much more focused idea on which to build a lyric.

Once you have your expanded title line, write down your song's central idea in a couple of sentences. Be sure you know what your title means and what you plan to write about. There will still be creative surprises along the way, just be sure they fit into your concept for *this* song.

Use your title line as a guide

You can now use your title to keep your lyric focused on a central idea. The following steps will show you how.

1. Create a strong film and TV title using the ideas in Shortcut 46. If your title is not a complete phrase, go ahead and expand it. Make it a statement that can stand alone.

2. Write a list of ideas, associations, images, phrases, and even dialogue lines related to your complete title line. Use some of the ideas in Shortcuts 53, 56, and 58 if you get stuck. Give yourself plenty of raw material to choose from.

3. Start with the chorus section in a Verse / Chorus song form. Use your title line as the first line of your chorus. Using the list you made, write three or four lines to follow it. Imagine that the title line is followed by the word "because" or the phrase "What I want to tell you is..." or "It feels like..." then write your lines.

   If you prefer, you can use your title as the last line of the chorus, a "payoff" line. Just be sure your opening line is equally strong. To keep you on track as you write, in your mind try ending every line of your chorus with the title. All lines should lead the listener to the central thought in the title line.

4. Keep adding to your raw material as you work and use it in your verse lyrics. When you feel you have a strong chorus, Shortcut 57 can help you develop your verses.

Exceptions? Sure.

There are songs that mention the title once somewhere in the third verse. Coldplay's "Violet Hill" is a good example. When these songs are used, there's often another line that *is* a powerful hook. (Coldplay's repeated line, "If you love me, won't you let me know?" is the one listeners remember.) When you're as famous as Coldplay, by all means, play around with your title. For now, though, give your song the best shot you can by making the title a strong focal point for the whole song!

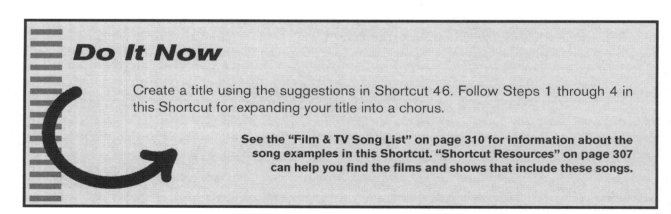

Do It Now

Create a title using the suggestions in Shortcut 46. Follow Steps 1 through 4 in this Shortcut for expanding your title into a chorus.

See the "Film & TV Song List" on page 310 for information about the song examples in this Shortcut. "Shortcut Resources" on page 307 can help you find the films and shows that include these songs.

Shortcut #57

Develop Your Lyric for Film & TV

Five ways to keep your lyric moving forward.

In a film or TV show, it's the scriptwriter's job to tell the story, not yours. What a relief! Finally… something you *don't* have to worry about! In the majority of today's placements, songs are used to create atmosphere, add energy, or deepen the viewer's emotional experience; songs are not expected to add information or move the plot forward. (This is the opposite of the way songs are used in the Classic stage musical style. For more on that use, read Shortcut 62.)

So, the only thing you need to do is keep out of the way of the scriptwriter. That ought to be easy, right? Well, I'd by lying if I said it was a total no-brainer, but there are a few simple tricks that can help you get the job done successfully.

Think deep, not wide

Sometimes the biggest problem can be finding enough material to keep your song interesting. If you're not telling a story and you've expressed the song's central idea in your chorus, what more is there to say? You can't just keep repeating yourself! The key to lyric development for the film and television market lies in going *deeper* into your theme, rather than creating a broad picture. It's all about putting one moment or idea under a microscope and increasing the magnification until you can see every detail, every raw edge.

Go deeper!

➢ **Write your chorus or refrain first and feature the title.**
Write a strong film and TV title and know what your central idea is going to be. Use the previous Shortcut to help you create a chorus based on your title. Keep your chorus lyric tightly focused on an emotion that viewers can relate to, then use the following ideas to build your verses and bridge section.

➢ **Zoom in for a close up.**
From a distance, a tree can look like a blob of green on top of a brown stick but, up close, it reveals a fascinating world of branches, birds' nests, and leaves in many shades of green. In the same way, a single situation, character, or emotion can contain enough material to fill many songs if you look closely. For a beautiful example, listen to "See the World" by Gomez. This character portrait was perfect for an episode of *House M.D.* Verse 1 describes the character's combative exterior, the side he shows the world. Verse 2 describes the emptiness of his inner life. I have the feeling the songwriter could have written many more verses and never run out of things to say. Look closely at your theme, look at it from different angles, ask questions about it and answer them in your verses.

Get up close!

> **Raise the stakes.**
> Increase the emotional risk in each verse. If the singer is willing to swim a river for love in the first verse, then how about sailing an ocean in the second. In the first verse of "The Climb" (Miley Cyrus), the singer has a goal but no idea how to reach it. In Verse 2, she struggles, takes chances and risks failure. The stakes have risen; the potential loss is greater. This lyric keeps the momentum going while staying focused on the central idea of "the climb."

Increase the risk.

> **Move from outside to inside.**
> Start with observations of what's happening in the world outside the singer, then narrow your focus and move inward. Listen to Dido's "The Day Before the Day" to hear an excellent example. She begins with clocks, flowers, and flags in Verse 1. She ends by telling us she "missed the most important thing you ever tried to say," a personal and very intimate revelation.

Try a different angle.

> **Pile on examples.**
> Give listeners examples of what you mean as the song moves along so they get a more complete picture. In "Cannonball," Damien Rice uses this technique very effectively. In the verses, he gives listeners detailed examples of where this relationship is at. Then, in the bridge, he creates a peak moment by revealing an additional angle to the situation: he doesn't want to scare her away with the intensity of his feelings. From the examples he gave, listeners already have a good idea of just how intense those feelings are.

Use examples.

Do It Now

Using the chorus you wrote in the previous Shortcut, write a first verse, second verse, and bridge using the tips in this Shortcut.

See the "Film & TV Song List" on page 310 for information about the song examples in this Shortcut. "Shortcut Resources" on page 307 can help you find the films and shows that include these songs.

Shortcut #58

Bring Your Idea to Life

*Use dialogue and character to turn your theme
into flesh and blood.*

The great power of songs lies in their ability to move people emotionally. One of the mistakes that inexperienced songwriters sometimes make is to tell listeners what they *should* feel, instead of giving them a chance to feel it for themselves. A song that preaches, or tries too hard to "sell" its central idea will drive listeners away rather than draw them in, and won't work well for the film and TV market.

Let's say your theme is "Success changes a person." While many of us know from experience that this is true, if you simply state it as a fact, you're not likely to convince anyone who doesn't already know it, or make anyone care very much. A better approach would be to make listeners *feel* the truth of the statement.

To evoke a strong reaction in your listeners, try bringing your theme to life the same way a screenwriter or playwright would. Give your audience a compelling, emotional experience by having a flesh and blood, believable character experience the truth of this theme firsthand.

*Use a character
to express your
theme.*

The singer is a character

Think of the singer of your song as a character in a scene. Mentally create a setting and a situation. This character is probably not alone; frequently, the singer is addressing the song to "you": "You've changed." "You don't treat me the way you once did." The second character in the scene is "you," even though "you" has no lines in the scene.

To make sure that the character is expressing his emotions, questions, and fears in a believable and honest way, imagine yourself in the situation and look for the words *you* would use to convince the other person of something that's important to you. You wouldn't just say, "You've changed." While that might be *one* of the things you'd say, you might also add things like …

> You finally got what you dreamed of,
> Now everybody wants pieces of you,
> More and more, there's less and less left for me to hold onto,
> But I don't want to let go. I'm not ready to let go.

By writing this "dialogue" in short phrases, the lines take on a lyrical quality that starts to sound like a song. You can carry on this dialogue, possibly bringing up the good times, and comparing the old relationship with the new.

Once you've written a list of lines your character wants to say, lay them out in a song structure. The lines that I just wrote suggest a chorus section to me but they could work just as well in a song that features a refrain instead of a full-blown chorus. Highlight one important point the character wants to make in each verse and the bridge. Like this:

Sketch out a song structure in a few lines.

Verse 1:   You've changed.
Chorus: I'm not ready to let you go.

Verse 2:   Look at what we've lost.
Chorus: I'm not ready to let you go.

Bridge: Success isn't worth the price if it means losing love.
Chorus: I'm not ready to let you go.

The title of the song? Obviously, "Not Ready to Let You Go."

Using a believable person, situation, and dialogue to bring your theme to life allows the lyric to grow organically. It helps you stay on track without much effort and gives your song believability. It's a creative and satisfying way to approach lyric writing and one that works well for film and television because it utilizes one of screenwriting's most effective tools: character.

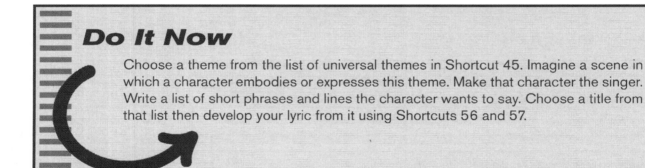

Do It Now

Choose a theme from the list of universal themes in Shortcut 45. Imagine a scene in which a character embodies or expresses this theme. Make that character the singer. Write a list of short phrases and lines the character wants to say. Choose a title from that list then develop your lyric from it using Shortcuts 56 and 57.

Shortcut #59

A Fresh Approach
Can Make Your Lyric Compelling

Try a new angle, a unique description, or an unusual point of view.

In the world of writing, "everything old is new again." Films like *O Brother, Where Art Thou?* and *Cold Mountain* rework the same themes that inspired the poetry of Homer 2,500 years ago. Today's hit love songs retell the same stories of love and loss as the troubadours did 800 years ago, and innumerable songwriters have been doing ever since.

There are just a few truly universal themes (see Shortcut 45) and these are recycled over and over again. An unskilled writer will turn out something familiar and predictable, however, in the hands of a good writer, these themes come to life, entertaining and moving audiences as they have for hundreds of years.

So, why is it that the very same core idea can succeed in one film or song and fail in another? What is the good writer doing that makes viewers want to follow the exploits of a Ulysses one more time or feel the pain of lost love in yet another ballad? The good writer turns the theme into a fresh, compelling experience by making audiences *experience it in a new way.*

Look for a fresh angle

Give a basic theme an unanticipated slant that will surprise your listeners. Write something they haven't thought of or heard before.

> **Do the unexpected:** Instead of "Life can be hard," try something like "Life can be hard but I embrace it." ("Let Go" — Frou Frou)

Don't settle for doing it the same way everyone else does!

> **Add a twist:** Rather than "I love you," try something like "I'm not sure if I love you… yet." ("Who Knows?" — Natasha Bedingfield)

> **Offer a creative solution to a familiar problem:** Turn "I lost my girlfriend" into "I lost my girlfriend but I'm going to get her back." ("The Man Who Can't Be Moved" — The Script)

Consider a different point of view

Often the usual reaction to a situation or idea is the one that gets used just because it's the first one that occurs to you. But dig a little deeper, put yourself into the situation. Look at *all* of your responses, not just the obvious ones. You may come up with a different reaction that's honest but unexpected, as Damien

Rice does in "Cannonball." He focuses on the fear of being too needy with a new love when many songwriters would focus on the feeling of new love itself.

Offer an original insight

Consider writing a lyric that gives listeners a different way to look at a thing... literally. In Rain Perry's simple, bluesy "Beautiful Tree" she takes the notion of a family tree a little further and makes the listener realize how similar family trees are to real trees. In Peter Gabriel's song "In Your Eyes," he describes what he sees in his lover's eyes—"the light, the heat"—and something more, something unusual: "the doorway to a thousand churches," associating love with worship, giving the song a powerful, unique resonance. A single image like this in a chorus or refrain line can touch listeners in a new way.

The common thread that runs through all of these techniques is the ability to put yourself inside your theme, experience it, and capture an honest, original reaction. Spend time looking at your theme from many angles. Make a list of associations that occur to you and choose one that stands out as original.

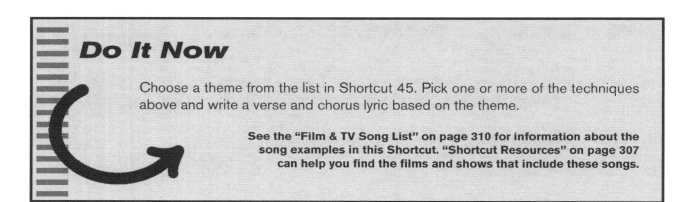

Do It Now

Choose a theme from the list in Shortcut 45. Pick one or more of the techniques above and write a verse and chorus lyric based on the theme.

See the "Film & TV Song List" on page 310 for information about the song examples in this Shortcut. "Shortcut Resources" on page 307 can help you find the films and shows that include these songs.

Shortcut #60

Be Credible and Authentic

Five ways to make your lyric completely believable.

Just as characters in a film have to speak and act in a believable way so, too, a song has to use lyric language that sounds authentic and credible. Whether a song is used as music underneath a scene, a featured performance by a character, or source music coming from a DJ's turntable, if the lyric sounds false, unnatural, or inconsistent, viewers will find themselves pulling away, mistrusting what the song is telling them.

➤ 1. **Use a conversational word order.**
Underneath the surface of a strong, believable lyric is the feeling that someone, a real human, is actually saying these words. Using the natural word order of speech is the best way to create that feeling. A conversational tone lends realism to your lyric, even if the lyric uses a lot of poetic imagery. For a great example of a lyric that sounds like the singer is actually saying the words, listen to The Script's "The Man Who Can't Be Moved" or Tina Dico's "One."

➤ 2. **Organize your thoughts.**
If you were explaining your thoughts or feelings to a friend, how would you say it in a way she could understand? You would probably go through your explanation in a certain order, giving her the information she needs to know before moving on. Approach your song lyric the same way. Try talking your idea through simply and honestly, as if you are telling a friend. Record your explanation and use those lines, in that order, as the basis for your song lyric. You can then replace some of them with more vivid language, but preserve the original order. "I Need to Wake Up" by Melissa Etheridge is a good example of a lyric that explains a feeling, making sure the listener hears the ideas in an organized way.

Keep the trust of your audience. Write a believable lyric.

➤ 3. **Mix direct statements with poetic language.**
Being conversational and organized doesn't mean you can't use poetic language. Images, action words, comparisons, and associations are part of our everyday language. As we saw when we looked at clichés (Shortcut 49), vivid, fresh language can keep things interesting and give the listener a more powerful experience. Try a mix of direct, clear statements *and* poetic language. John Mayer's "Gravity" is a good example of a mix of poetic language with direct statements.

➤ 4. **Make the style of language consistent with the use.**
A 13-year-old schoolgirl with a crush doesn't use the same language style, expressions, or vocabulary as a 25-year-old single woman looking for love. Each of these characters has a style of speaking that comes from her experience, age, and social surroundings. This holds true for song

lyrics as well. For example, a song in a Disney Channel show needs to speak believably to a youthful audience. These viewers have a fine-tuned detection system for adult messages and dated language. Watch the shows, listen to how the characters speak, study the Teen Pop music genre. You can hear the kind of language that works well for this style in the *Camp Rock* song "This Is Me" recorded by Demi Lovato and Joe Jonas.

A show like *Grey's Anatomy,* on the other hand, with characters in their 20s and 30s and a college-educated audience, favors songs that use language in interesting ways, mixing poetic devices with a conversational tone, like Beck's "Youthless" or Mat Kearney's "All I Need."

MTV's reality shows often feature songs with more aggressive language aimed at older teens. A good example of this type of lyric can be heard in "Top of the World" by The Pussycat Dolls, used as the theme song for the reality series *The City.*

> **5. Maintain a natural word order while rhyming.**
>
> Rhymes are an essential songwriting tool; they can draw attention to an important word or add closure to a thought. But, if you violate the natural, conversational word order of a line to accommodate a rhyme, you can lose believability. The audience is suddenly made aware of song craft and they take a step back. You'll have to work hard to earn their trust again.
>
> Using near rhymes like "speak" and "sleep" or "fine" and "night" (the vowels are the same but the final consonants are not) will give you a large selection of rhyming words to choose from; you should be able to find the rhymes you need and sound natural at the same time. You can hear rhymes of this type in all of the song examples in this Shortcut. Visit wikirhymer.com for lists of near rhymes.

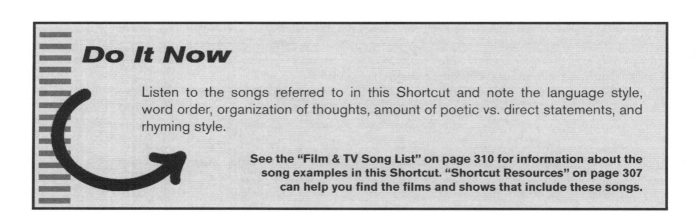

Do It Now

Listen to the songs referred to in this Shortcut and note the language style, word order, organization of thoughts, amount of poetic vs. direct statements, and rhyming style.

See the "Film & TV Song List" on page 310 for information about the song examples in this Shortcut. "Shortcut Resources" on page 307 can help you find the films and shows that include these songs.

Shortcut #61

Film & TV Musicals: Lyrics Say What Dialogue Can't

Let your lyrics reveal the real feelings of your characters.

Have you ever looked someone straight in the eye and told that person exactly how you feel? If you have, then you know how hard it is. Instead of saying "I love you," it's easier to buy a Hallmark card, a bouquet of roses, or just shorten the phrase to "Love you!" It's even harder to say, "I *don't* love you!" In real life, people often find ways to avoid expressing their deepest feelings. Insecurity, habit, and painful lessons all work together to keep us silent.

To be believable, film and television characters have to behave the way real people do. So, just like us, they hide their feelings or fail to say what they mean. Viewers, however, need to know what a character *really* feels. They can't be left in the dark wondering who's in love, who is jealous of whom, or what the hero truly feels. This is where a song can perform an essential job because *in a lyric* characters can come right out and declare their feelings. When words are wedded to music, listeners accept heightened emotional statements. For instance, in the musical *Dreamgirls,* a character sings the lines "Tear down the mountains. Yell and scream and shout!" If she had spoken those words, listeners would not have found them credible; it's not something a person would actually say. But in the song "And I Am Telling You I'm Not Going," it's a blockbuster moment and audiences love it!

A lyric can convey strong emotion more effectively than dialogue.

Use your song lyric to go deep into the heart of what the character is feeling. Try combining direct statements of feeling with images and action words, just as Effie does in the quote above. Help the audience feel what the character feels. Shortcuts 53 through 55 can give you plenty of suggestions on how to do this.

Know your characters

When you write a song for a character to sing, be sure you learn everything you can about that character first. What kind of vocabulary and expressions does he or she use? What is the character's motivation? What does the character know about the situation and other characters? Get a feel for the way the character speaks then incorporate that "voice" into the early lines of your song to transition smoothly into the images and emotions of a chorus.

Characters change

Just like real people, characters learn, grow, and change. Over the course of a musical, they move from one attitude or situation to another. Your lyrics will need to reflect the character's thoughts and feelings as the story unfolds. To see how a character's growth can affect lyrics, watch *Hannah Montana: The Movie.* Notice the way the lyric themes change along with the language style as the story progresses. A song like "The Good Life" at the beginning of the film has a lyric "voice" that's quite different from "Butterfly Fly Away," which occurs later in the film.

Give your character the last word!

When people talk to each other, they rarely utter memorable, pithy sayings, even in highly-charged, emotional situations. Those lines are more often the things they *wish* they'd said. The wonderful thing about songs is that you can put those "wish-I'd-said" lines into your lyric! Give your character the final word. Imagine what it is *you* would most like to say in that moment. Try out different phrases. Experiment until you find the killer line.

Write a character song right now

You can turn any film or TV drama into a musical. It's fun to do and will provide you with excellent practice in writing lyrics for today's musicals.

Practice writing lyrics for musicals.

1. Choose a scene in a TV drama or dramatic film, one in which a character is feeling a strong emotion. Look for a moment when the character reaches an emotional peak.

2. Freeze the scene and write short phrases that express what the character is feeling. What's going through his or her mind? What hasn't been said? Choose one of these phrases as your title, the one that strikes you as the most honest, the most emotional.

3. Surround that line with others that support the statement. Use images, action words, sense experiences, and emotional details (Shortcuts 52, 53 and 54).

4. Watch the scene again, then freeze it at the same point. Sing what you've written. Does it feel as if it speaks for the character? If so, continue writing.

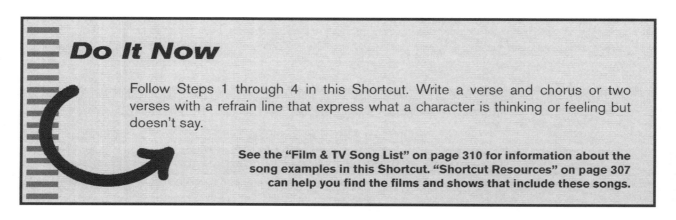

Do It Now

Follow Steps 1 through 4 in this Shortcut. Write a verse and chorus or two verses with a refrain line that express what a character is thinking or feeling but doesn't say.

See the "Film & TV Song List" on page 310 for information about the song examples in this Shortcut. "Shortcut Resources" on page 307 can help you find the films and shows that include these songs.

Shortcut #62

Film & TV Musicals: Your Lyrics Have a Job to Do

Get the most from Plot, Patter, and Performance song lyrics.

The stage musicals of the 1940s and 1950s set the standard for lyric writing in the musical genre and defined the way songs are used. Many stage musicals that become movies, like *Chicago* and *Dreamgirls,* carry on that tradition and today's made-for-TV, film, and animated musicals continue to build on that foundation.

➤ **Plot songs:** Audiences need a certain amount of background information in order to quickly grasp what's happening, where the action takes place, and what the characters' relationships are. Letting them in on this information, called "plot exposition," is crucial. It can take many pages of dialogue to explain. Or it can be done in a quick, interesting, entertaining way with a song!

To write one of these songs, identify the information the audience needs to know. Express it using examples, images, and details. Keep it action-oriented. Avoid *telling* the audience what you want them to know, instead, show it to them. You can hear a good example of plot exposition in the song "Best of Both Worlds" in *Hannah Montana: The Movie.* It's a fun, pump-up-the-energy song that fills the viewer in on the double life Hannah Montana leads. Without that song, the script would have to convey the information in dialogue, which could sound contrived and slow the pace of the story.

➤ **Character songs (lead characters, sidekicks, and villains):** Songs can explain a character's motivations, personality, and background to the audience. The lead character/hero can express aspirations that will move the plot forward, as Simba does in the song "I Just Can't Wait to be King" from *The Lion King.* The bad guy can let the audience know how he will try to stop the hero, just as Scar does in the song "Be Prepared," also from *The Lion King.*

In musicals, songs have a job to do.

As in plot songs, lyrics should rely on examples, action, and vivid details to get the information across. Listen to the two songs I've just mentioned and notice how the lyrics tell the audience what the character is doing or expects to do, what the outcome will be, and how others will react. Getting that same information across in dialogue wouldn't be half as much fun!

➤ **Patter songs:** Scar's "Be Prepared" is a type of song called a "patter song." For a lyric writer, patter songs are the chance to compete in the songwriter Olympics. These lyrics push rhyming and language skills to the limit. Audiences expect to be dazzled with verbal gymnastics and you need to deliver. The word pace is fast; the rhymes are fresh and surprising, while the content remains focused. The big challenge here is to keep the language authentic while writing clever rhymes. It takes discipline to work with a rhyme until the line sounds natural and it takes even more discipline to throw away a smart rhyme that isn't working.

A little mental warm-up is a great idea when writing patter songs. Spend time listening to (and singing along with) patter songs from Gilbert and Sullivan operettas and Disney's animated musicals. Every successful Broadway musical has at least one humorous song in this style. A search of the Internet for "patter songs" will turn up several suggestions. You're not looking for rhymes or ideas to copy. Rather, listening to these songs will turn on a switch in your brain, get you thinking and talking in rhyme and meter. Just beware: Once that switch is on, it's hard to turn off! You'll be dreaming in rhyming couplets.

Warm up before working on a lyric for a patter song.

➤ **Performance songs:** Many of today's movie and TV musicals feature a fictional band or artist. Obviously, this affords plenty of opportunities for song performances. To write these songs, aim for the lyric style of the genre in which the character is supposed to be working, such as Pop, Rock, Country, or R&B. If the character is supposed to be a singer in a successful Pop/Rock band, then study current Pop/Rock hits for the lyric style in that genre. The same holds true for Country and R&B. Your lyric needs to be credible in order for the character's performance to be believable.

A note on rhyming

The musicals of the '40s and '50s demanded clever wordplay and perfect rhymes (rhymes in which both the vowel sound and final consonant are exactly the same). While perfect rhymes are still used in some stage musicals today, in film and TV the trend has been toward a more relaxed Pop style, in which an authentic, conversational tone is emphasized and "near rhymes" are used (rhymes in which only the vowel sound is the same). A good rule of thumb: In patter and humorous songs, perfect rhymes add strength. In songs that express strong emotion or a serious theme, put the emphasis on content rather than rhyme. Keep the language authentic for the character and use vowel rhymes to add color and emphasis.

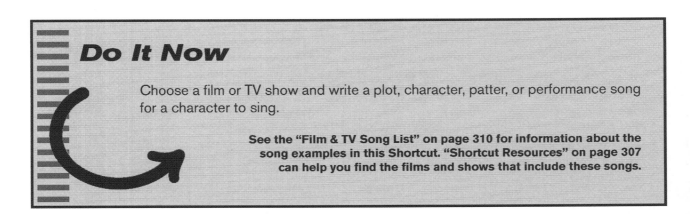

Do It Now

Choose a film or TV show and write a plot, character, patter, or performance song for a character to sing.

See the "Film & TV Song List" on page 310 for information about the song examples in this Shortcut. "Shortcut Resources" on page 307 can help you find the films and shows that include these songs.

Shortcut #63

Evoke a Location or Era in Your Lyric

Seven techniques you can use to set the scene for viewers.

A song lyric can give viewers a lot of information about where and when the action in a story takes place. Writing a song for this use allows you to dodge a few of the lyric guidelines for film and TV songwriting, such as avoiding place names, but adds others you need to know about. While there are fewer opportunities for these songs than there are for songs with more universal lyrics, you'll have fewer competitors for the spot.

Tell the viewer *where* it happened

➤ **Use a place name.**
If you've been itching to use a place name in a song then this is your chance. However, merely mentioning Chicago or San Francisco in your lyric won't be enough to set a location for the viewer. If you're going to summon up a location, then focus your lyric on the look, the feel, or the lifestyle of the place. Recreate the essence of the city; bring it to life with fresh insights and vivid images. "I Left My Heart in San Francisco" is a good example of this type of song. It has been used in dozens of TV shows and films.

Use place names, landmarks, and dialect to convey location.

➤ **Focus on local interests and attractions to capture location.**
To evoke a location for viewers, try using famous landmarks, specialty foods, activities, or celebrities identified with the area. Marc Cohn did a great job of recreating the feel of a visit to Memphis in his hit "Walking In Memphis," used effectively in the film *Graceland*.

➤ **Use local dialect and idioms.**
In most cases, using local idioms, dialect, or a foreign language in your lyric would be risky—your audience may not understand you—but if you're attempting to create a location rather than convey information, it can work. A good example can be heard in Beausoleil's "Zydeco Gris Gris," featured in the film *The Big Easy*. The lyric is in both English and Cajun. Rap lyrics are exceptionally good at painting dramatic images of urban locations. In these songs, street slang adds authenticity.

Tell the viewer *when* it happened

➤ **Study the lyric style of the era.**
Today's lyrics are conversational, the word order generally reflects the way people speak, but this wasn't always the case. In popular songs of the 1890s, the word order was often mannered and stiff. A line like "Their love no change ever knew," from a hit song of 1908 was not unusual for the time. Tin Pan

Alley songs of the 1930s used word play and rhymes to dazzle the listener. The late 1960s reveled in lyrics with plenty of imagination, double meanings, and colorful imagery. Be aware of these period approaches to lyrics and take them into account when writing.

Use lyric style, attitudes, and catch phrases to evoke an era.

➤ **Know the themes and attitudes of the time.**
Over the decades, songwriters have handled the same themes in many different ways. The innocent novelty songs of the Gay Nineties reflected the Victorian ideals of courtship and marriage that were prevalent at the time. The songs of the 1970s disco era took a very different approach, reveling in sexual freedom and redefining relationships. The 1950s fell somewhere in between these two: innocent but tentatively exploring. Listen to the popular hits of an era and note the themes that are used and how they're handled.

➤ **Beware of anachronisms.**
An anachronism is something that is misplaced in time. For instance, if you're recreating the British Invasion sound of the early 1960s, you don't want to mention cell phones, CDs, or video games! These objects belong to later time periods; they're a dead giveaway that the song is not authentic.

➤ **Use slang and catch phrases of the time.**
A catch phrase or slang expression can quickly set a time period in the audience's mind. "Groovy, baby," summons up the 1960s, while "Shake your booty" evokes the mid '70s. Do your research. Period films, TV series, and documentaries are good resources. To attract the attention of a music supervisor looking for a period song, use a slang phrase in your title. This is the opposite of what you would do if you were writing a universal lyric to pitch to a wide range of scenes, but it can work here.

To hear film and TV songs that use the lyric styles of earlier eras, listen to "Dance With Me Tonight" (British Invasion, 1960s) from the 1996 film *That Thing You Do!,* "You Will Be My Ain True Love" (Civil War, 1860s) from the film *Cold Mountain,* and "Razzle Dazzle" from the film *Chicago,* a musical set in the 1920s.

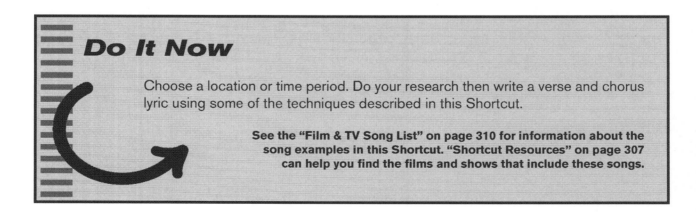

Do It Now

Choose a location or time period. Do your research then write a verse and chorus lyric using some of the techniques described in this Shortcut.

See the "Film & TV Song List" on page 310 for information about the song examples in this Shortcut. "Shortcut Resources" on page 307 can help you find the films and shows that include these songs.

Shortcut #64

The Film & TV Lyric Checklist

Ten ways to give your lyric a final film/TV polish.

Before you spend your time, energy, and money recording your song to pitch to film and TV, make certain your lyric is as strong as it can be and fills the needs of this market. Go through this checklist and strengthen any weak areas using the Shortcuts.

THE LYRIC CHECKLIST

1. **Did you use a theme that's film and TV-friendly?**
   To increase your chances for a placement, choose a theme that's frequently used in film and TV scripts. Shortcut 45 includes a list of common themes or you can use the exercise in that Shortcut to identify themes by watching movies and TV shows.

2. **Does your title suggest potential uses for your song?**
   A title that conveys a situation or character can make it easier for music users to find your song and identify scenes in which it might work. Be sure to give your song this extra edge! Read Shortcut 46 to find out how.

3. **Is there a universal situation in your lyric?**
   Be sure to reach out to viewers by using a situation with which they can identify. If you're writing about your own experience, try taking a step back, eliminating details that are too specific. Shortcut 48 includes five categories of universal situations.

   Refer to the Shortcuts for ideas on how to strengthen your lyric.

4. **Did you focus on an emotional peak in your lyric?**
   Highlight the moment when emotions reach a climax, the point where a song is most likely to be used. Shortcut 51 can help you locate and support that crucial spot.

5. **Are there plenty of images and emotional details in your lyric?**
   Use images, associations, and action words to convey emotion in a way that's compelling and original. Fine-tune your lyric with the suggestions in Shortcuts 52 and 53.

6. **Does your lyric support your title and develop effectively?**
   Once you have a strong title that lends itself to a film or TV use, keep it in focus as you write your lyric. Shortcuts 56 and 57 can show you how to build your lyric on your title and develop it moving forward.

✍ 7. **Is your lyric believable?**
Remember that your song is a character in the scene; like the actors, it needs to be believable. Use Shortcut 60 to help you maintain a conversational word order and organize your thoughts in a natural way.

✍ 8. **Have you identified and reworked any clichés?**
Go through your song and identify any cliché phrases. Use Shortcut 49 to help you replace or rework them using fresh ideas, comparisons, and twists.

✍ 9. **Did you replace specific names and dates?**
Avoid using proper names, place names, and dates unless you're planning to evoke a specific location or era with your song. Try replacing them with descriptive phrases as described in Shortcut 50.

✍ 10. **Are your music and lyrics supporting each other?**
Your words and music will have a far greater impact on the listener if they're working together to express a single emotion. Try the suggestions in Shortcut 43 to get your whole song—tempo, rhythm, melody, and lyrics—in tune!

PART SIX

Shortcuts to Song Production for Film & TV

Make a broadcast quality recording of your song

to pitch to film and television.

Arrange, produce, record, and mix

using top-notch resources and talent

on an affordable budget.

Shortcut #65

You Can Make Broadcast Quality Recordings

The industry needs recordings they can use "as is."
You can make them!

Back in the days of the great Hollywood movie musicals, songwriters could audition their material for producers and publishers with a simple live performance—just a singer and a piano. If a song made the cut, the movie studio orchestra would record it. But times have changed and today's productions want something more from you, the songwriter; they need a fully produced, broadcast quality recording they can use *as is* in their project. While this might sound daunting at first, it's entirely doable. Broadcast quality recordings are being made every day in home studios, in demo production houses, and in inexpensive commercial studios.

Here are a few questions about broadcast quality recordings that frequently come up.

> **What does "broadcast quality" mean?**
> A broadcast quality recording is the result of several things, all working together and working well:
>
> • Instrumental arrangement and performance
>
> • Vocal arrangement and performance
>
> • Recording and mixing quality

What is broadcast quality"?

> **Can I record broadcast quality tracks at home?**
> Let's start with a *reality check*. Can broadcast quality recordings be made in a home studio? The answer is an emphatic YES! That's the "reality" part. Now, here comes the "check" part. If you have never recorded anything before and you want to end up with something that sounds like a slick Pop/Rock radio hit, then the answer is no, that's not going to happen right away. However, if you want to record an "unplugged" version of your song—just guitar and vocal—that's something you *can* do at home with a little knowledge and some basic equipment.
>
> You can also select from the many resources that are available to help you create your tracks, including demo production services and commercial studios. You'll still need to do some careful preparation and be sure you clearly communicate what you want. If you've done that, you should end up with a good quality recording you can pitch. The following Shortcuts will help get the most from a home studio, demo service, or commercial studio and use available resources to strengthen your recordings.

There are many options for making broadcast quality recordings.

> **How good does my recording have to be?**
The short answer is: It needs to be as good as other songs in a similar style that have been used in film and TV. Why? Because that's your competition.

Listen to songs that have been used successfully in commercially released movies and TV shows. You'll find a list on page 310. These can give you a good idea of the type of arrangement and the quality of the performance and recording needed in a wide range of styles. You'll be surprised at how simple some of these recordings are.

> **Can I perform my own song?**
The film and TV market emphasizes emotion over perfection, so if you've got a voice that's expressive, connects with listeners, and you record it well, then you should be fine. But if a vocal performance is not emotionally convincing or in the wrong style for the song, if your rhythm guitar plays a roaming beat, or the drums and bass sound stiff, you'll end up with a weak track. In Shortcuts 78 through 81, you'll find tips and techniques that will help you strengthen your own performance or get a great performance from other musicians and singers.

> **Where can I hear broadcast quality recordings?**
Go through the "Film & TV Song List" on page 310 and listen to a variety of songs. You'll hear simple productions, like The White Stripes' "We're Going to Be Friends," productions that are slightly more involved, such as Rain Perry's "Beautiful Tree," and Ingrid Michaelson's "Keep Breathing," as well as the more complex arrangements of songs like The Fray's "Never Say Never."

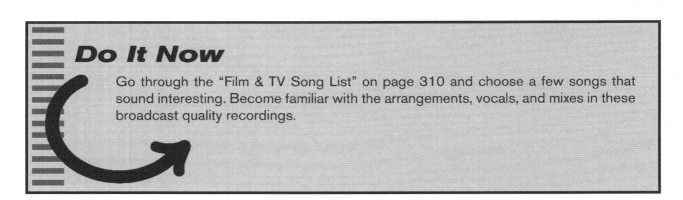

Do It Now

Go through the "Film & TV Song List" on page 310 and choose a few songs that sound interesting. Become familiar with the arrangements, vocals, and mixes in these broadcast quality recordings.

Shortcut #66

Be Your Own Music Producer
Three essential tools you need to get the job done.

If you ask 20 people in the music industry what a music producer does, you'll get 20 different answers. This isn't really as odd as it might seem. Every music project is different; each has unique challenges and strengths. It's the producer's job to overcome the challenges, make use of the strengths, and create the best result possible. So you can see why it might be a little hard to pin that down.

You've worked hard on your lyrics and music. If you're a musician and singer, you've spent time practicing the guitar or keyboard part and going over the vocal. However, you might not have thought too much about the job of producing. In this Shortcut and the one that follows, I'll show you how to sharpen your producing skills so that you end up with the best recording possible.

Tool #1: Your Resources

Create a list of the people and businesses that can be helpful to you as a music producer. Check out local studios, equipment rental places, and music stores. Not only are these good resources on their own but they can also provide referrals to engineers and musicians. Include any good musicians you've worked with, along with the instruments they play and contact information. Do the same for singers. If you've used someone on a previous project, make a note of that. Keep your eyes and ears open for more contacts to add to your database. Is there a college in your area with a music department? Find out which students have home studios and who the good singers and players are. Read Shortcut 81 for more potential resources you can add to your database.

Start collecting your resources now!

Tool #2: Your Organizational Skills

Budgeting, scheduling, preparing rough demos, checking to see what key the song should be in, and hiring musicians: these may be unglamorous tasks but they're crucial to the success of your production. Planning your session can help you avoid problems and keep spending under control. Shortcut 85, at the end of this section, will take you through a list of pre-production tasks.

Planning your production can save you money.

Organizational skills can also extend to the creative realm: How will you turn the arrangement you have in your mind into a reality? For instance, will you record a live drummer, or sequence the drum parts, or use rhythm loops? Which track should you record first? Planning in advance can solve these problems, allowing you to focus on being creative when the time comes to record.

Tool #3: Your Vision

I don't mean "vision" as in eyesight, but "vision" as in concept. As the producer and songwriter, you're the one who knows what the final recording should sound like. Make certain the vision you have of your song is clear and focused. What is the effect you want to achieve?

Communicate your vision to others.

To help you answer this question, look for existing commercially released songs that sound like what you have in mind. This is a vital step in the production process and one that creative people often undervalue. "I don't want to sound like anyone else" is a common excuse. But choosing reference tracks can help you avoid some big problems down the road: 1) It will keep you focused on the sound you're aiming for and 2) it's a useful way to convey to others what you hear in your head. Talking about music is difficult. It's hard to describe a sound or a feel. You end up saying things like "I want a kind of empty sound... but full, knowhatImean?" If you play an example of something similar to what you have in mind and point out which element in the track you like, then you've got a solid place to start.

It's a good idea to identify three or four different recordings that embody the arrangement, style, or sound you want. You'll probably find that you prefer one for the sound of the mix, another for guitar performance or drum style, a third for the vocal. Keep these reference recordings with you while you arrange, record, and mix your song—whether you're doing these things yourself or having the recording done by someone else—and refer to them often to keep you headed in the direction you *want* to go, not the direction that just *happens!* In the following Shortcut, I'll show you how to listen to and analyze reference recordings.

Producing music is a job and, like any other job, the more knowledge you have and the more groundwork you've laid, the easier the job becomes and the more successful you'll be at doing it.

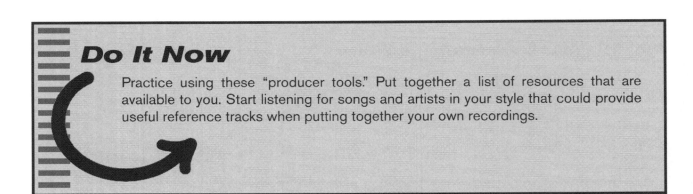

Do It Now

Practice using these "producer tools." Put together a list of resources that are available to you. Start listening for songs and artists in your style that could provide useful reference tracks when putting together your own recordings.

Shortcut #67

The Best Advice: Train Your Ears

Don't just listen. Learn what makes a track tick!

As a producer, you'll be depending on your ability to hear details that the average listener doesn't even notice. You can, in fact, learn to focus your ears the same way you focus your eyes. You can listen to the overall sound and feel of a track and zero in on the individual elements that combine to create that sound. Then you can use that knowledge to create similar effects when you produce tracks of your own.

Start by choosing a song you like by an artist whose albums have been released commercially. Independent releases by unsigned artists and bands can have high quality production but it's hard to be sure. So I recommend starting with an artist on a major label or established small label.

As you listen, go through this list of questions. Focus on each one until you can answer it.

Arrangement
What instruments are playing?
What part is it playing?
How do the instruments or parts change as the song goes along?
What do you like about the arrangement?

Train your ears to listen like a producer.

Vocal performance
What emotion is the singer expressing and how?
What is unique or distinctive about the vocal?
Is the singer hitting the correct pitches? For the whole note or just part of the note?
Are there harmony parts? When do they occur?
What do you like about the singer's performance?

Instrumental performance
Listen to the individual instruments. Are the individual players strong?
How does the ensemble sound? Is it tight or somewhat loose?
Does the drum or rhythm track sound like a live performance, a loop, or a drum machine?
Do any of the parts sound stiff or mechanical?

Recording and mix
Can you hear each instrument and the singer clearly?
Is the singer in front of or surrounded by the instruments?
Can you hear effects like echo, filtering, or delay?

Can you clearly hear the low instruments, such as bass guitar?
Is there a balance between low and high sounds?

You could call this "listening on a molecular level." It's an invaluable tool for a producer. With it, you can discover how successful arrangements work, how to make changes in a vocal performance that will add interest and emotion, how to locate a problem area in a mix. Whether you're recording your song yourself—playing and singing everything—or hiring a musician, singer, or engineer, you can improve the end result by knowing what it takes to create a successful recording.

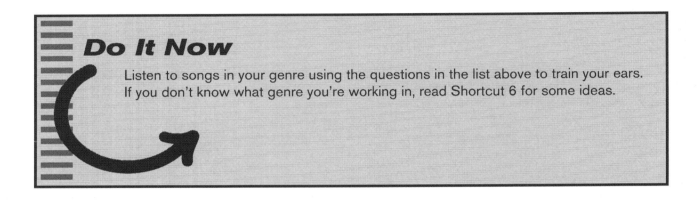

Do It Now

Listen to songs in your genre using the questions in the list above to train your ears. If you don't know what genre you're working in, read Shortcut 6 for some ideas.

Shortcut #68

Make a Rough Demo as a Foundation and Guide

Seven uses for a rough demo and tips on how to make a good one.

It's easy to overlook the lowly rough demo, to brush it off as something that's just a byproduct of the songwriting process, a mere suggestion of what you have in mind. Nevertheless, your rough demo is one of the most important tools in your production toolkit. It can be a map, a foundation, and the keeper of your vision as you move through the arranging, recording, and mixing tasks ahead. Respect the rough demo!

What is a rough demo?

A rough demo can be as simple as a guitar and vocal or piano and vocal recording made on a handheld recorder. Or it can be as elaborate as a concept for a complete track with drums, bass, vocal, keyboard, and guitar recorded on multiple tracks. Simple or elaborate, to be truly effective it needs to convey the essential energy and feel as well as the complete melody, lyric, and chord progression of the song. (See points 6 and 7 in this Shortcut for non-chord demos.)

Why you need a rough demo

➤ 1. **To test your song ideas:** One of the most important uses for a rough demo is to record your structure, melody, and lyric ideas so you can hear them as a listener would. When you're involved in the physical effort of singing and playing your song, it's impossible to get a listener's perspective. Recording a rough demo allows you to walk away then come back later to listen with fresh ears, as an audience member would hear the song. Note your reaction as you listen. Where does the song lose energy or focus for you? Did the melody become too complicated to follow? Did that double chorus at the end feel too long? Go back and change those things, record a new demo, then walk away and come back to listen again after an hour or so. Go through the same process.

➤ 2. **As a reference for yourself:** When producing a song in your home studio, use the rough demo to keep in touch with your original inspiration. At some point in the process, you're bound to reach a point where nothing seems to work, you're sick of the song, and you're thinking about speeding up the tempo because you're soooooooo bored. That's the time to go back and listen to the rough demo. It's not unusual for the original feeling you loved so much to slip away during the production process. Your rough demo can be a lifesaver. In fact, there have been instances when the rough demo ended up on someone's album because they were never able to reproduce that feel!

> 3. **As the basis for a final recording:** You can continue to build on and refine your rough demo to create a final master recording. If you used a simple, repeated rhythm loop for the rough demo, create variations, fills, or add and subtract extra percussion and drum sounds. Replace a keyboard part with a better performance or a richer sound. Replace a synthesizer bass line with a real bass player. Keep what you like, change or improve what you don't.

> 4. **For musicians:** If you're bringing in a musician to play on your recording, a rough demo can be a huge help. An idea of how you hear the song can give the player a direction. You'll get something that's close to what you want but better, without having to say things like "I want something sort of smooth but punchy and kind of lonely." (A good musician will nod like he understands, but he really doesn't. Would you?)

Melodies are hard to remember. Don't forget yours!

> 5. **For vocalists:** First, record the melody to make certain *you* remember how it goes! Phrasing that seemed obvious one day may be totally forgotten the next. That cool bridge you wrote could be gone with the wind after an hour or two.

If you're hiring a singer, most will ask to hear a demo. A lead sheet with the melody written out is a big help to any singer who reads music but there are many who don't. Hearing a demo with the melody ahead of time will allow a singer to hear your interpretation, suggest ideas, and speed up the learning curve. It can save a lot of time. If you can, give the singer a copy of the demo several days before the session.

> 6. **For a demo service:** If you're hiring a demo service to produce your song, your rough demo will give them an important starting point. Include as much information as you can in your demo: tempo, rhythmic feel, melody, lyric phrasing, chords, and any instrumental riffs or parts you want.

Most important of all, make an accurate recording of the melody. If the note pitches aren't clear when you sing, record a chorus, verse, and bridge using a keyboard to play the melody. Send two versions of your demo, one with the vocal melody and one with the keyboard melody. The keyboard will convey the correct pitches of the melody and your voice will communicate the phrasing of the lyric, something a keyboard can't do.

Some demo services offer to write chords to your melody. You can send them a vocal-only demo. It's a good idea to sing the melody to a rhythm loop or a click track (metronome) to keep a steady beat and convey the tempo you want. A rhythm loop and vocal can give them a good idea of the feel of the song even without chords.

➤ 7. **For the U.S. Copyright Office:** The copyright office defines a song as "words and music." They don't care about chords. They will accept a voice-only recording, singing melody and lyrics, without any accompaniment at all.

Making a rough demo

If you used the songwriting process laid out in Part Three and Part Four of this book, then you already have a good start on a rough demo of your song.

Convey the rhythmic feel — You can choose a drum or percussion loop, or strum a guitar, or use a piano to play a rhythm part. If you're not using a loop, record your demo to a click track or metronome. All music software has some form of click track that will play a steady beat as you record. The vast majority of contemporary songs keep a steady beat of some kind.

Include all the sections of your song — The rough demo should be a complete representation, including all verses, choruses, a bridge (if there is one), intro and ending. If you think you want a double chorus at the end, put it on your demo. If you want to repeat a refrain line before the bridge, be sure it's on your demo.

A strong demo =
Rhythm
Song structure
Chords
Melody
Lyrics
.

Play the chord progression — Change chords exactly where you want them to change and be consistent. If you play a chord early in one verse, then play it early in the next. Don't be sloppy about this. You may end up using your rough demo as a foundation for building your final tracks. If you bring in a bass player (or play bass yourself), you'll be using those chord changes as a guide.

Sing the melody and lyrics — Come as close as you can to the performance you want, even if you won't be the final singer. Go for energy, mood, and phrasing. Get your interpretation of the song on tape so you can refer to it later. If you'll be hiring a singer, read point 5 "For vocalists" above.

Do It Now

Write a song or use one you've already written and create a rough demo using the suggestions in this Shortcut.

Shortcut #69

Put Together a Basic Home Studio

Acquire the minimum equipment needed to record broadcast quality songs.

Let's say you've got a nice, comfy, quiet room in your house where you like to write. Now that your song is done, you'd like to record there, too. To compete in the film and TV music market, do you need to have a fully tricked-out, professional, top-of-the-line home recording studio? No. While you do need a few things that won't come with your family home entertainment system, you certainly don't have to buy a big array of expensive pro gear. You can put together a successful, broadcast-quality home studio with a minimum investment of time and money by keeping one important concept in mind: *Keep your projects within the capabilities of your gear and your ability to use it.* In other words, you have a better chance of ending up with a broadcast quality track if you stick with a barebones, unplugged arrangement than if you try to record a live Rock band or orchestral simulation. Layers of synthesizers and multiple live instruments are harder to handle than an acoustic rhythm guitar and solo vocal.

With that in mind, here's a list of the basic pieces you'll need in order to record broadcast quality tracks at home. I won't be comparing the pros and cons of specific brands because there are so many Internet sites and magazines where you can find that information. You'll find a list some of them later on in this Shortcut.

> **Computer** — PC or Mac, either will work fine. Choose the one you're most comfortable with. Most of today's computers have enough muscle and memory to get you started. For those of you who really want to push the envelope with big files and loads of audio tracks, choose your audio recording and sequencing software first and check the system requirements. The more bells and whistles you want, the more processing power and RAM you'll need. In general, a 1.5 GHz processor with 2 GB of RAM is recommended but you can work with less. If you have an older computer, check into processor and memory upgrades that are available. Audio tracks eat hard drive space for breakfast so store your completed projects on CD, DVD, or flash drive to free up hard drive space. Keep your hard drive clean and defragmented to maintain speed when recording. I like to keep my music software on my computer's internal hard drive and record to a separate FireWire (or IEEE 1394) hard drive.

> **Audio recording and sequencing software** — A good music software program can turn your computer into a complete recording studio, including all recording and mixing functions. There are many audio recording and sequencing programs to choose from with a range of prices and features. If you're already familiar with home recording, you probably have one of the well-known programs like Sonar (PC), Cubase (PC or Mac), Logic Pro

(Mac), Digital Performer (Mac), or Pro Tools LE (PC or Mac). These can be pricey ($500 and up) and come with a steep learning curve but they are miracles of musical computing filled with an endless supply of playthings (pitch correction, surround sound, beat detection) for your enjoyment.

If you're just starting out, decide how much time you want to spend learning to use a program before you actually make any music. If you want to get to the music part right away, try an entry-level program like Apple's GarageBand (included free in the iLife suite) or Music Maker Premium by Magix (around $100). Both are made for ease of use. Other programs worth checking out are Ableton Live and ACID Pro (in the $300 range). Take your time making a decision. Download free demos and try them out.

Before buying, be sure your computer has the speed and power to handle the larger programs. Watch video tutorials. Read the forum discussions on the maker's website to find out what users are asking about or wrestling with. The more informed you are, the better decision you will make and the quicker you'll learn the program.

➤ **A really good audio interface** — Consider spending some extra dollars here. Your computer's built-in sound card is fine for recreational music listening and gaming but *not* for broadcast quality recording. Everything you record into your computer, from vocals to guitars to external synthesizers, has to go through an audio interface in order to be turned into digital bits your computer can understand. The interface can raise the sound quality by adding presence and clarity to some of the most important elements in your track, especially the vocal! Focusrite, Apogee, and M-Audio all offer good audio interfaces priced from $300 to $500. Be sure the interface includes at least one microphone pre-amp and one pair of instrument jacks for stereo keyboard or guitar recording. If you're recording one vocalist at a time and one guitar or keyboard, then you don't really need more than this number of inputs. Put your money into good quality, not extra inputs.

A good audio interface is important!

➤ **Two microphones (or maybe just one)** — Mics can range from inexpensive ($100 to $300) to high-end "wallet busters" ($3,000 and up). The good news is you don't need to bust your wallet. You can record broadcast quality vocals and acoustic guitars on mics in the $100 to $300 range. (But you can't do it on a $25 mic unless a lo-fi sound is what you're after.) Eventually, you'll want to buy one "dynamic" mic for vocals and one "condenser" mic for recording instruments such as acoustic guitar. The truth is, if you're strapped for cash, you can get started with just one mic. Try a legendary workhorse: the SM57 or SM58 from Shure. For around $100, this mic will handle most of what you need to do. Pick up a mic cable and mic stand at the same time.

➤ **Keyboard with MIDI capabilities** — Besides recording vocals and live instruments, you'll want to be able to play and arrange or "sequence" the sounds and samples that reside in hardware synthesizers and in your computer. Although the entry-level programs will let you do this on your computer's typing keyboard, you'll get the best results if you use a piano-style keyboard with MIDI (Musical Instrument Digital Interface) capability. If piano is an important part of your sound, get a full 88-key model. However, if you're primarily using the keyboard to input data and play chord pads, riffs, bass lines, and drum parts, then a low-cost 61-key or 76-key keyboard should work for you. While you're at it, you may need to pick up a box called a "MIDI interface" for around $150. It acts as a translator between your keyboard and computer. Some keyboards, like M-Audio's Keystation, come equipped with a built-in MIDI interface. They lack some stand-alone playing features, however. To learn more about these keyboards, research "MIDI keyboard controllers" on the Internet.

> **Studio monitors** — It's essential that you have a good idea what your track sounds like while recording and mixing. For this, you'll need a pair of "near field" monitors. "Near field" simply means that you'll get the most accurate sound by listening to them within a range of three to five feet. If you send audio to your speakers from your audio interface unit or the audio output of your computer, you'll need to buy powered (also referred to as "active") monitors. Brands like KRK, M-Audio, and Alesis all offer powered, near field monitors in the $200 to $300 range.

Do your research before you buy

Spend time before you spend your money! Do your research.

Magazines like *Recording, Keyboard, Mix,* and *Electronic Musician* offer extensive advice on miking, recording, and mixing, plus excellent reviews of new gear. Websites like Tweakheadz Lab (www.tweakheadz.com) can help you compare features. Check out the forums on manufacturers' websites to hear what equipment users are saying about their experiences with the gear. If you live in a city with an active music scene, try renting equipment for a day or two; this is a great idea if you're interested in checking out some of the more expensive studio gear.

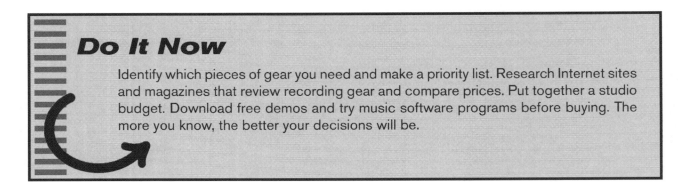

Do It Now

Identify which pieces of gear you need and make a priority list. Research Internet sites and magazines that review recording gear and compare prices. Put together a studio budget. Download free demos and try music software programs before buying. The more you know, the better your decisions will be.

A Basic Home Studio Set-up

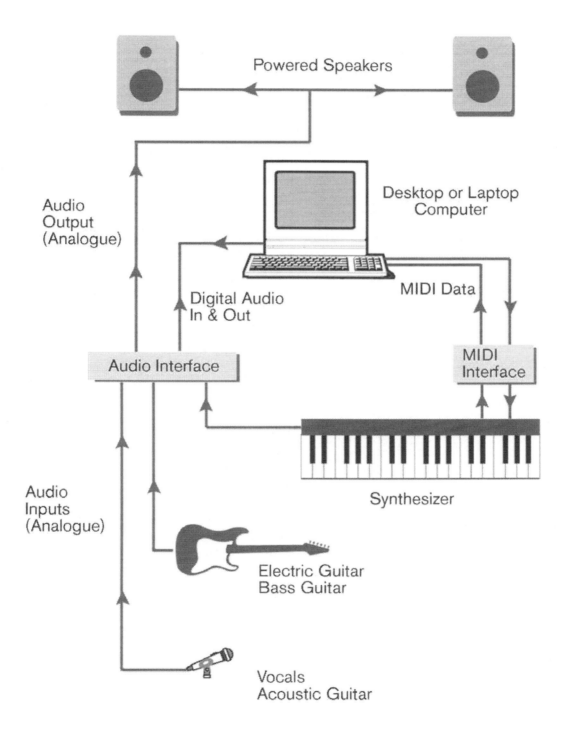

Powered Speakers

Audio
Output
(Analogue)

Desktop or Laptop
Computer

Digital Audio
In & Out

MIDI Data

Audio Interface

MIDI
Interface

Audio
Inputs
(Analogue)

Synthesizer

Electric Guitar
Bass Guitar

Vocals
Acoustic Guitar

Shortcut #70

Get the Most from a Demo Production Service

For the best results, prepare ahead of time and communicate clearly.

What do you do if you don't have a home studio? Or the production you have in mind for your song exceeds the capabilities of your home equipment? Let's say you've written a Pop/Rock song in the style of Daughtry. A marketable recording is going to need a driving, urgent, live band sound. Recording (and playing) those layers of tight, punchy electric guitars and finding a drummer who can slam home a performance (not to mention recording that performance) takes the kind of skills and equipment that few songwriters have in their bedrooms. An "unplugged" version might be a possibility but sometimes a song's just gotta rock! Fortunately, there are solutions to this problem.

Using a demo production service

A demo production service will make a complete recording of your song for a fee. A good service can create solid, broadcast quality recordings; a poor service will give you something you can play for your friends and family and that's all. It's important to do your research, use your ears, and choose carefully. Anybody can put up a website touting his or her demo production skills. It's up to you to decide whether they've really got those skills or they're just blowing smoke.

➤ **Assess the quality of their work:** Before you do anything else, listen to examples of their work. (If they don't offer any, flee!) Compare their samples with current, commercial releases in the genre you're interested in. Do the examples sound dated? Are the vocals out of tune? Is the mix muddy? Use the list in Shortcut 67 to analyze the arrangement, vocal, performance, and mix.

➤ **Check their rates:** Most demo services offer package rates depending on the number of instruments and vocal tracks you want. For a simple guitar and vocal or piano and vocal demo, you should see a price of $300 to $400. A full band with no vocals (drums, bass, acoustic guitar, electric guitar, keyboard) should be in the $600 to $750 range. Add a vocalist for another $125. In fact, each instrument will cost on average about $125.

For a look at a good demo production service, check out Studio Pros (www.studiopros.com). Listen to their demos in all styles, research their rates, and get familiar with their demo process.

Get the most from the service

➤ **Give them a good rough demo:** You'll need to give the demo service a rough demo or "sketch" of your song. This is where a simple but accurate home recording will be crucial. Be sure the melody, chords, and lyrics are accurate. For more on what goes into making a good rough demo, read Shortcut 68. Have a lyric sheet available with chords written above the words.

➤ **Discuss style and share examples:** A good production service will talk with you about your vision for your song. Give them examples of what you have in mind—commercial releases that include sound or mix elements you'd like to hear in your own song. Here's the reason why this is so important: Talking about music is like talking about color. If I tell you that a jacket in my closet is blue, you have no idea what shade of blue. It could be sky blue, royal blue, baby blue, aquamarine, turquoise, or azure. But if I show you the jacket then we both know which blue I'm talking about. It's the same with music. If you tell a producer you'd like your song to be "upbeat and danceable," you have no idea what that means to him, what he's hearing in his head. *Never* assume it's the same thing you're hearing. The best thing to do is to play examples of commercial releases that are similar to what you have in mind in terms of groove, instrumentation, vocal performance, and overall sound. In Shortcut 66, I suggested that you find reference tracks to use for production ideas. Now is a good time to whip them out.

Discuss commercial releases with the sound you want.

➤ **Your budget can make a difference:** Adjust your expectations to your budget. You may not be able to afford stacks of vocal harmonies in the chorus. But, guess what, while those vocal stacks could work well on an R&B/Pop song they could sound dated on a contemporary Rock track. You might decide to forego the extra vocals on a Rock song and use just one vocal harmony part; you'll save money and sound more contemporary. On the other hand, if your song is in the R&B/Pop genre, where vocal harmonies are an important part of the sound, you might decide to keep the vocal harmonies and sacrifice something else. Discuss what you can afford and the best way to deal with expensive arrangement ideas.

Work within your budget.

➤ **Know your feedback and approval points:** Find out at what point you'll have an opportunity to hear your track in progress and give feedback. You should have the chance to give feedback and request changes at least once before the recording is final. More than once is better. This should be included in the price.

➤ **Clarify your rights and ownership:** Before you pay for the completed recording, get a signed release form stating that you own and control all the rights to the completed recording, including the vocal, instrumental performances, and arrangement. See Shortcut 82 to find out more about the importance of these waivers. Nashville demo services often use musicians who are members of the Musicians Union, working under a special demo contract. This contract *does not* give you all the rights you need for the film and television market. If you're recording in Nashville, be sure to discuss this with the demo service. Ask if the musicians and vocalist will sign a waiver granting you full control and ownership of all performances. If not, you may need to look for another production service.

➤ **Instrumental version:** Request an instrumental version of the song (instruments only, no vocals). Read Part Seven "Shortcuts to Instrumental Opportunities" for more information on editing and pitching instrumentals in the film and TV market.

➤ **A couple more thoughts:** The best demo production services only do one thing—produce songs—and they do it well. No career consultation. No "Gee, we'll make you a star!" No "let us write your melody." If you write lyrics only and pay a service to write your melody, be sure that you own and control all rights to the music. Get it in writing. I don't recommend paying someone to write a melody for you. Instead, look for a good collaborator who works in your genre. The two of you can share the costs of the demo and you'll know exactly who wrote the song. It's okay, though, to pay the service to write a chord progression.

Customize your track

➤ **Singer-songwriters** – If you want to sing the song yourself, have the production service create the instrumental track only, then add your vocal in your home studio or in a commercial recording studio. You can mix at home or in the studio.

➤ **If you play an instrument** – Ask the demo service to record the track minus your instrument and add it yourself later. Some services will let you send the track back after adding an instrument or vocal for a final mix.

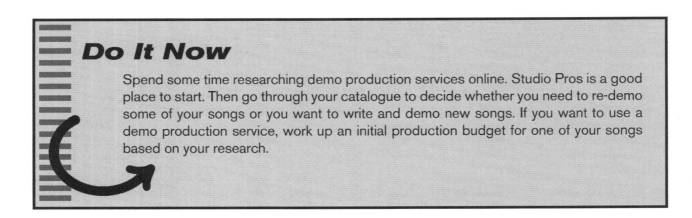

Do It Now

Spend some time researching demo production services online. Studio Pros is a good place to start. Then go through your catalogue to decide whether you need to re-demo some of your songs or you want to write and demo new songs. If you want to use a demo production service, work up an initial production budget for one of your songs based on your research.

Shortcut #71

Know When to Use a Pro Recording Studio

For live band tracking and special gear,
a pro studio is worth the money.

Commercial recording studios have lost a lot of business to the home studio revolution. As a result, they've focused their efforts on providing equipment and services that are hard to find or too expensive for the home studio market. There are times when a commercial studio is just what you need to get the high quality or special sound you want.

➤ **Live band recording:** Recording your band in your garage can be an iffy proposition, especially if you're trying to make broadcast quality tracks. A good pro studio has the big selection of microphones, isolation between the instruments, and the engineering know-how to get a good sound from every instrument. Just as important, it allows you and your band to focus on making music and encourages a get-down-to-work attitude.

➤ **Piano tracking:** If wedging a nine-foot Steinway grand into your closet-sized home studio doesn't appeal to you, try recording your piano tracks at a commercial studio. Studios know they can attract clients by offering a special instrument like this; there's just no substitute for the real thing! Not only that, they know how to record it well. They'll also have it tuned before your session. (Be sure to ask them to do that.) If you're adding piano to a pre-existing track, bring a mix of the track with a count-off at the beginning (two bars of click) so you can start playing on the first note of the track.

➤ **Drum tracking:** Drums are another instrument that can be a real challenge to record at home. If you want live drums on your recording and you know a first-rate drummer, you can rent a studio with good drum acoustics and a large mic selection and have the drummer play to your pre-recorded track. Be sure the track itself doesn't have any drums on it. Mix all the instruments on one side of the stereo field and record a click track on the other (or put them on separate tracks) so the volume level of the click can then be adjusted separately from the rest of the track. Drummers like it *LOUD!*

➤ **Mixing:** If you recorded your tracks at home, consider doing the final mix at a pro studio that offers an array of good outboard gear and the kind of mixing board you couldn't possibly afford in your wildest dreams. These boards can add presence and clarity and a big, fat sound that's a challenge to get in a home studio.

Read Shortcut 81 for another way to add live drums to your track.

> **Analogue tracking and mixing:** If the warm analogue sounds of the pre-digital era appeal to you, there are studios that specialize in this type of gear and know how to maintain and use it. A multi-track analogue tape machine can add its own sound to a project. Some producers even record on tape, then transfer the tracks to digital, reusing the tape as they go. To save money, consider recording your tracks at the studio then mixing on your digital gear at home.

But I can't afford a commercial studio!

The big drawback to recording in a commercial studio is cost. That's why we all bought home recording studios in the first place! A good recording studio can cost from $100 to $250 per hour. This may or may not include the engineer's fee. The trick to using a recording studio is to get the most out of every minute you pay for.

Discount rates: You can save money on studio rates by booking a block of time, two or three days in a row, an entire weekend, or ten-hour blocks during the week. Some studios offer extra discounts during off-peak hours. These rates vary from studio to studio, so ask about the special deals they offer.

Ten ways to save money

#1: Rehearse before you go into the studio. If you're working with a band, be sure the ensemble playing is as tight as possible. Have the arrangement down cold. Know the intro and ending and every other part of the song.

#2: Rehearse with a click track! Except for the very rare ballad, all of today's film and TV songs keep a steady beat. Practice with a click track so you're used to it. It's a good idea to use headphones while rehearsing for the same reason. Get used to them. Once you're in the studio, you don't want anything to distract you from your primary job: making the best music you can.

#3: Record when you're rested and alert. There are a lot of myths about crazed musicians recording masterpieces at 4 a.m. Yup, those are myths. Those great takes happened in spite of the situation, not because of it.

#4: If you and your band feel tense at the start of a session, go ahead and jam for 10 minutes. Get a feel for the sound of the room. Make yourselves at home musically. Don't make yourselves at home in other ways.

#5: Most studios don't charge for set-up time. Come as early as they will allow and set up your gear so you're ready to start recording on time. Make every minute count.

#6: Don't rewrite your song in the studio! It should be completely written before you go in. If it's not, then you've booked the session too soon.

#7: Don't settle for a weak take. Spend the time to get it right. It's much faster than trying to fix something in the mix.

#8: Record and mix songs with the same basic instrumentation and performance style at the same time. The engineer can use a similar set-up and save time.

#9: Bring a reference CD with tracks that are similar to the sound you have in mind for your own tracks. Refer to it whenever you feel you're losing touch with the sound you want.

#10: Get an instrumental-only mix and a vocal-only mix. It can save you a lot of money down the road. If you need to change a lyric line or even a whole verse, you can come back into the studio, sing what you need, drop it into the vocal-only mix and then sync it up with the instrumental. No need to go through the whole mix process again. Plus, you'll want those instrumental tracks for film and TV pitches! Read Part Seven "Shortcuts to Instrumental Opportunities" to learn more.

Find a commercial studio in your area

Start your search by asking local bands and artists for their recommendations. Find out what projects were recorded at each studio and, if possible, listen to one or two tracks at home. (Sometimes big studio speakers can fool you into thinking something sounds better than it does.) *Music Connection* magazine publishes an annual list of recording studios. You can order this issue of *Music Connection* on the website or view the digital editions online (www.musicconnection.com).

Do It Now

Look for a professional recording studio in your area. Find out about their equipment and rates. Even if you're not planning to record there, a pro studio can be a good resource for finding the top musicians and good recording engineers in your area.

Shortcut #72

Get to Know the Basics of Arranging

Support your song with an effective instrumental arrangement.

The first and most important thing to remember about arranging your song is this: No matter how cool your guitar chops are, no matter how interesting that bass line is, in film and TV, *the vocal is the star of the show.* You'll be supporting the vocal with an instrumental arrangement, showcasing it like a diamond in the perfect setting.

But what will that setting be? What instruments will you use? What will they play? Some songwriters depend on a producer or on the musicians for arrangement ideas. While you could end up with a good arrangement, there's a chance that you might run into problems. The arrangement may not be what you had in mind when you wrote the song, or it may not support the song as effectively as it could.

If you kept tempo and rhythmic feel in mind as you were writing your song (Shortcuts 19 and 20), you already have a good start on your instrumental arrangement. Learning more about how instrumental arrangements work can help you communicate with producers and musicians or create a strong arrangement on your own in your home studio.

What is an instrumental arrangement?

An arrangement can consist of a single instrument or many. The goal of the arrangement is to focus attention on the singer and create a compelling sonic environment that supports the song. It consists of five elements:

What is an arrangement anyway?

1. **Dynamics:** Dynamics are variations in intensity. They can be created by adding or subtracting instruments, changing the volume level at which the instruments are playing, or changing the playing style. Read Shortcut 73 to find out more about creating and using dynamics in your arrangement.

2. **Structure:** An arrangement supports and defines the song's structure by creating transitions and changes in dynamics, letting listeners know when they're hearing one section, for instance a verse, rather than another, such as the chorus.

3. **Rhythm:** Rhythmic feel, energy, and pace are created and supported by a variety of instruments in the arrangement. It may be something as simple as a strummed acoustic guitar or as complex as a drum kit mixed with ethnic percussion loops.

4. **Chords:** Chords can be played by a range of instruments including acoustic rhythm guitar, keyboards, electric guitar, horn or string sections, and more. The instruments you choose will depend on the overall effect you want to create and how they interact with one another.

5. **Melody:** Solos, riffs, harmony parts, and counterpoint (melody lines that weave around and through the lead line) all contribute to the melodic component of your arrangement. It's important to ensure that they complement each other and support the lead melody.

The first two elements—dynamics and structure—are the result of the whole arrangement working together to sustain and build interest. We'll look more closely at those in the following Shortcut.

The next three—rhythm, chords, and melody—describe the function of individual instruments. An electric guitar might play a chord on the first beat of each bar and hold it for several beats, fulfilling the chord function. Sometimes the same instrument can fill two roles: a piano or acoustic guitar might play chords in a rhythmical way, covering both the chord and rhythm function.

Each instrument has a function: rhythm, chords, or melody.

The bass guitar performs a rhythm function and also anchors the chords, so it can be categorized as both a rhythm and chord instrument. (Although bass lines can be melodic, the note range is generally far below the lead melody line and listeners don't perceive it as a melody, so I don't include it as a melody instrument.)

A guitar solo, a slow moving string line, or a sax riff, all add to the melodic or harmonic (by adding harmonies) aspect of the arrangement. A background vocal can function in a similar way, adding riffs, harmony parts, and fills, so think of these secondary vocals as part of your melodic/harmonic instrumental arrangement. The trick is to keep all of these elements from conflicting with the primary melody line and each other. If a part is busy and draws attention to itself, like a riff, try limiting it to the spaces in between the vocal. Harmony parts and countermelodies need to be handled carefully to make certain they don't rub against the lead melody or the chords, creating dissonance.

Practice using your "arranger ears"

While you can learn about things like instrument timbre, note ranges, and harmony from books, ultimately it will be your ear that tells you whether your arrangement is working or not. Just as you learned how to train your "producer ears" in Shortcut 67, you can also train your ear to hear and analyze instrumental arrangements. Producer and arranger listening skills often overlap, so when you work on one, you improve both.

To train your arranger ears, listen to and analyze the arrangements of successful film and TV songs to learn how the arrangement is created. In the following Shortcut, you'll learn how to create an arrangement layout sheet that can help you keep track of ideas, ones you can use when building your own instrumental arrangements. To get started, pick a song from the "Film & TV Song List" on page 310 and listen to it a few times as you do the following steps.

Study an arrangement by listening, focusing on the role of each instrument.

✆ Listen for the most noticeable instruments, the ones that are easiest to hear (excluding the lead vocal).

✆ Determine the function of each of the instruments or accompanying vocals. Is it rhythm, melody, harmony, or chords, or does it have more than one function?

✆ Listen for instruments that are less noticeable and determine if they're playing rhythm, melody, harmony, and/or chords.

✆ Now go back and focus on each instrument or vocal part, starting with the most noticeable ones. Where does each one start playing? Does it stay in all the way through the song or drop out and come back in? Where?

Do It Now

Choose a song from the "Film & TV Song List" on page 310 and listen to the arrangement using the steps in this Shortcut. "Shortcut Resources" on page 307 can help you find the films and shows that include these songs.

Shortcut #73

Add Dynamic Energy to Your Arrangement

Use these techniques and layouts to create a successful arrangement.

Arrangement dynamics—raising and lowering the energy of the instrumental track—play a crucial role in any successful recording. Whether subtle shifts or sudden leaps, dynamic changes keep listeners interested by adding variety and supporting the emotional rise and fall of the song. An arrangement that lacks dynamics feels static and lifeless.

Five ways to change dynamics

It's not difficult to change dynamic levels in your arrangement, merely a question of choosing how and when you want to do it. Here are five techniques that work well:

➤ Play louder in one section and softer in another.

➤ Add or subtract instruments. Bring in a second guitar or keyboard, or drop out a drum part or synthesizer pad.

➤ Increase the complexity of a part by playing more notes per beat or more fills or riffs.

➤ Change the way an instrument is played. For example, go from fingerpicking to strumming a guitar.

➤ Raise or lower the note range of an instrument.

Try these five ways to raise or lower the energy level.

A good arrangement uses a combination of these five techniques. Simply raising the volume level of an instrument is not enough by itself to create a compelling change of energy level. However, if you increase the volume *and* add a new instrument *and* change the way an instrument is played, it's likely to increase the intensity for the listener.

Organize your arrangement ideas

On the following pages, you'll find two arrangement "road maps" derived from successful film and TV songs. Listen to the songs and follow along with the map. I've also included a blank layout sheet for you to copy and fill in with your own arrangement ideas as you write and record your songs.

Instrumental Arrangement Layout #1

To hear an arrangement like this, listen to "One Day" recorded by Jack Savoretti, used in the end credit role of the film *Post Grad*.

Song structure: Verse / Chorus / Verse / Chorus / Bridge / Chorus

Song Section	Instrumentation	Function (See Shortcut 72)
Intro at :00	Acoustic Guitar #1	Rhythm & Chords
Verse 1 at :14	Acoustic Guitar #1 **ADD:** Light Percussion	Rhythm & Chords Rhythm
Chorus 1 at :43	Acoustic Guitar #1 Light Percussion **ADD:** Bongo Drum **ADD:** Bass **ADD:** Acoustic guitar #2 (on right)	Rhythm & Chords Rhythm Rhythm Rhythm & Chords Rhythm & Chords
Verse 2 (first half) at 1:11	Acoustic Guitar #1 Light Percussion **SUBTRACT:** Bongo Drum **SUBTRACT:** Bass **SUBTRACT:** Acoustic guitar #2	Rhythm & Chords Rhythm
Verse 2 (second half) at 1:26	Acoustic Guitar #1 Light Percussion **ADD:** Bongo Drum	Rhythm & Chords Rhythm Rhythm
Chorus 2 at 1:40	Acoustic Guitar #1 Light Percussion Bongo Drum **ADD:** Bass **ADD:** Acoustic guitar #2 (on right) **ADD:** Acoustic guitar #3 (on left)	Rhythm & Chords Rhythm Rhythm Rhythm & Chords Rhythm & Chords Rhythm & Chords
Bridge at 2:08	**SUBTRACT:** Acoustic Guitar #1 Light Percussion Bongo Drum Bass **SUBTRACT:** Acoustic Guitar #2 & #3	Rhythm Rhythm Rhythm & Chords
Break at 2:22	**ADD:** Acoustic Guitar #1 Light Percussion Bongo Drum Bass **ADD:** Acoustic Guitar #3 (on left)	Rhythm & Chords Rhythm Rhythm Rhythm & Chords Melody
Chorus 3 at 2:36	Acoustic Guitar #1 Light Percussion Bongo Drum Bass **ADD:** Acoustic Guitar #2 (on right) Acoustic Guitar #3 (on left)	Rhythm & Chords Rhythm Rhythm Rhythm & Chords Melody Melody

Instrumental Arrangement Layout #2

To hear an arrangement like this, listen to "Come Back When You Can" recorded by Barcelona, used in the TV series *The Vampire Diaries*.

Song structure: Verse / Chorus / Verse / Chorus / Chorus

Song Section	Instrumentation	Function (See Shortcut 72)
Intro at :00	Drum kit Bass Piano Electric Guitar #1 (on left)	Rhythm Rhythm & Chords Chords Chords
Verse 1 at :15	Drum kit Bass Piano **SUBTRACT:** Electric Guitar	Rhythm Rhythm & Chords Chords
Verse 2 at :44	Drum kit Bass Piano **ADD:** Electric Guitar #1 (on left) **ADD:** Strings	Rhythm Rhythm & Chords Chords Chords Melody (counterpoint)
Chorus 1 at 1:12	Drum kit Bass Piano Electric Guitar #1 (on left) Strings **ADD:** Electric Guitar #2 (on right) **ADD:** Background Vocals	Rhythm Rhythm & Chords Chords Chords Melody Chords Melody ("Oh" phrase)
Break & Verse 3 at 1:41	Drum kit Bass Piano Electric Guitar #1 (on left, lower note range) Strings **SUBTRACT:** Electric Guitar #2 (on right) **SUBTRACT:** Background Vocals	Rhythm Rhythm & Chords Chords Chords Melody
Chorus 2 & 3 at 2:24 At 2:54	Drum kit Bass Piano Electric Guitar #1 (on left) Strings **ADD:** Electric Guitar #2 (on right) **ADD:** Background Vocals **ADD:** Electric Guitar #3 (center)	Rhythm Rhythm & Chords Chords Chords Melody Chords Melody ("Oh" phrase) Melody
Tag/End at 3:22	Drum kit Bass Piano Electric Guitar #1 (on left) Strings **SUBTRACT:** Electric Guitar #2 (on right) **SUBTRACT:** Background Vocals **SUBTRACT:** Electric Guitar #3	Rhythm Rhythm & Chords Chords Chords Melody

Instrumental Arrangement Layout: Blank

Song structure: Verse / Chorus / Verse / Chorus / Bridge / Chorus

Song Section	Instrumentation	Function (See Shortcut 72)
Intro at :00		
Verse 1 at		
Chorus 1 at		
Verse 2 at		
Chorus 2 at		
Bridge at		
Chorus 3 at		
Tag/End		

Shortcut #74

Arranging: Use Similar Artists or a Genre as a Guide

You don't have to reinvent the wheel. Build on what's already out there.

What will your finished recording sound like? Will it have layers of electric guitars, powerhouse Rock drums, and a gritty vocal? Or will it be filled with punchy Dance/Pop synthesizer sounds, a programmed drum part, and a lead vocal with rhythmic chops? Whether you're writing Rock, Blues, Dance/Pop, or Americana, if you want to give your song an edge in the film and TV market, focus on identifiable, characteristic aspects of the genre's sound in your arrangement.

Why it's important to arrange in a genre or style

➢ **You make it easy to categorize and find your song:** In the two examples I just gave—Rock and Dance/Pop—the arrangement clearly conveys the sound of a genre and many of the artists working in it, making it easy for music users to categorize it correctly for potential uses. If your song features several of the elements of the contemporary Dance/Pop genre in its arrangement, it will be easy to classify. When a producer shouts, "Quick! I need a Dance/Pop song in the style of Lady Gaga!" a music supervisor or music library will easily find yours.

See Shortcut 6 for more on finding "in the style of" artists.

➢ **It helps you plan your recording:** The genre you choose will affect the decisions you make regarding your recording. For example, can you record a complex Dance/Pop arrangement in your home studio or will you have to find a producer with the knowledge and equipment it takes to create broadcast recordings in this style? Just what goes into a good Dance/Pop arrangement anyway? Do you have the skills needed? If you want to record and mix your tracks in your home studio, choose a genre that plays to your strengths and to the knowledge, equipment, and skills you already have. Maybe the barebones production of the singer-songwriter or the more acoustic, organic Americana style would work better for you than contemporary Dance/Pop.

Study a song arrangement in a style

Each genre has a sonic landscape and arrangement style of its own. Some are easy to spot: a Country song sounds different from a Hip-hop song in some obvious ways. But it's not always easy to discern the difference between a Hard Rock song and a Pop song. The lines can become blurred and one style can cross over into the other. Unless you already know a genre well, the best approach is to choose successful artists who are firmly established in a genre and use their work as a guide. Choose a couple of songs with a sound that's similar to the style you envision for some of your own songs and let the arrangements suggest musical directions you might follow.

See Shortcut 72 and 73 for more on instrument functions and dynamics.

> **Listen for the sound palette.**
> Make a list of the instruments used in the arrangement. Which instruments are featured? Which instruments are handling rhythm? Which are handling chords? Are there any instruments playing melody? How are the arrangement dynamics being created? Listen to the sound of each instrument. Does it sound organic and real? Or synthetic and electronic? Do you have equivalent sounds and effects in your studio or will you need to work somewhere else?

> **Listen for the performance style.**
> Do the performances have plenty of variety and subtle detail, the hallmark of live musicians? Are there some performances that sound highly repetitive as if they were looped or sequenced? This is characteristic of styles like Hip-hop and Dance/Electronica and needs to be handled well. Is the ensemble performance tight or loose? Can you play in this style or will you need to hire musicians?

No hard and fast rules, just a guide

Studying arrangements is simply a way of getting to know the elements of a good arrangement and the sound of a genre or group of artists. Being creative within your genre is a must. Have fun! But don't go so far that you lose the essential heart of the sound. A Rock song with a harmonica works fine, but a Rock song played by a Bluegrass band doesn't; it loses its essential sound and quality. This is an extreme example, of course, but you get the idea. The limits of the characteristic sound of a genre can be reached.

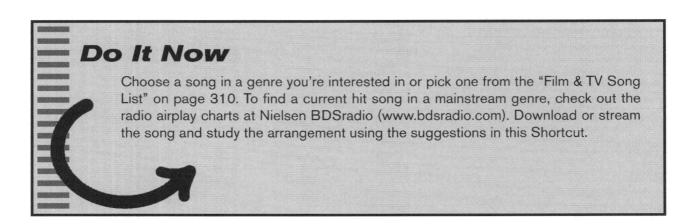

Do It Now

Choose a song in a genre you're interested in or pick one from the "Film & TV Song List" on page 310. To find a current hit song in a mainstream genre, check out the radio airplay charts at Nielsen BDSradio (www.bdsradio.com). Download or stream the song and study the arrangement using the suggestions in this Shortcut.

Shortcut #75

Try a "Bare Minimum" Arrangement

Craft guitar/vocal or piano/vocal arrangements that work.

In the world of film and television music, less can definitely be more. Often a simple, barebones arrangement can be as effective as a full band recording with layers of electric guitars and synthesizers. A single instrument, such as acoustic guitar or keyboard, plus a vocal may be all you need. Adding a bass to anchor the bottom keeps the arrangement spare and yet fills plenty of space. A single percussion part, like a shaker, preserves the feel and adds another texture. Basically, what you're aiming for is an arrangement that uses the minimum number of instruments to get the essence of the song across and create a mood.

Three good reasons to record a barebones arrangement of your song

#1: A minimal arrangement allows the singer to be the focal point of the song, creating an intimate, emotional sound that works well under scenes with or without dialogue.

#2: For home studio recording, a simple arrangement is likely to give you the best outcome. The less you have to juggle in the recording and mixing process, the better!

#3: A stripped-down arrangement moves any song toward the singer-songwriter style, which is very popular in the film and TV market.

Listen to some examples

Really simple production ideas!

The best way to get an idea of what barebones arrangements sound like is to spend some time listening to them. Here are just a few of the many tracks that have been successful in film and TV, tracks that rely on one or two instruments plus vocal.

Song	Artist	Instrumental Arrangement
"From the Morning"	Nick Drake	guitar
"Cannonball"	Damien Rice	three acoustic guitars, vocal
"Daydreamer"	Adele	acoustic guitar, vocal
"Songbird"	Fleetwood Mac	piano, vocal
"Hero"	Regina Spektor	piano, vocal
"Hide and Seek"	Imogen Heap	vocal through a Vocorder
"Say It to Me Now" (soundtrack)	Glen Hansard	guitar, vocal
"Rise"	Eddie Vedder	mandolin, vocal
"We're Going to Be Friends"	The White Stripes	acoustic guitar, vocal, foot taps

Five keys to a simple production

1. **Use dynamics.**
   Even in a minimal arrangement, you still need to change the dynamic level of the track in order to keep listeners involved. Adding a single vocal harmony part can build energy in the chorus. Adding a second guitar or bass can boost the interest level. Try changing the part you're playing: increase the number of notes per beat or raise the note range. Add a rhythm part: a shaker, tambourine, ethnic drum, kick, or snare drum to lift the energy. Consider a solo instrument like violin or cello. Remember that every sound counts so get the best performances you can.

2. **Fill space with the instrumental arrangement.**
   Determine the note range of the vocal melody then build your instrumental arrangement around it. The vocal will usually fill some portion of the midrange so, when working up your guitar or keyboard part, pay special attention to the high and low note ranges. The low notes can anchor the arrangement much as a bass part would. The high note range will add color and fill space above the vocal range. Adele's "Daydreamer" and Nick Drake's "From the Morning" are good examples of guitar arrangements that surround the vocal and fill a lot of sonic space.

3. **When a steady rhythm is needed...**
   A rhythmic strumming style on acoustic guitar can lay down a groove that eliminates the need for a drum track. Listen to Damien Rice's "Cannonball" to hear a two-guitar strummed style that sets up a steady beat. Eddie Vedder's "Rise" nails the rhythm on mandolin. Piano can set up a rhythmic feel using arpeggiated chords (playing the notes of a chord one after the other instead of together) or by playing a steady, repeated rhythmical phrase. Both acoustic and electric piano sounds will work. A percussion instrument, like shaker or conga, can keep the beat and still preserve the minimal feel.

4. **The vocal is the centerpiece.**
   In this style, the vocal is king and everything else is there to give it support. These vocals are very present, unadorned, direct and honest, almost as if the singer is speaking directly to the listener. Singing close to the mic and using very little reverb on the vocal is a good approach. Read Shortcut 79 for a whole host of ideas on how to deliver a strong vocal performance.

5. **Fill space with your mix.**
   For a good mix in this style you need to fill the entire sonic spectrum with a very few elements (instruments and vocal) from high to low end and left to right. For this type of work, where a fat sound is crucial, I recommend

spending the money on a good commercial studio. Have your arrangement all worked out and make certain you (or your singer) have worked on the vocal parts so you don't waste any time. Specific advice on recording and mixing in your home studio is outside the scope of this book. If you're working at home and you need help, try Studio Buddy (www.studiobuddy.com), a free, easy-to-use, downloadable reference that answers many basic recording and mixing questions.

Do It Now

Listen to the instrumental and vocal arrangements in the examples listed in this Shortcut. Go through your catalogue and choose a song or write a song and record a rough demo in the barebones production style.

See the "Film & TV Song List" on page 310 for information about the song examples in this Shortcut. "Shortcut Resources" on page 307 can help you find the films and shows that include these songs.

Shortcut #76

Produce Arrangements in Period and Niche Styles

From the Jazz Age to the Disco era, from the Blues to the Bayou, can you sound like that?

The film opens in a celebrity-filled nightclub. The disco ball is spinning like it's 1975, which it is. The crowd is grinding on a packed dance floor as the DJ drops the needle on another LP. So, what's playing? The drumbeat is unmistakable—four-on-the-floor and "pea-soup, pea-soup" on the high hat. The electric bass is fat 'n' slappy and has all the nuances that only a live player can bring to a performance. The Fender Rhodes electric piano is richly tonal and the electric guitar is cookin'. The sampled horns are playing a repetitive, edgy, looped riff and... What? STOP! This can't be 1975. The scene is ruined! Why? Because, of course, sampled horn riffs weren't used in 1975.

Because movies and TV shows must maintain the audience's belief in the reality of the story and characters, everything that's used, from the smallest prop to the cars and costumes must appear to be authentic. If the audience detects, even unconsciously, something that's out of place, they'll begin to doubt the story. Once that happens, the entire effect is blown. You *don't* want to be responsible for that!

What's true for time periods is also true for locations. If you want to transport the audience to a faraway place—and music is a very good way to do that—then be sure the arrangement, instruments, and performances sound authentic to the locale.

Be sure your arrangement, instrumentation, and performance are authentic.

If you're working in a niche style—a style that's limited to a region, time period, or has an identifiable, non-mainstream sound like Blues or Southern Zydeco—spend time studying and absorbing the sound so you can reproduce it convincingly. Films like *Music and Lyrics, That Thing You Do!, Paris 36,* and *O Brother, Where Art Thou?* include great examples of song arrangements in period and regional styles.

Do your research

Listen to recordings from the period or locale in which you're interested. Specialty record labels that carry historical and regional styles are good places to start. You can use your "arranger ears" to study the instrumentation and dynamics in niche styles in the same way as mainstream, contemporary styles. Read Shortcut 72 for ideas on how to listen to and analyze arrangements.

Focus on your strengths

Get a head start on the competition by making use of your strengths. If you play Blues guitar, get to know the arrangements and instrumentation of various Blues styles and eras. Make your guitar the centerpiece of your arrangement and get as close as you can to an authentic sound and performance.

Give yourself an edge. Use your strengths.

Get together with local musicians who have knowledge of regional or period styles and work up a few arrangements of original or public domain songs. When you have four or five well-rehearsed arrangements, go into a commercial studio and record them in a day or two.

If you've got a few vintage synthesizers and you just love the Pop music of the 1980s, by all means, go for it! As with many musical eras, the arranging style grew out of the cultural shifts and new technologies that were available. Try to capture that sense of excitement and exploration in your arrangement. Show respect for the period; don't parody it.

To be safe, keep it simple

The more instruments you use in your arrangement, the greater the risk that one will strike a false note with the audience. Keep your recording as simple as the style will allow. Strip down the arrangement to its basic elements and concentrate on making those as effective and credible as possible.

What about sampled sounds?

While those sampled horn riffs in the Disco track certainly didn't work, there are excellent sampled horns, string sections, woodwinds, and ethnic instruments that can be used in period and regional arrangements. The trick is to get as close to a realistic *performance* as possible. No matter how good the sound quality of a sample might be, if it's not played like a real musician would play it, then it's not likely to work. Pay attention to volume rides, variations in note attack and decay, and other nuances that make the difference between a stiff or inauthentic performance and one that sounds believable.

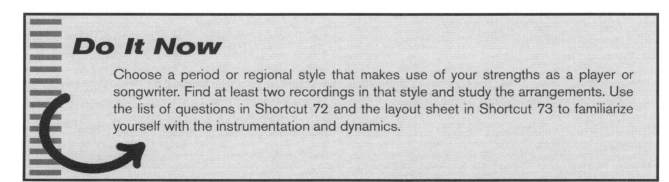

Do It Now

Choose a period or regional style that makes use of your strengths as a player or songwriter. Find at least two recordings in that style and study the arrangements. Use the list of questions in Shortcut 72 and the layout sheet in Shortcut 73 to familiarize yourself with the instrumentation and dynamics.

Shortcut #77

Shape Your Intro, Tag, and Ending to Add Appeal

*Little things can make your song more useful
to the film and TV market.*

While the verses, chorus, and bridge are the big guns of your song, the little things, like a final scene-ending chord or body-grooving introduction, can have a subtle but memorable effect. And it isn't just the audience that will appreciate these touches; intros and endings can make a big difference when it comes time to edit your song to picture. As you create your arrangement, take some time to give the beginning and ending a little TLC.

Use a "button" ending

*Button endings
are important!
Check this out.*

When you give the end of a song a recognizable stopping point, finishing it with a final chord, phrase, or note, this is referred to as a "button ending" or "definitive ending." This is in contrast to the fade outs used in many radio hits, where the song volume is simply lowered until the music is no longer audible, usually while the chorus repeats. With a button ending, the listener clearly knows the song is over.

A well-defined end point can create its own unique moment for viewers. In a sad song, it's like a final goodbye; in an upbeat song, it provides one last kick of energy. These moments can be very effective, especially when they land at the end of a scene, giving it a memorable wrap up. You can see a good example of this in the TV series *Life Unexpected*. In the closing scene of the first episode, the song "Can't Go Back Now" by The Weepies hits its final note just as the scene ends, giving the viewer a clear sense of finality.

To create a strong sense of completion, try ending a song by landing on the "home" chord, the I (one) chord of the key in which the song is played, as The Weepies do in "Can't Go Back Now." For a more unsettled ending, you can end on a note or chord that suggests the song is unresolved, like the IV chord. Listen to the final notes of The Fray's "Never Say Never" to hear this type of button.

While a gradual fade out at the end of a song can work for film and TV, consider this: A music editor can create a fade at just about any point in a song simply by lowering the volume, but it's very difficult, technically, to create a real button ending. (The final notes need to sustain and then release with a natural sound.) If you're not sure whether you want to use a button or not, try recording your ending both ways, then you can give music users a choice. Believe me, they'll appreciate the professional touch!

Use your intro to set the tone

The first thing the listener hears, before the vocal melody or lyrics, is the introduction—the first few bars before the vocal starts. This is a great spot to set up the overall energy and mood of your song. Is your song bright and upbeat? Set up a bouncy, energetic tone right from the opening notes. If the song's theme has to do with loneliness or solitude, try opening with a solo instrument, use a slow tempo, or feature a minor key feel.

A long intro of eight to sixteen measures would be unheard of in a hit radio single, but could be acceptable in the film and television market. The music editor might use your intro to create a smooth transition, setting up the tone of the song instrumentally before the vocal comes in. (Ray LaMontagne's "Be Here Now" is a song with a one-minute intro. In the film *27 Dresses*, all of it is used!) However, music supervisors are very busy people. When auditioning your song, they want to get to the vocal quickly. So, here's a useful trick: Mix two versions, one with a long intro and one that gets to the vocal within four measures or less. Pitch the version with the short intro. If there's interest, let them know about the other version.

<= Good idea...
Mix two versions.

Add a "tag"

A tag section consists of a repeated line at the end of a song. It may be an emotionally moving refrain line or one of the lines in your chorus, maybe a strong first or last line. The repeated line reinforces the central feeling or idea of the song. Repetition gives it a special significance and can create a haunting, memorable effect. In the Verse / Chorus song form, the tagline generally follows a single or double chorus at the end of a song. In the Verse / Verse / Bridge / Verse form, it can follow the third verse or replace it altogether, as it does in Ingrid Michaelson's "Keep Breathing."

To create a tag section based on your chorus, try varying the melody as The Fray does in "Never Say Never." The Fray's chorus is a series of repetitions of the line "Don't let me go." If the singer simply continued to repeat the line in exactly the same way in the tag section, it could become unbearably monotonous. Instead, the melody changes to a rising line, intensifying the emotion and building the dynamics of the song. You can hear another great example at the end of "Let's Not Pretend" by 16 Frames. You'll hear a double chorus with a tag based on the final line shortened and altered to maintain interest. Like the Fray's song, it also uses a button ending.

Try a tag at the
end of the song.

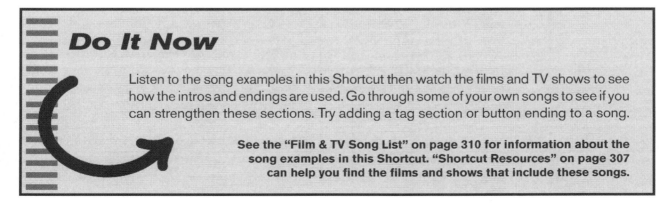

Do It Now

Listen to the song examples in this Shortcut then watch the films and TV shows to see how the intros and endings are used. Go through some of your own songs to see if you can strengthen these sections. Try adding a tag section or button ending to a song.

See the "Film & TV Song List" on page 310 for information about the song examples in this Shortcut. "Shortcut Resources" on page 307 can help you find the films and shows that include these songs.

Shortcut #78

Get Your Instrumental Performances in Shape

Support your song with a good performance that has solid energy and feel.

The quality of the instrumental performances on your recording is crucial to your success in the film and TV market. Confident playing, good ensemble work, and a solid rhythmic feel provide a strong foundation that helps your track create the all-important mood and energy that music users look for. An uneven or messy performance can undermine the very things you've worked so hard to achieve in your song.

A confident performance is key

Listeners can sense when a performer is uncertain, even if there are no obvious mistakes. A small hesitation or stumble in the rhythm can tip them off. If the overall feel or emotional commitment in the performance is weak in spots, they'll sense it even though they might not be able to tell you exactly why.

"Confident" doesn't mean "perfect" but it does mean really, really good!!!

Practice, practice, practice. The best way to ensure a strong performance is to rehearse. Whether you're playing solo piano or working with a band, be sure that everyone knows what to play! If you're thinking about what you're supposed to be playing, then you're not focused on expressing energy and emotion. Audiences can sense the difference.

Use a chord chart. A chord chart can be a big help. It provides an easy road map to the song that allows musicians to focus on feeling and interpretation instead of wondering what chord comes next. Even if you're the only musician, write out the chords of the verse, chorus, bridge, intro, and ending for yourself. The simplest chord sheet consists of the lyrics with each chord change indicated above the word where it occurs. A more elaborate chord chart includes the bar lines with the chords indicated for each measure. These are helpful if there are a lot of chord changes or the chords change in unexpected places. If you're working with other musicians, try numbering each measure for easy reference. Jotting down a lyric line at the beginning of each section can make it easy to locate a verse, chorus, or bridge. If you alter your chord progression while you record, be sure to update the chart.

Record when you're fresh and alert. Energy and inspiration tend to ebb fairly quickly, resulting in performances that are sloppy and less than inspired. The takes that are likely to yield the best results are the ones you record after you're warmed up but before you start to lose energy.

Comp tracks: Combine the best from several takes

To create the best possible performance on an instrument, you may want to compile (or "comp") the strongest parts from many takes. Let's say you're playing a piano part. You might record several complete takes, choose the best parts from each one, and combine them on a single track. Make certain your edit points are smooth and natural sounding, and that the combined portions match each other in terms of musical energy, style, and flow. If your playing loosened up as you did multiple takes, you may hear a difference when you try to comp an early take with a later one.

Comp the best parts of each take for the strongest performance.

If you're recording at home where you can afford to spend a lot of time, try recording a few takes, comp the best portions, then take a break. Come back when you're fresh and see if you can beat what you recorded earlier. You may decide to use portions of your new takes, make a whole new comp track, or stick with what you had.

Keep the ensemble tight

Whether you're playing all the parts yourself, bringing in a couple of additional players, or working with a full band or combo, all the performances need to work together to create a seamless overall sound.

Chords should change at the same time. Check to be sure that all instruments with a chord function are working together. Don't let one guitar change chords at a different time than another. All instruments, including bass and drums, should support "pushes." These are chord changes that are played on the upbeat before a strong beat; they create a sense of rhythmic anticipation.

Organize riffs and instrumental hooks. These instrumental attention-grabbers should be placed where they can shine on their own and avoid conflicting with the vocal. If you've got a ton of great ideas for riffs and licks—*too many* great ideas—try saving a busy, overplayed take for an instrumental mix. (Read Part Seven for more on instrumental mixes of your song.) For the vocal version, record a simpler take or do some creative editing and muting in the mix.

The elements of a good performance.

Lock into the rhythmic feel. Every instrument must work together with every other instrument to create a single overall rhythmic feel. Bass, drums, guitar, and keyboards should all be playing in sync. Focus on one instrument as your rhythm guide and check to make certain that all others are locked into the same tempo and groove. Avoid a stiff or programmed sound. Simply using the quantization function in your music software to sync up the instrumental performances won't work! Music is about energy and feel. Good musicians know how to nail the beat and still create a body-moving rhythm.

Your instrument

Tune it up. Nothing can wreck a good performance like a tuning problem. Tune up before every take. Use an electronic tuner to provide a consistent tuning reference. *Guitar players:* Be a pro and change your strings a few days before a recording session. New strings stretch and go out of tune quickly. If you're working with a band, be sure everyone is in tune with each other. If you're recording in a commercial studio, using their acoustic piano, ask them to have it tuned before the session begins.

If you need a better instrument, rent one.

Use an instrument with a good sound. If your instrument has problems that cause rattles, buzzes, or other noises during a session or if it has a thin sound or is difficult to tune, consider renting something better from a music store or equipment rental service. Do it a few days before your session to give yourself time to get used to it. Remember, though, even the best instrument won't mask a weak performance. If you don't feel comfortable on a rental, then consider investing some money in improving the instrument you have.

Hire first-rate musicians

If you can't nail the performance yourself, bring in someone who can. Use the resources in Shortcut 81 to find pro musicians. Talk to local studio owners about the top musicians in your area. Studios are likely to have heard these musicians and will know whether they're experienced in recording work. Listen to their work before hiring them. Be sure they are familiar with and can play in your style.

Play to a click track

Learn to work with a click track.

The click track is loved by producers and hated by musicians but, love it or hate it, it's a powerful tool that can help you deliver a solid performance. The trick to working with a click is to learn how to lock into the beat and still keep a human feel. A pro musician will have this skill down. Practice until you can play comfortably in time to the click. Your goal is to play so tightly with the click that you make the click sound disappear.

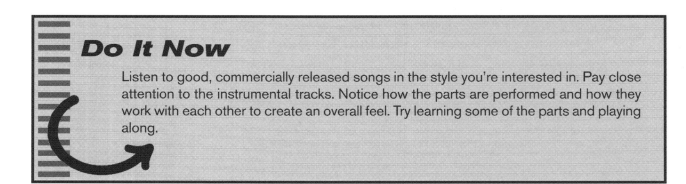

Do It Now

Listen to good, commercially released songs in the style you're interested in. Pay close attention to the instrumental tracks. Notice how the parts are performed and how they work with each other to create an overall feel. Try learning some of the parts and playing along.

Shortcut #79

A Strong Vocal Performance Brings Your Song to Life

Eight tips producers use to get a great vocal performance.

Music supervisors gauge the impact of a song by their own response to it. They may call it a *ping* or *resonance*. Whatever word they choose, they're talking about the direct, heartfelt response that a good song evokes in them. The vocal performance is responsible for much of that *ping*. If the singer sounds unsure or uncommitted, if the vocal is hidden under layers of reverb, if the singer is missing that high note, then the melody and lyric may never have a chance to work their magic.

Secrets of a strong vocal performance

Whether you're recording the vocal yourself or producing a singer, here's a list of vocal tips that will add strength to any vocal performance.

Tip #1: **Pitch is important.** That seems obvious, doesn't it? But notice I didn't say, "Pitch is *everything.*" A great vocal performance doesn't have to be pitch perfect. There are ways to play with pitch as part of a singer's style. You can scoop up to a note (start low and rise to the pitch) and you can fall off the pitch at the end, but the "meat" of the note should be on pitch. Think of it this way—the vocal pitch needs to be *accurate enough that it never becomes a distraction for the listener.* A good rule of thumb: If you record a note that makes you wince a little every time you hear it, or draws your attention in any negative way, fix it! If you're not sure, fix it!

Should you use auto pitch correction? Many music-sequencing programs come with a tuning function that can be applied to a recorded vocal. Use it sparingly. If you tune a vocal note more than a small amount, it becomes very noticeable and artificial. If a note is flat, the best solution is to re-record it. In the R&B and Hip-hop genres, obvious auto pitch correction is currently an acceptable effect but could soon become dated.

Tip #2: **Focus on phrasing.** "Phrasing" can make the difference between an adequate vocal performance and a very good one. "Phrasing" refers to the rhythm of a singer's delivery. Within the rhythm of the melody as it is written, the singer has some leeway: stretching out a word to add emphasis, rushing a few words to create energy, taking an unexpected breath to set up a word, or grouping words in a way that underlines their meaning. Phrasing also refers to the way the singer relates to the underlying beat of the song, sometimes dragging the words a little, at other times getting ahead of the beat. Above all, effective phrasing

Good phrasing can make a vocal shine!

expresses the meaning of the words, keeping them from becoming just syllables that are sung.

All good singers use phrasing to keep listeners involved in their vocal. Listen to tracks by John Mayer, Christina Aguilera, Sheryl Crow, or Kings of Leon; you'll hear great phrasing. Try singing along with some of your favorite vocalists to learn their phrasing patterns and techniques.

Try speaking first then singing the lyric.

Tip #3: **Add emotion to your performance.** A strong vocal performance makes the audience believe that the singer is feeling the emotion embedded in the lyric and melody. Here's a tip that can help: Imagine yourself saying the lines to someone as you sing. Even better, speak the lines out loud, with feeling, just before you record your vocal. (Interestingly, when you focus on the meaning of the words, pitch problems are often reduced or disappear entirely. Try it!)

Tip #4: **Be yourself.** Besides singing with good pitch, phrasing, and emotion, and having to do it all into a microphone, you need to do one more thing: Be yourself. Your personality and character need to come across. One of my favorite tricks for getting that last piece of the puzzle to slip into place is to record until you've got a strong complete take or a compilation of several takes (Tip #7 below), then go for a "party track." I don't mean literally have a party, just record a few takes in which you let go of thinking and just feel it. These takes can often be more spontaneous and inspired than earlier ones, providing single lines or whole sections that are better than what you already have.

Don't hide!

Tip #5: **Don't be embarrassed to be naked.** Trying to hide a weak voice by doubling it, slathering a lot of reverb on it or adding a chorus effect rarely works. With each additional effect or double, more of the intimate, personal presence of the singer is lost. Instead, try doing the opposite! Emphasize the personal quirks and idiosyncrasies by singing close to the microphone, perhaps a half inch to one inch away. Avoid pops by positioning the mic just above your lips or to the side of your mouth. (Singing so close to the mic will add extra "oomph" to the low end of your voice. It's called the "proximity effect." Roll off some EQ in that range to compensate.

Tip #6: **Choose the right note range.** Decide on the note range *before* you start recording your final track. If you're doing the vocal, make certain you can comfortably reach the highest note of the song. Never let listeners know you're pushing your limit; it makes them uncomfortable. Always keep something—extra volume, one more note—in reserve. If you're working with a singer, talk to him or her ahead of time to determine the note range so you can record your track in the right key.

Tip #7: **Record multiple takes and comp your vocals.** There are many ways to record vocals and different singers prefer to work in different ways.

The complete take: It's a wonderful thing to record a vocal from beginning to end in a single pass. It gives you a chance to create a strong emotional performance with an organic flow. If you like to work this way, try recording three or four complete takes. Each one may have sections that are stronger and those that are weaker. Listen to each and make notes on the sections, and even individual lines, you think are the most effective. Then compile the strongest parts of each take onto a vocal comp track.

The punch-as-you-go take: Unfortunately many of us don't have the stamina to make it through a complete take and still have as much energy as we'd like by the final chorus! If that's you, consider warming up with a couple of complete takes. Keep what you like from those, then start at the beginning and record a strong first verse, then a good chorus, then the second verse, and so on. The trick to doing this is to sustain the emotional energy as you go. Speak the words before singing. (Use Tip #3 above.) Listen to your rough demo or earlier takes to stay in touch with your original feeling. If you haven't gotten a good take in one hour, stop! Take a break and come back when you're fresh.

Three ways to approach a vocal recording session.

Get close, then fix-as-needed: Sing two or three complete takes. By the third take, chances are you'll be warmed up and still fresh. That's the sweet spot! Listen to your third take. If you like most of it, go back and record only the individual lines or words that need to be fixed. Make certain that you choose a good place to punch in (start recording) and punch out (end recording). Don't chop a breath in the middle or cut off a word. (*Hint:* The best spot to punch in is at the beginning of a word, keeping any intake of breath that's already there.)

Tip #8: **Take a few lessons with a vocal coach.** There are plenty of major artists who do this; they just don't tell anyone! A good vocal coach can show you how to breathe so you can produce a sound that's natural, how to reach for the high notes without straining, and help you find a variety of phrasing choices. Explain what you want to do, play some of your own songs and artists you think are similar in style. Sure, there will be some vocal exercises involved, but you'll still end up sounding like you, only better.

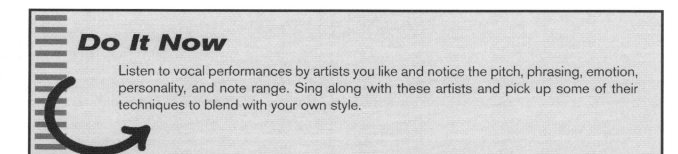

Do It Now

Listen to vocal performances by artists you like and notice the pitch, phrasing, emotion, personality, and note range. Sing along with these artists and pick up some of their techniques to blend with your own style.

Shortcut #80

Choose the Right Singer for Your Song

Will you sing your song or hire a vocalist?
Use this guide to vocal style.

Even a great singer doesn't handle every style equally well. A killer vocalist with jaw-dropping Dance/Pop chops may not be able to deliver the emotionally revealing, raw sound of the singer-songwriter style. A voice that sounds great on a Jazz song could turn in a weak Rock performance. Some voices have a very contemporary sound; others are more retro. Whether you'll be singing on the track or hiring a vocalist, it pays to research the vocal sound that will work best for your song.

Know the vocal style you're aiming for

Look for artists with songs that are similar to yours in style. (If you don't know which artists are similar, Shortcut 6 can help you.) Make a list of songs by two or three of these artists. Listen closely to the vocal performance on each and answer these questions:

Identify the characteristics of a vocal style with this list of questions.

Q: Does the singer have a wide or narrow note range? What are the highest and lowest notes the singer hits? If the notes are more than an octave apart, then the singer has a reasonably wide note range.

Q: How is the singer starting and ending notes? Are there scoops at the beginning? A little riff on the end or a fall off in pitch? How is the pitch overall—on pitch, sometimes off pitch?

Q: Does the singer have a gritty voice or a clear tone?

Q: Is the singer hitting high notes with a lot of strength or using a thinner, more fragile "head voice"?

Q: Is the singer relying on a powerhouse performance with plenty of vocal chops to get the song across or using a more intimate, conversational style?

Q: Is the singer using a lot of rhythmical feel (Dance/Pop and R&B/Pop are good examples) or is the rhythmical feel of less importance than putting the words across?

Q: Is the singer using vibrato (a small, rapid fluttering in pitch) on sustained notes? Or are the notes held without vibrato?

Q: What interesting vocal tricks is the singer using that catch your attention? How often? Where?

Q: Do you feel that the singer believes what he or she is singing?

Q: Is there a lot of emotion in the vocal? Or is there more focus on attitude and personality?

The vocalist you use for your recording should have many—and preferably most—of the characteristics you've identified from listening to artists and songs that are similar in style to yours.

Will you be the singer?

You wrote the song. You know every emotional nuance you put into the lyric and melody. When you sing the song, you feel an emotional connection to it. Friends and fans have told you how much they like your performance of the song. *But* are you going to be the singer on the recording you pitch to music users? Here are some things to consider.

➤ **Compare your vocals with the vocals of similar artists.**
Use the answers to the questions on the previous page and compare them with your vocal style and ability. If the style demands a lot of a singer, do you have the chops? Are there some techniques you need to work on? Try singing along with some of the songs on your list to get a feel for the style. Does it feel comfortable for you?

Would you hire yourself for the gig?

➤ **Does your voice have the right sound for the song's genre?**
You may be a very good Rock singer, but if you've written a Billie Holiday-style 1930s Jazz/Blues song, your track will have a better chance of success if you bring in a vocalist who has a tone that's reminiscent of Holiday, Norah Jones, Joss Stone, or Madeleine Peyroux. It's not all about chops; vocal tone and timbre play a big role.

➤ **Can you get enough distance from the song to produce yourself?**
Songwriters tend to sing lines over and over as the song is being written, locking in much of the interpretation before the song is finished. Discovering new and effective ways of delivering a line is a tough challenge. A singer who is exploring the song for the first time may discover new interpretations you never even thought of. It happens!

➤ **Tailor your songs to take advantage of your vocal style.**
If you really want to sing your songs yourself, then take a step back and assess your vocal style and strengths. If your song has a wider note range than you can handle, you could consider reworking the melody so you can sing it more easily. If you sound like Tom Waits, write a song in the Americana genre and deliver it with plenty of grit and feeling. If you've got a soft, breathy voice, aim for the intimate singer-songwriter style of Meiko or Jack Johnson.

Will you hire a singer?

If the song is in a style that's not your strength, if the melody is outside of your range, if you've written a song for the opposite gender, or you just don't feel like singing this one, there are many vocalists who can do a great job for you. Unsigned artists are often interested in recording demos for songwriters because it gives them one more opportunity to be heard! Shortcut 81 has some excellent resources for finding singers to record your demo.

Be sure you choose a singer who's right for the style of your song. Listen to samples of his or her work and compare them with the characteristics you identified in the list of questions.

When you find a singer you like, check to see if he or she has studio experience; a talented but inexperienced singer can turn your recording session into a marathon.

If you find a singer you like, consider collaborating on a song. Build it around the singer's strengths. You'll save the cost of hiring a vocalist and end up with a lead vocal that you know is in the right style!

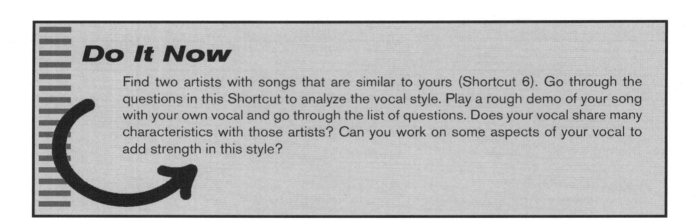

Do It Now

Find two artists with songs that are similar to yours (Shortcut 6). Go through the questions in this Shortcut to analyze the vocal style. Play a rough demo of your song with your own vocal and go through the list of questions. Does your vocal share many characteristics with those artists? Can you work on some aspects of your vocal to add strength in this style?

Shortcut #81

Try These Pro Musician and Singer Resources

Top session players and singers deliver tracks over the Internet.

No one can do everything! Even the best major label singer-songwriters surround themselves with pro engineers, excellent producers, and experienced musicians. You, too, have access to pro resources that you may not even know about and they're just a mouse click away.

Drums

Guitars, bass, and vocals can be handled fairly easily in a home studio. But what about a live drum track? Not just any drum track but a great sounding track with a solid groove and tasty fills. It takes multiple mics, cables, inputs, and a room with good acoustics to handle a full drum kit. It also requires a great kit, an excellent drummer, and the know-how involved in mic placement and recording. This is a big investment of time and money, and wouldn't you rather be writing, anyway? Well, you can have good drums and still have a life! Consider hiring one of the excellent session drummers who offer to record to your track in their own studio for $125 to $200.

It works like this: You send the drummer your track via mp3. He records the drum part and sends it to you as a file (or multiple files). Then you line up the drums with your original track and continue with your project. You'll find more information on each drummer's website, including details on click tracks, count offs, and the forms in which the final tracks can be delivered to you (file types, drums mixed or separate). Here are a few websites to get you started. All of these drummers give you complete ownership and control of the recorded drum tracks.

Hire a session drummer to play and record drum tracks for you.

> Drums For You (www.drumsforyou.com)
> Brian McRae (www.drumoverdubs.com)
> Craig Sowby (www.myonlinedrummer.com)
> Shay Godwin (www.edrumsessions.com)

More instruments

A mix of live instruments with your MIDI sequences can be your ticket to a great track. MIDI performances, even with authentic sounding samples, often lack the feel and energy of live players. Try adding just one live trumpet to a section of sampled horns or one real violin to a synthesized string section and suddenly your whole arrangement sounds totally *real*. It's amazing what a single live player can do to add energy and authenticity to a track.

If you live in an area with an active music scene, ask local studios to recommend the top players in your area. You're looking for musicians who have plenty of experience with studio tracking, not necessarily those who can wow an audience onstage. Live performance and studio chops don't always go hand-in-hand. Studio players need to be able to learn a song quickly, play the part consistently and without mistakes, and maintain spontaneity and emotion while doing multiple takes.

While top session drummers have discovered the Internet, other musicians have been slower to pick up on the idea. Here are two websites where you can audition a variety of session players who offer long distance tracking on a Work for Hire basis, meaning you own and control the recorded tracks.

> Studio Pros (www.studiopros.com)
> Online SongMasters (www.onlinesongmasters.com)

Finding the right singer

Shortcut 79 can help you capture a good vocal performance.

The vocal is the most important single element in your track and there may be times when you need to bring in a singer who can really nail the style. Ideally, you want to be in the studio while the singer records your vocal so you can give feedback. That means that local singers will be your first choice. Again, a recording studio in your area can be a good source of leads. If that fails, then try local clubs and music venues. Look for a lead singer in a band or a solo artist who has the sound you're looking for. While a singer with studio experience is a plus, an authentic, emotional sound is essential so focus on that first. If you can't find someone local, try these online resources.

> Online SongMasters (www.onlinesongmasters.com)
> Studio Pros (www.studiopros.com)
> CD Baby (www.cdbaby.com)
> At CD Baby, click on "Explore Music." In the "Sounds like" box, fill in the name of an established artist whose vocal style would work well for your song. Listen to samples until you find a few singers you like. A quick search will usually turn up a website with contact information.

Very Important: Both Studio Pros and Online SongMasters state that all performances are done on a Work for Hire basis. To learn more about Work for Hire, read the next Shortcut.

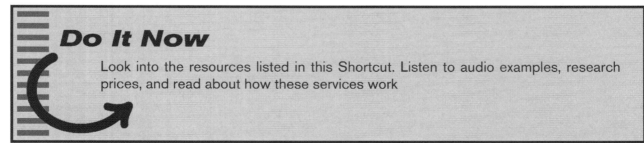

Do It Now

Look into the resources listed in this Shortcut. Listen to audio examples, research prices, and read about how these services work

Shortcut #82

Get Release Forms from Musicians and Singers

Avoid problems later by getting Work for Hire waivers up front.

If you're the only singer on your recording and you played all the instruments, then, clearly, you're the owner of that recording and you control the rights. This will be important when you're ready to make a deal with a music supervisor or film and TV music library. However, at some point, you're likely to write some songs that require the services of a musician or singer other than yourself. Let's say you want a bagpipe solo or an acoustic rhythm guitar performance that nails the part better than you can. Or you need a vocalist in a style you can't cover. What then?

If someone else, a musician or singer, performs on your recording you may not have the right to do everything you want with the final recording, and that extends to placing it in film and television productions. To ensure you have all the rights you need, have all the performers sign a short release form in which they declare their performance to be a "work made for hire." In this Shortcut, you'll find an example you can adapt for your own use. Get the form signed up front or when you pay for their work. Don't wait until later!

To learn about the rights you need, read Shortcut 100.

What is a "work made for hire"?

Under the U.S. Copyright Act, a "work made for hire" is defined as a work that is "commissioned"—specially made at your request—and is the subject of a written agreement. When a work is made for hire, the person who pays for the work (that's you) is considered the author and owner of the work. In other words, when you apply to the Copyright Office for a copyright, you'll indicate that *you* are the author of the "sound recording/performance," as well as the music and lyrics.

While the use of Work for Hire agreements has grown along with the increased use of unsigned songs in the film and TV market and the rise of music libraries, the musicians you work with may not have signed one previously. It's important to discuss this with them early on and make certain they agree.

Lead singers may need a special deal

Until recently, most demo singers could safely assume that their performances would only be used to pitch a song to publishers and artists (a purely "demonstration" use). However, with the rise of film and TV placements for independent songwriters, there are times when a singer may contribute a lead vocal to a recording that is then used in a primetime TV series or national commercial, generating sizable fees for the songwriter but nothing for the singer. As a result, many singers won't agree to a total waiver of their rights to the performance.

If you're hiring a singer to handle the lead vocal be sure to discuss your plans for pitching the song. If the singer feels that her role in the eventual success of the track is worth more than a single upfront payment, you might consider offering 10% of whatever you receive in master use fees. (If you make a deal with a music library to pitch your song, they'll keep a portion of the fees so be sure you only promise 10% of what *you* receive.)

The singer might also be interested in a release of the track as a music CD single or download. Make this a separate deal, just as a soundtrack album for a film is a separate deal. Since you paid to record the track you will be the record label, paying the singer an artist royalty. Consult a music business attorney if you and the singer decide to go this route. There are demo services such as Studio Pros (www.studiopros.com) and Online Songmasters (www.onlinesongmasters.com) whose lead singers will waive all rights to their performances.

Samples

Samples have rights, too!

Avoid using any samples you've recorded from another artist's work. Even if you obtain a clearance it will probably only cover music CD sales and downloads; these clearances don't extend to film and TV placements. Sampled sounds from a commercial sample library that you own should be fine as long as they're used in the context of a production. Check the licensing agreement that came with your sample library.

Nashville demo services

Nashville is a special case.

There are many studio production facilities in Nashville that offer high-quality demos. The musicians are excellent and, in fact, many of them play on albums by the Country genre's biggest stars. They work under a special Musicians Union contract called a "Demonstration Contract" that allows demos to be recorded inexpensively but *doesn't* allow the recording to be used for commercial purposes such as film and television broadcast. For that, you'll need to upgrade to a "Master Contract" at a higher rate. (You can read both contracts and see the rates on the union's website at www.nashvillemusicians.org.) You'll have to decide whether the song has a chance of paying back your investment if you choose the higher rate.

Producers

If you work with a demo production service or producer who creates some or all of the tracks for you and you pay a fee for the work, treat the producer as you would a performer and get a signed Work for Hire agreement. Make it clear that there is no participation in the master recording or songwriting.

WORK FOR HIRE AGREEMENT

This letter of agreement confirms that your work (the "Performance") on the recording titled _____ ("Recording") shall be considered a work made for hire as defined in Section 101 of the U.S. Copyright Act. You irrevocably grant to _____ ("Employer") all rights of every kind in and to the Performance(s) rendered hereunder, including the sole and exclusive right to copyright the Performance in Employer's name as the sole owner and author thereof.

Employer agrees to pay the sum of $_____ upon completion of the Performance in a recording satisfactory to the Employer. No additional royalties, residuals, re-use fees, new use fees or other payments required under any collective bargaining agreement shall be payable to or on your behalf for services performed hereunder. It is agreed that Employer may license the Recording for all synchronized uses, including all visual media now or hereinafter devised, without additional payment of any kind.

You hereby grant to Employer the worldwide right in perpetuity to use and publish and to permit others to use and publish your name, likeness, voice and other biographical material in connection with your services and performances hereunder.

Accepted and Agreed:

_____   _____
            Performer   Date

_____   _____
            Employer   Date

Shortcut #83

Make Broadcast Quality Mixes

The five essential features of a successful film/TV mix.

Film and TV songs stretch across an enormous range of styles and sounds. Still, there are some basic mixing concepts that apply across the board. Clearly, these will give you a competitive edge when pitching in this field.

5 Features of a Broadcast Quality Mix

➢ The mix emphasizes the vocal performance without losing the rest of the instruments, even at low volume.

➢ It has a crisp, clean top and bottom end and a smooth, even mid-range (no nasal or honking frequencies that jump out at the listener).

➢ All the sounds are well defined, each occupying its own sonic territory.

➢ It fills the sound space, both across the stereo field (width) and front to back (depth).

➢ The mix is stable (it retains these features) on many different types of speakers.

Check your instrumental arrangement

Before you dive into your mix, check to be sure that your arrangement is well thought out. If an electric guitar is riffing over the vocal, you may have to mute parts of it. If a string line is conflicting with a guitar chord, fix it now. Be sure you built dynamic changes into your arrangement. Don't rely on the mix for this. If you didn't do so already, go back to Shortcut 73 and make an arrangement layout of your song.

Clean up your tracks

Listen to each track in solo mode. Clean up any noises or noticeable edits. Check the vocal track to be sure that all breaths sound natural. Mouth noise in between words and talking should be muted. At the same time, get to know what's on each track. Like a juggler, learn what it is you're going to have to keep in the air.

Feature the vocal

Many engineers begin by muting all the tracks, then working on the drums first, followed by the bass, then guitars and keyboards, and finally the vocal. For film and TV mixes, consider getting a good vocal sound first, then bringing in the other instruments around it. Create a "pocket" for the vocal by rolling off EQ on the other instruments that are in the vocal range. This will allow you to keep the volume higher on those instruments without overwhelming the singer.

<= Do this!

Compare your mix with similar tracks

Continually refer to successful film and TV songs that are similar to yours. Stop every 30 minutes or so and play a reference track. Check the vocal sound and the relative level of other instruments, as well as the EQ, use of effects, and the stereo spread of the bass, drums, guitars, and keyboards.

The highly polished sound of a Dance/Pop track is very different from the raw edge of a Garage Rock song, so be sure the reference tracks you choose share vocal, lyric, and musical qualities with the track you're working on.

Gather information

Bring in an experienced engineer to create a basic mixing set-up for you, setting EQ, compression, reverb, and stereo panning. Take a "snapshot' of this basic setup. Most music software applications will let you create a template that will automatically bring up these settings when you start recording a new song. Whenever you record a track in this style, you can use the template to start your mix, then change as needed.

Hire a pro to help you get a good sound. Then use it as a template.

For specific suggestions on EQ, effects settings, and stereo panning, check out Studio Buddy, a free application offered by TAXI (www.studiobuddy.com) or any of the books on home recording available at Amazon.com or in your local bookstore. Read the manuals that came with your software and hardware. Then get in the sandbox and play!

Keep your ears fresh

As every mixing engineer knows, it's easy to get lost in the details; before you know it, you've spent hours messing with a snare sound. Chances are you've gone way past getting a good mix by that point. Stop. Take a break. Come back to the mix with fresh ears. Play your reference tracks to get some perspective, then play your own track. Make notes as you listen, make the changes you want and then take another break.

Mixing on headphones: When your neighbors need their beauty sleep but you need to work late, headphones can be the best solution. Just be aware: headphones cause ear fatigue more rapidly than speakers, so take breaks frequently. They also exaggerate the stereo effect, so it's a good idea to check the mix at low volume on your speakers. Some top engineers prefer to mix on speakers at low volume, feeling they get a better balance that way.

Test your mix on many speakers

Give your mix the speaker test!

A film and TV mix has to sound good on a wide range of speakers, from cheap built-ins to pumped-up home entertainment surround-sound systems. The best way to test your mix is to play it on many types of speakers. Car stereos, home stereo systems, and computer speakers are great places to listen. Don't forget to enlist your friends. Their cars, computers, and home stereos will give you even more ways to hear your mix. And, by all means, play your mix through your TV speakers. Many DVD players will play CDs. Just pop a music CD in the player and see how your mix will sound on TV!

How to listen: To get a reference on all these different speakers, first play one of the reference tracks you've been using during your mix. Notice how the speakers affect the sound: Does the vocal still sound clear, are the other instruments still present, what's happening to the low end and high ends? Then play your own track. Does it undergo the same sonic changes? Or did something else happen? If your vocal suddenly disappeared or the high end became an irritating, spitty mess (and it can happen), your mix may not be as close to the reference track as you thought. Make a note of the differences and go back into mix mode.

Keep this in mind

A great mix can't save a poor performance so, before you invest time and money in your mix, be sure that all the recorded performances are strong.

And remember: *Match your project to your capabilities.* If you don't have much experience as a mixing engineer, you'll want to keep your projects simple at first and work up to more complex mixes. Try a barebones arrangement to start with (Shortcut 75). A good guitar and vocal performance with a clean mix… you could get a placement with that!

Do It Now

Go through the "Film & TV Song List" on page 310 and look for songs in the style you want to work in. Buy the song (CD quality is preferred) and listen for the five features of broadcast quality mixes. Choose one song to use as a reference track and try mixing a song of your own to match it. Take special care to get the vocal sound as close as you can.

Shortcut #84

Mastering Is Not Needed for Film & TV Tracks

Pay attention to the peaks and overall sound levels during your mix.

Mastering is a process that's used to ensure all the tracks on a recording are perceived to be at a similar volume level and co-exist in the same world as far as overall sound. In other words, from a listener's perspective, on a mastered recording, even tracks that don't have the same instrumentation or vocal sound will flow smoothly from one to the next. For radio airplay, tracks are mastered to give them the maximum overall volume, hoping they'll grab the listener's attention. This has led to tracks that are heavily compressed so that every instrument is pushed to the maximum possible volume level.

Although mastering can be very useful for commercial CDs, digital releases, and radio singles, it isn't necessary for film and television uses. Here's why: The volume level at which a song will be played in a film or TV show will be determined by the type of placement. If a song is played under dialogue, it will be at a very low level. If it's used to create emotion or atmosphere over a montage of scenes, it might be played at a much higher volume. In other words, it doesn't need to match surrounding tracks as a CD or radio single does. Professional mastering or excessive compression isn't needed. As long as you create a clean, well-balanced mix with instruments and vocals that are clearly defined and fill the appropriate space, you'll be in good shape. You don't need to have the loudest mix on the block.

In film and TV, the volume is determined by the use.

However, this doesn't mean that you can submit a track that's far below the average volume level. Just like any listener, music supervisors don't like to manually crank the volume to the max just to hear your song. It suggests that the mix is amateurish, a perception that could rub off on the song.

Master your track while you mix

For film and TV, you can add some mastering tweaks to your track while you mix. You want to aim for the best *overall* level for your track. One brief peak can prevent you from raising the level of the entire track, so focus on the peaks.

➤ Look for those instruments that contribute the most volume and lower them during the peak.

➤ Try removing an instrument that won't be noticed at that point.

➤ Instruments in the low end, like bass, can add a lot of volume. Try extra compression on the bass track.

➤ Boosting EQ adds volume so try rolling off EQ on some individual instruments where it won't be noticed.

➤ Put a master compressor or limiter on your final mix. You can do this right on your master fader. Or, if you prefer, you can run a final stereo mix then make adjustments to EQ and compression on that mix, giving you two final mixes—one mastered and one not.

Your master is only as good as your song

Mastering can't save a poor quality song or performance. Be sure you focus on lyrics, melody, production, and performance before you even think about mastering. It's the last link in the chain and certainly not the most important one. There isn't a music supervisor out there who will say, "Gee, this is mastered so well, I think I'll use it!" They're looking for heart and soul. If raising the overall volume level and tweaking the EQ can help to put that heart and soul across, then go back to your mix and do it.

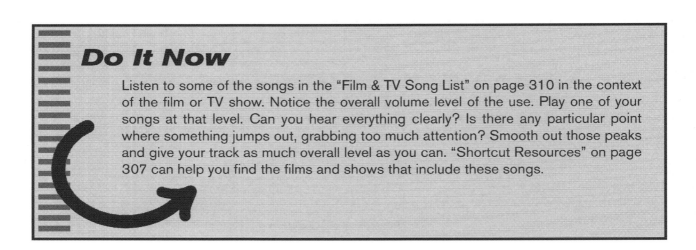

Do It Now

Listen to some of the songs in the "Film & TV Song List" on page 310 in the context of the film or TV show. Notice the overall volume level of the use. Play one of your songs at that level. Can you hear everything clearly? Is there any particular point where something jumps out, grabbing too much attention? Smooth out those peaks and give your track as much overall level as you can. "Shortcut Resources" on page 307 can help you find the films and shows that include these songs.

Shortcut #85

Use This Pre-production Checklist

*Lay the groundwork for your recording
and get the results you want.*

Pre-production is something that creative types, like songwriters, tend to avoid like the plague. Nevertheless, I'm urging you to put on your producer hat, move your songwriter-self off to the corner for a while, and focus on one of the most important jobs of record production. While it does have its slogging-through-mud aspects, it will pay off in time and money saved and a final product that lives up to your expectations.

What is pre-production?

The pre-production process ensures that you have all the resources you need to complete your recording within your budget before you commit money and time. If you'll be recording at home, do you have the equipment and expertise to finish the job? If you're going to be using a demo production service, can you afford all the musical bells and whistles you envision? Do you need to rethink your arrangement? You want this project to go as smoothly as possible from beginning to end. Use this checklist to give yourself the best chance of getting exactly what you want.

The Pre-Production Checklist

Assess the commercial potential of your song. Have you heard songs in a similar style used in film and TV? Is your song competitive? Go through the Music and Lyric Checklists one last time.	☐
Record a rough demo of your song at the tempo you want. Be sure the vocal lead hits the right notes and sings the final lyric (Shortcut 68). Check to make certain the chords are correct, then write the chords on a lyric sheet or make a chord chart (Shortcut 78).	☐
Choose reference tracks. Look for songs that are similar in style. You might select different reference tracks for arrangement, performance, vocal style, and mix.	☐
Work up an instrumental arrangement. Decide what instruments you'll be using and write up an arrangement layout sheet (Shortcut 73).	☐

*Use this
checklist to help
you get the best
results.*

Set a maximum spending cap for your budget. As you go through the checklist, try to keep the total cost under this amount.	☐
Decide on your recording strategy. Where will you record? Where will you mix? Will you use some combination of home studio and commercial studio? Get a cost estimate from the commercial studio (Shortcut 71). Check your home studio equipment to see whether you need to invest in additional equipment (Shortcut 69).	☐
If you're using a demo production service, contact them. Play your rough demo and discuss your arrangement ideas. Give them the titles of your reference tracks and talk about them. Get a cost estimate (Shortcut 70).	☐
If you'll be producing this yourself, choose the musicians and singers you'll be using. Contact them. Work out a price. Confirm it in an email.	☐
Project your final budget costs based on the information you have so far. If you're over your limit, rethink your production. Could you do this with fewer musicians? Less studio time? Simplify your arrangement?	☐
Get release forms from musicians, singers, and producers signed and returned to you (Shortcut 82).	☐
Make certain your arrangement is complete. Intro, ending, riffs and hooks, instrumental breaks. If you're using a vocalist, confirm that the song is in the right key for him or her.	☐
Create a recording schedule. Contact any musicians or singers to make certain they're available. Aim for a realistic completion date.	☐

If you've laid a strong foundation based on this checklist, you're much more likely to end up with a successful, broadcast quality recording. Save time! Save money! Do it right!

PART SEVEN

Shortcuts to Instrumental Opportunities

There are not just thousands but millions *of opportunities to place instrumental tracks in film and television! Multiply your placements and your income by pitching your song tracks as instrumental music.*

Shortcut #86

Song Beds: You've Got Instrumental Music

Use your song's instrumental track to create more pitching opportunities.

While you're arranging and recording your song, you're creating something more, something that can provide many additional pitching opportunities for you and earn extra income. It's a "song bed," also known as a track-only mix, instrumental mix, or TV mix. Your song's instrumental track, minus the vocal, is a stand-alone piece of music that can be in scenes, commercials, promo spots, and trailers.

Television uses millions of pieces of instrumental background music, or "cues," each year. While feature films have a music budget that allows instrumental music to be written expressly for a scene, many television shows and networks rely on music libraries to fill their needs. These music users need everything from powerhouse Rock instrumentals to intimate, solo piano pieces. The track you created to accompany your song can be edited, rearranged, stripped down, and remixed to fill the needs of this market.

An instrumental cue may be a track-only mix of a song!

Although a performance royalty for a background instrumental cue is a fraction of what you would make for a featured song performance (a one-minute cue pays about 20% of what a similar featured song use would earn), when you place multiple instrumental tracks, those royalties can really add up. Unlike most song uses, a single cue may be used more than once during a movie or TV program. Each time your cue is played, it earns a royalty payment. And keep this in mind, too: Instrumental cues earn royalties by the minute. A two-minute cue will earn twice as much as a one-minute cue.

Once you have your song bed, you can create instrumental cues of different lengths, add or mute instruments to vary the texture and dynamics, or replace the lead vocal with an instrument. I'll tell you more about all of these options in the following Shortcuts, but first, let's lay some basic groundwork.

Listen to examples

Instrumental song beds are used in many commercials and TV shows. You might not even realize they're the accompaniment for a song; they stand on their own as complete, usable instrumental music cues. Here are a few:

➢ A series of television ads for the Ford Fiesta uses an instrumental mix of "Janglin'," by Edward Sharpe and the Magnetic Zeros, minus the lead and group vocals on the chorus. To see it, do an Internet search for the phrases "Ford Fiesta," "It's a Pretty Big Deal," and "video."

> The dance film *Step Up 2: The Streets* uses the vocal version of Kevin Michael's "We All Want the Same Thing" about 19 minutes into the film. It follows that up with a short instrumental mix of the same song less than two minutes later, giving a sense of unity to the scene.

> MTV's *The Hills* reality show uses the instrumental track from Vaughan Penn's "Bring on the Day" as the opening background cue. This rhythmic instrumental provides the music that plays under recaps of the previous episode. (You can see episodes of *The Hills* on MTV's website.)

> Cadillac ads have been very successful in using instrumental portions of songs. In some cases these are instrumental intros and breaks from the actual song track rather than a mix minus the vocal. You can hear this type of use in 2009 Cadillac ads featuring the song "1901" by Phoenix. Here, the 27-second intro jumps straight to the one-word, repeated hook line. In other ads, only the intro was used. You can find the Cadillac ads at YouTube.com.

How to make a song bed

The easiest way to create a track-only mix is to mute all the vocals, including any vocal doubles, harmonies, and background vocals, then run your mix. If you still hear a "ghost" of the vocal, check to see that all the vocal effects, like reverb and delay, are muted.

> **Create a button ending:** While you're working on your track, spend a few extra minutes on the ending. Make certain your track has a clear, well-defined end point. Avoid long instrumental fade-outs. Instead, use a chord or riff with a clean finish (instruments end at the same time). Leave a couple seconds of silence at the beginning and end of your track. (For more on button endings, read Shortcut 77.)

No SFX allowed!

> **No sound effects in your mix:** If you include the sound of ocean waves in your track, you limit its uses. Put it in a desert scene? No way. When creating a song bed, remove all sound effects such as crowd noise, nature sounds, car horns, or laughter, anything that might conflict with the content of a scene and distract the viewer.

Have a "track-only" mix ready to go

If you recorded and mixed your song in your own studio, run an instrumental mix immediately after your final vocal mix. That way, you can be certain that the two mixes are identical in every way except the vocal.

If you're working in a commercial studio or using a demo production service, be sure to ask them for a track-only mix. They should be happy to do this for you. There may be a small extra charge but it's well worth the money. If you're able to do some editing on your home computer, you can ask for various sub-mixes (or "stems") that will allow you plenty of editing flexibility at home. To learn more about stems, read Shortcut 87.

> **Don't keep them waiting:** When your song is placed, the music supervisor will ask for your instrumental mix. Why? Because it can be used to adapt your song to the demands of a scene, replacing a portion of the vocal with the instrumental to avoid conflicts with dialogue, looping it to extend the song, or adding a few seconds to make certain a lyric line falls in the right place. A music library will ask for a track-only mix when they make a deal for your song. You don't want to find yourself saying, "Gee, I haven't got one" or "I'll see what I can do." Be ready to rock 'n' roll. Get your instrumental mix done ahead of time, have it clearly labeled, and ready to go out the door.

Always get an instrumental mix of your song.

> **Be sure you have all the rights you need:** If there are musicians other than yourself playing on your track, make certain you have Work for Hire releases from them. If your track was recorded under the Nashville Musician's Union "Demonstration Contract," you will not be able to pitch the instrumental version to film and TV. See Shortcut 100 for more information on recording rights you need for film and television.

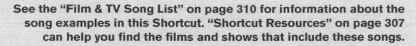

Do It Now

Listen to some of the instrumental uses above. The commercials can be found on YouTube.com. You can also check the website at Splendad (www.splendad.com) for commercials that use songs. Look for a song name next to the ad. Given the tight time constraints and the importance of the voice-over message, many of these commercials use instrumental versions and breaks from the songs.

See the "Film & TV Song List" on page 310 for information about the song examples in this Shortcut. "Shortcut Resources" on page 307 can help you find the films and shows that include these songs.

Shortcut #87

Add Flexibility to Your Mixes with "Stems"

Make sub-mixes of your track for versatility and ease of editing.

A "stem" is a sub-mix. It includes some of the instruments or vocals in your full mix but not all. It can consist of a single instrument, a vocal, or a group of related instruments or vocals along with any effects, such as compression, reverb, or EQ, that are applied to those tracks. Stems allow you to easily change the relative levels of groups of instruments without remixing, use only some elements of your final mix, or make a difficult edit easier.

Let's say you have a full track mix that includes a vocal, two acoustic rhythm guitars, bass, a drum kit, and piano. If the acoustic guitars are playing the same part, they could be considered a single instrument group. One is probably panned to the left and one to the right. Both have a little reverb, some EQ, and perhaps other effects. The acoustic guitar stem would consist of a stereo mix of both guitars plus their effects. The drum kit is actually made up of several different instruments: cymbals and high hats, snare, toms, and kick drum. You could create a stem of the entire drum kit or turn the drum kit into two stems: one consisting of high-end percussion (cymbals and high hats) and the other snare, toms, and kick drum.

These mixes are made by muting and un-muting tracks depending on which instruments you want to record. You can record a mix of each individual instrument, if you like. Don't forget to record the lead vocal as a stem and give the background vocals their own sub-mix.

Choose your instrument groups

Make sub-mixes of similar instruments.

When grouping instruments, generally you want to keep together instruments with a similar function and sonic range. So you might include a shaker and tambourine with the drum cymbals and high hats—all are high-end percussion instruments. If you have several layers of dark synthesizer pads, you could group those together. However, if there are bright synthesizer strings featured in the chorus, you wouldn't include those with the dark synth pads. To allow flexibility, try grouping those with an instrument that isn't playing in the chorus.

If you're working in a commercial studio, consider making fewer sub-mixes as these will take extra time. Decide on what will be most useful—maybe drums on one stem, bass and guitars on another.

Things you can do with stems

> **A stem can become a stand-alone cue:** An acoustic rhythm guitar stem that creates a folksy mood could work as a cue. A dark synthesizer pad might become an atmospheric, ambient cue. If the stem feels incomplete on its own, you can use it to build up new ideas and arrangements.

> **Change the relative levels of instruments within a mix:** Let's say a music supervisor feels that the lead guitar in your song mix should be at a lower volume and the vocal should be louder. You can quickly reassemble your mix changing the levels of those elements. Or perhaps a mix without drums would provide better support for a scene. Reassemble the stems sans drums.

Customize your mix quickly and easily!

> **Stems provide a useful back-up:** While today's music software and automated boards make it easy to recall a mix, there's no guarantee you'll get exactly the same result! Changing one piece of gear in your studio may mean that you'll never be able to recapture exactly the same transparent synth sound! If you recorded in someone else's studio, you may not be able to get back in or they may have changed their gear. If you have stems, you can reassemble, remix, or replace parts without having to worry about whether everything is exactly the same as it was.

> **Stems can be helpful when editing:** Even with the convenience and accuracy of digital editing, there may be times when a music editor just can't find an edit point that will work. Editing the stems individually can solve that problem.

Important things to remember!

> **Add a reference sound at the top:** A single short click or beep in the same spot on each stem before the track begins will help you line up your tracks when reassembling the mix. Or you can just make sure you start all your sub-mixes at exactly the same point. Adding four to six clicks or drum hits to set the tempo before the track begins will make it possible to add new instruments at the beginning.

<= Don't forget to do this!

> **Keep the silent spaces:** As you record your stems, you'll notice long periods of silence in many of the tracks. For instance, if the background vocals only come in on the chorus, there will be long stretches during the verse sections when you won't hear anything. That's fine. Just stay in record mode and let it roll. When you put the stems back together to recreate your mix, those long silent stretches will keep everything in the right place.

Shortcut #88

Texture: Keep Your Instrumental Tracks Interesting

Add dynamics and create new cues with this simple idea.

In a full song production, the vocal is the focus of the track. The content of the lyrics, distinctive phrasing, and tone of voice all work together to keep the song interesting. When you remove the singer, you lose an important piece of the puzzle. A track that was created to support a vocal may sound repetitive and monotonous without it.

While background cues can get away with a certain amount of repetition, too much of it creates a static feel. On the other hand, if your track changes too radically, it could be difficult to place. A high-energy cue that works well for a chase scene won't be very useful if it suddenly becomes thoughtful and introverted! Your goal is to keep the instrumental mix evolving and changing enough to sustain interest without altering the core energy or feel. You can do that by playing with sonic textures in your arrangement.

Avoid being static and boring!

Here's an example of what I mean: If you keep the tempo and rhythmic feel of your track unchanged but shift the tone of a bright electric guitar to a more muted, percussive sound, you'll create a very noticeable difference in the sound of your track. However, as far as the audience is concerned, you haven't changed the energy. That's because texture relies on sound, not rhythmic feel or pace, to work its magic.

Changing textures

Like a painter with a palette of colors, you can mix and match sounds according to your taste. You could change an acoustic rhythm guitar part to rhythmical fingerpicking, then return to the full guitar part. You could drop out the drum kit for a few measures and replace it with another percussive instrument, like a shaker. Play with these ideas, experiment. If you don't like the result, return to where you started and try something different.

Here are four changes you can make to individual instruments within your arrangement that will alter the texture of your track.

Five ways to change texture!

- Change the sound: bright to muted, distant to present.

- Change the playing style: smooth to percussive, chords to single notes.

- Change the note range: low to high or vice versa.

- Add, subtract, or replace instruments.

- Adjust an instrument's volume level or panning.

Use what you already have

If you mixed the full track in your home studio, you can go back to the unmixed tracks and make changes there. If you mixed somewhere else but you have some basic home recording gear, you can use the stem mixes (Shortcut 87). Line up the stems so they're playing in sync then try muting one or more at some point. One of the simplest ways to vary the texture of a track is to start simple and add instruments. Begin with just the drums then bring in the guitars, then bass, and finally everything else.

Sometimes a small change in the mix can make a big difference: Bring one of the instruments closer to the center and raise the volume slightly to draw more attention to it. Adding a single, sustained note on a synthesizer, doubling an electric guitar with piano chords, or muting an instrument for several measures can subtly change the sound. When you've got something you like, run a new mix. Be sure to label your mix. Give it a descriptive name that will help you find it later, like "My Title: version with piano."

Start using those stem mixes.

Tips for enhancing cues with texture

➢ **Don't overdo it:** Give listeners a chance to absorb and react to changes in texture. When you make a change, consider sticking with it for at least four to eight bars, longer if you feel that it supports the energy of the track.

➢ **Keep your track organized:** Choose a logical spot to make changes, like the beginning of a song section, where listeners might expect to hear a difference in tone. If you're making changes to more than one instrument in the section, either have the changes occur at the same time or gradually build them. For instance, mute the bass and keyboard at the beginning of a verse and let the drums and a guitars carry on, then bring the keyboard back in at the beginning of the pre-chorus, and the bass at the beginning of the chorus to create a dynamic build.

➢ **Make a clear statement right at the start:** If your Rock track starts with a low-energy intro and first verse before slamming into a big, powerhouse arrangement for the rest of the track, you can improve your chances for a placement by starting your cue with the chorus. A music supervisor will hear a single, focused feel right from the start.

➢ **You've got related cues:** Don't give up on the intro and first verse of that track, though! Create a separate cue. Although it's less energetic and intense, it shares similarities with the hard rockin' cue. A music editor can mix and match the two as needed. By splitting them up, you give the editor more flexibility while creating two cues you can pitch. And don't forget that you can make two or three versions of *this* cue, too!

➢ **Watch out for the dialogue zone:** As you add texture to your cue, try to avoid busy, melodic parts in the middle to upper ranges. These could conflict with character dialogue or narration. (Read Shortcut 89 for more about the dialogue zone.)

➢ **Try a mix with background vocals:** You don't have to eliminate all the vocals. If you have "ahhh" and "oooh" vocal hooks in your arrangement, run a mix that includes them. To hear this type of mix, watch Sharpie's "Self Expression" commercial featuring "Mister Sister" by The Tender Box. You'll find it at YouTube (www.youtube.com).

Test as you go

While you work on your cue, keep a DVD or videotape handy, one with a scene that you feel would work well with your cue. Test your changes by playing the cue with the scene or with several similar scenes. Did the changes you made enhance the effectiveness of the cue or diminish it? Think like a music editor as you work on your cue to give it a competitive edge.

Do It Now

Listen to the music cues in TV dramas, reality shows, news programs, and commercials. Notice how they create energy, vary it, and build it. Try texturing and editing a few instrumental cues from your own song instrumental tracks for uses like these.

Shortcut #89

Replace the Vocal Melody
with an Instrument

Fill the space without getting in the way of dialogue.

Removing the lead vocal from your track can have a big effect on your mix. All those midrange frequencies you rolled off to create a "pocket" for the vocal are now empty and the stereo field has a hole in the center where the vocal was. Some tracks can survive the loss of a lead vocal better than others. A good Dance/Pop track with a cool groove will probably do fine with just a few volume adjustments. However, if texturing or changing volume levels doesn't effectively fill the gap, you may want to consider replacing the vocal melody with an instrument.

Replacing a lead vocal

The majority of instrumental cues are played under dialogue. Here are some tips that will help you create a music cue with a melody that won't get in the way of spoken lines.

Truth is... dialogue is more important than music!

➤ A busy melody line with a lot of motion, especially in a high or middle note range, is likely to conflict with dialogue. Try smoothing out the melody. You can convert a series of short, repeated notes to a single long one or simplify a fast up or down run of notes by eliminating some.

➤ Use an instrument that's characteristic of the genre, one that blends into the track. Again, this helps to keep the melody line from drawing attention to itself and away from dialogue or voice-over narration.

➤ Keep the volume of the melody line at or below the loudest instrument in the mix and keep the playing consistent. A note that's louder than the average volume level could be distracting.

➤ Unless you're creating a very high-energy cue, this is not the place to show off your athletic ability on your instrument! Keep the performance restrained. Stay away from fast runs and trills.

➤ After you record a mix with an instrumental melody, run a mix without the melody. A music editor could use the melody version to lead into a scene then cut to the non-melody version when dialogue or narration begins.

Keep it real

Remember, you're replacing a vocal track so try to preserve some of that human feel. Avoid a stiff, programmed sound in your melody line. Even if you're not a top-notch musician, you can still turn in a workable performance. This isn't about dazzling listeners. You want to fill the space with something that feels natural. Practice the part ahead of time then record several takes and compile the best from each. You can also record one or two phrases at a time, stop, practice the next few lines then record those. Be prepared to do whatever it takes to get the performance you need.

Use your stem mixes

Read Shortcut 87 for more info on stems.

This is where stem mixes can really come in handy. Line up all your stem mixes except for the lead vocal. Record the instrumental melody line and place it in the center where the vocal would have been. Blend it into the mix with a little EQ and reverb and you're done!

If you recorded and mixed the project in your home studio, you don't have to use the stems. You can go back to your unmixed tracks and add the instrumental melody then run a mix.

To hear a great example of an instrumental track with a melody line, watch the Ford Fiesta commercial called "It's a Pretty Big Deal." You'll hear a zany marching tune that is, in fact, the instrumental version of "Janglin'," by Edward Sharpe and the Magnetic Zeros. (See the ad at YouTube.com.) The song's chorus includes the melody line from the song played on brass.

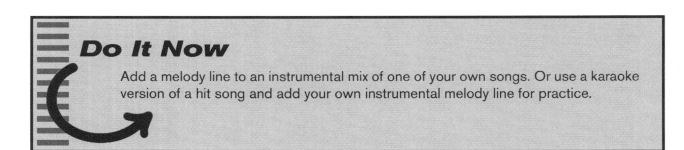

Do It Now

Add a melody line to an instrumental mix of one of your own songs. Or use a karaoke version of a hit song and add your own instrumental melody line for practice.

Shortcut #90

A Simple Solo Track Can Get a Placement

An acoustic guitar or piano track may be all you need.

There's no rule that says film and TV tracks must be complicated, filled with layers of instrumentation, or require 250 tracks of digital magnificence in order to be effective. You don't need to record the London Philharmonic or a squad of ocarina players. Often, a single instrument is enough to suggest a warm homecoming or evoke the sensation of wonder or love.

A good solo performance on piano, acoustic guitar, accordion, harmonica, or violin can be a strong, pitchable track in the film and TV market. Solo acoustic guitar tracks are always in demand. Hartford Insurance commercials use solo piano in one ad, solo guitar in another. An Oreo commercial uses synthesizer bells and tuned percussion sounds. Sometimes simple is best.

Check your individual tracks

If you recorded a barebones arrangement of your song—just piano and vocal or guitar and vocal—you may already have an expressive solo instrumental. Mute the vocal then listen to the accompaniment to see if it will work as a stand-alone track.

Go through the stem mixes of your more complex arrangements to see if you have a single track that evokes an emotion or mood on its own. You don't need a full three-minute, song-length track; anywhere from 30 seconds to two minutes will be enough for a cue. (See the following Shortcut for information on editing your tracks for length.)

When working with solo tracks, any ambient noise or leakage from other tracks will be difficult to mask. Listen carefully to identify any problems. If there's unwanted noise, try using a different section of the song or, if necessary, re-record the track.

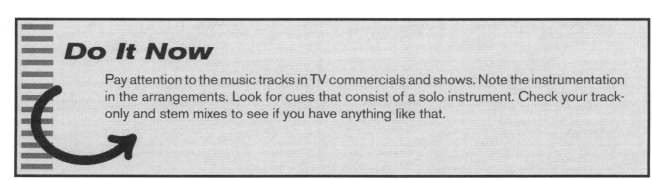

Do It Now

Pay attention to the music tracks in TV commercials and shows. Note the instrumentation in the arrangements. Look for cues that consist of a solo instrument. Check your track-only and stem mixes to see if you have anything like that.

Shortcut #91

Edits: Turn One Track into Many Cues – Bumpers, Stings, & Transitions

Be prepared to give them a range of track lengths they can use.

So far, I've been showing you how to create a variety of instrumental cues from your arrangement by texturing, soloing, and replacing the melody. But, there's another way to turn one track into many cues: editing the length. Commercials and TV shows use hundreds of short cues every day, millions per year. The standard lengths of 30, 60, and 90 seconds are the most common.

Obviously TV commercials are big users of the 30- and 60-second lengths but TV shows of all kinds use these cues, looping them to create longer pieces of background music.

Instrumental music for commercials

:30, :60, :90 are standard music lengths for some cues.

Because a television station works on an exact timetable, weaving hundreds of commercials and TV shows in and around each other every day, TV commercials must stick to predictable lengths. When they ask that a music cue run for 30, 60, or 90 seconds, they really mean it! Small errors can add up, eventually causing evening programs to be late and possibly moving some commercials into or out of the time slot they paid for. There's no room for error, no forgiveness for "a couple extra seconds." When you work in this market, you have to get used to working within fractions of a second.

In fact, a 30-second music cue must end at 29.5 seconds to be used in this market. That means the reverb has tailed off and there is complete silence *at exactly* 29.5 seconds. If the cue ends earlier than that, it will be too short for a standard 30-second commercial; if it ends later than that, it will have to be edited. Unless the cue is very desirable or unique, the music editor will simply use a different cue. The same holds true for all standard cue lengths. For instance, a 60-second cue must end at 59.5 seconds, a 90-second cue at 89.5 seconds.

Bumpers, stings, and transition music

While commercials are the primary users of 30- and 60-second cues, there are music uses that depend on even shorter lengths—15 seconds or less. Watch a TV news program or segmented show of any kind and you'll hear numerous "bumpers," "stings," and other transition cues. These are short bits of music that start, end, or link segments of the program.

Bumpers are used when a program transitions to a commercial and then again from the commercial back to the program. Often the bumper consists of a quick distillation of the show's theme music, from five to ten seconds long. However, for shows that use a lot of them, like news programs, this would quickly become predictable. So bumpers are also selected based on the energy and mood they create. A bumper must make a quick, highly focused musical statement that communicates energy or mood to the viewer. News programs, for example, try to transition to a commercial break with a high-energy bumper. When returning from a commercial break, they will use a bumper that sets a mood for an upcoming story.

Stings are even shorter than bumpers, as short as one or two seconds in some cases. They provide a kind of musical punctuation mark. Like bumpers, they can be used at the end or beginning of a scene.

You can hear transition music in TV dramas, smoothing the changeover from one scene to the next. These music cues can be used to suggest the passage of time, a move to a different location, or a shift in content.

The job of bumpers and other transition music cues is to prepare the audience for what's coming next. These musical transitions are very important for creating and maintaining a sense of flow and forward momentum, keeping viewers from tuning out or changing channels.

Transition cues are an important music use.

Button endings are the general rule

A well-defined button ending is the norm for all of the cues I've mentioned in this Shortcut. While there are occasional exceptions, you'll find that the majority of music used in transitions and commercials have a clean, intentional ending: a chord, a note, a drum hit or riff. As I've pointed out previously, a music editor can create a fade at any point but creating a button ending is much harder. Read Shortcut 77 to learn more about button endings.

Things to remember about short cues

➤ **Short cues require editing.** If you've got a computer with a music software program, you can handle the editing involved in these cues yourself. It takes some practice and it can be laborious at times but, with a little work, you can master it. You'll have more control over your edits if you use your individual, unmixed tracks or stem mixes, rather than trying to work with your entire instrumental or vocal mix.

➤ **Make a safety copy of your original tracks and stem mixes.** This type of editing is not always reversible. Don't work with the only copy of your tracks or stem mixes!

➤ **Take advantage of natural edit points.** An average chorus length is around 45 seconds. Tack on half of your intro in front of the chorus and the button

Edit your tracks for commercials, bumpers, and stings.

ending and you should be close to a 60-second cue. Adjust to reach the exact length you want by repeating or cutting individual measures.

> **Look for ultra short cues at the beginning or end of your track.** Often, you can create a five-second cue from the last few notes of your track, especially if you have a button ending. The button itself can work as a short cue and can also be edited onto the ends of other cues from your song. Try using the first few notes of your intro and adding the button for an ultra short cue.

> **Make several mixes.** Just as you did with your full track, you can make many different mixes, some with multiple instruments, some solo for these short cues. Don't forget to include any texturing and melody replacement (Shortcuts 88 and 89).

> **Try recording a few of these during the session.** Keep these ultra short cues in mind during your tracking session. You might record the last measure of the arrangement as a separate take; the intro as another. Avoid the time it takes to make edited cues by intentionally recording them.

> **Organize your cues.** Creating many cues of different lengths can turn into an organizational nightmare. Be sure to label your cues with a descriptive phrase and the cue length. Try making a folder for all the cues derived from a particular song with sub-folders for cues of various lengths.

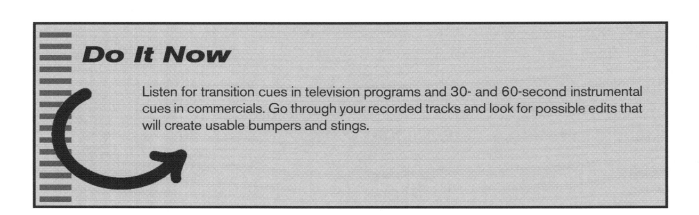

Do It Now

Listen for transition cues in television programs and 30- and 60-second instrumental cues in commercials. Go through your recorded tracks and look for possible edits that will create usable bumpers and stings.

PART EIGHT

Shortcuts to Getting Placements in Film & TV

Your song is written.

The music and lyrics create mood, energy, or atmosphere.

The recording supports the song with strong performances

and a solid mix. Now it's time to take it to market!

Shortcut #92

The Giant Step to Getting Your Songs Placed

Do this and the rest will follow.

You're pumped! Ready to take on the business of getting your songs out into the film and television market! Perhaps you even skipped over the song craft Shortcuts in this book and started reading right here. You might be saying, "I've got a whole CD filled with great songs that are ready to go." Or "I've been writing and recording for years—I know my music is great."

Congratulations! And I sincerely mean that. There's nothing wrong with either of those statements, but if you really want to successfully target the film and TV market and create an income-producing business for yourself, try shifting your thinking just a little. How do you know if your songs are what *they* are looking for? How do you know whether your songs will fill *their* needs? *Changing your point of view from "I" to "they" is the most powerful and productive way to approach this business.*

Shift your thinking from "I" to "they"!

Not all good songs will work for them

Let's say you and your band play live shows that absolutely slay your audiences. You've got a song that your fans are crazy about and you feel it ought to be a shoo-in for some TV show or film. Keep this in mind: Some of your song's appeal is based on the energy you put across in your performances. Will that energy still be there when your recorded track is played at low volume underneath a scene with dialogue? Will it move a TV audience if all they hear is the chorus? Will the lyric and music work together to increase the impact of a scene?

To learn the answers to these questions, study how songs are used in film and TV productions then try playing your own songs in a similar way under a few scenes. Was your song as effective in enhancing the scene as the song that was used? If not, you might have a song that works well for *your* purposes, but may not work as well for *theirs*.

Think beyond your album

If you've already recorded an album, go ahead and start getting your songs out into the market. *But don't stop writing and recording!* You'll have the best chance of success if you can become an ongoing resource for the industry. Use the Shortcuts in this book to help you give your songs a competitive edge as you move forward: Sharpen your choruses. Add tightly focused energy. Create atmosphere. You don't have to spend a lot of money on recording new songs. Keep costs low by taking a barebones approach to production. A simple arrangement with a featured vocal will work for this market as long as it has emotional integrity, solid performances, and a clean mix.

9 Tips for Taking the Giant Step

Start taking the giant step to film and TV success now!

1. Study how the film and TV market uses songs (Part Two).

2. Use tempo, rhythm, and melody to create mood and atmosphere (Shortcuts 38 through 40).

3. Write a universal lyric (Shortcuts 47 through 50).

4. Focus your lyric on a peak moment and use emotional details (Shortcuts 51 and 52).

5. Define your song structure. Music editors will thank you (Shortcut 26).

6. Record solid performances in your genre (Shortcuts 78 and 79).

7. Make a clean, well-balanced mix that features the vocal (Shortcut 83).

8. Fit into a genre or artist style (Shortcuts 6 and 74).

9. Always make an instrumental mix of your song (Part Seven).

Do It Now

1. Go through your songs and identify the ones that are most likely to work for the film and TV market. List potential uses for each one based on the Shortcuts in Part Two of this book.

2. Choose a song to work on. Go through the music, lyric, and structural Shortcuts and note any elements that could be strengthened for those uses. Go ahead and make the changes. If you decide to make changes to a song that you already recorded for your album, consider recording an inexpensive "unplugged" version with the changes for film and TV use.

Shortcut #93

You Are a Music Publisher

Understand the business you're in and make things happen!

As a songwriter, unless you're already signed to an exclusive staff writer deal with a music publisher, there's something you need to think about:

> **The moment you begin writing a song…**
> *you* are the *publisher* of that song.

Songwriting is so much more creative and fun than reading contracts and filing copyrights, no wonder songwriters like to avoid the publishing part of their job. But that's not all a publisher does. It's the publisher who keeps one eye on the market, who looks for new opportunities, and often it's the publisher who makes that one suggestion or asks for one last rewrite that makes the difference in getting a song placed.

When you write a song, you become a music publisher!

You don't have to be a rocket scientist or earn a law degree to be a publisher. Plenty of songwriters publish their own songs. With good advice, you can learn as you go and avoid mistakes. You may wind up being the publisher from a song's inception through years of royalty payments or you may only act as publisher until you are signed with a music library or established music publisher. Whichever way you go, you should know what to do… or what the other person is supposed to be doing for you. You owe it to your songs!

What does a publisher do?

The following is a list of the basic tasks a publisher performs. You can find out more by reading the referenced Shortcuts.

Task #1. **Guide the songwriter** — Take a step back from your song and look at it as a publisher would: that is, someone who is going to invest time and money in the song. Could the song be strengthened for the film and TV market with some rewriting? Would it have a better chance if the style, emotion, or energy were clearer? Does it have a competitive advantage over other songs? Read the next Shortcut for more ideas on how to think like a publisher.

<= The jobs you need to do as a publisher.

Task #2. **File for copyright** — If you're going to be using a demo production service, musicians and singers other than yourself, or a commercial studio to make your recording, I suggest that you copyright your song in rough demo form, then copyright it again when the final recording is complete so you have a copyright of the song early on, as well as the final sound recording later. If you're recording in your own home studio, you can copyright words, music, and sound recording when your demo is completed. (See Shortcut 95 to learn more about copyrighting songs and sound recordings.) Remember, you can save money by copyrighting groups of songs rather than one song at a time.

Task #3. **Research the film and TV market** — Never stop doing your research. Stay current with what's happening in the market by watching films and TV shows that use songs. Whether you're publishing the song yourself or working with a library or established music publisher, this information will help you focus on creating songs that get placements and make money for you!

Task #4. **Make demo decisions** — The decision to make a demo and how much to spend on it is one that should be made based on your research of the film and TV market and an honest assessment of the song. Decide whether it has a good chance of being placed before investing your publishing money.

(!) Important!
Know your song's genre, mood, tempo, and style.

Task #5. **Know your song catalogue** — Be able to describe the songs you're going to be marketing. Know what genre they're in, the tempo and mood, and which artists they are "in the style of…" If you're not sure, use the suggestions in Shortcut 6 to help you identify the genre and similar artists. If the genre is unclear, you may need to rework some of your existing songs to clarify the style.

Task #6. **Pitch your songs** — "Pitching" a song means sending a song via CD, mp3, or emailing a link to a song to someone who places music in film and television productions. You'll need to decide on the pitching strategy that works best for you. Will you do it yourself, go through a music library, use a pitch service like TAXI, or a combination of all three? For more on these approaches, read Shortcuts 97 through 99.

Task #7. **Keep complete records** — Create a "Song Pitch" database. Include all the information you have on the company and contact person you pitch to, list the songs pitched, date of the pitch, and result (even if you didn't hear back from them). Recordkeeping may be boring but it will pay off as your contacts accumulate. Repeatedly sending a song when they haven't shown interest or forgetting which song your sent when they do show interest is just not professional.

Task #8. **Negotiate fees and contracts** — Read and understand all contracts thoroughly. Find out if there's room to negotiate and, if so, on which points. Fees for the use of songs in film and TV are negotiable although as an unknown songwriter or artist you may not be in a position to bargain. The same holds true for music library deals. Keep things in perspective. Judge your value to the company or project offering the deal and proceed accordingly. Shortcuts 100 and 103 have more information about the deals you're likely to see. Shortcut 106 can help you find an attorney to advise you as needed.

Task #9. **Collect royalties and fees** — Fees are collected by the publisher from the music user. If you are both publisher and writer, then you will keep the entire fee. Performance royalties are collected by the performing rights society with which you're affiliated (ASCAP, BMI, or SESAC, for example) then paid directly to the publisher and writer. You can read more about fees in Shortcut 101, about performance royalties in Shortcut 102, and about music library and film/TV publisher deals in Shortcut 103.

Do It Now

Go through the list of nine tasks in this Shortcut. Ask yourself which tasks you are already doing and which ones you still need to work on. Read the referenced Shortcuts to help you understand the tasks. Start thinking about the best way to pitch your songs and how you can strengthen the rest of your capabilities as a publisher.

Shortcut #94

Get Your Creative and Business Sides Working Together

Encourage mutual respect between your songwriter-self and publisher-self.

You are both a creative artist and an entrepreneur in the music business. You make *and* market music. The part of you that makes music, let's call your "songwriter-self," is a creative, skilled craftsperson who is dedicated to communicating an emotional idea. The part of you that takes your completed songs out into the marketplace we'll call your "publisher-self." This person keeps an eye on trends, assesses the marketability of your songs, and watches for opportunities that make use of your songwriting strengths, as well as doing the recordkeeping jobs.

Working together, your creative and business sides can achieve what neither of them can accomplish alone. To create rapid, long-lasting success, they need to respect and listen to each other. If your songwriting-self belittles the music business as a sell-out and something that requires you to "dumb down" your songs, then you can't expect your publisher-self to be very effective. If your publisher-self is slacking off, failing to research the market, unable to give you good advice on targeting your songs, then your songwriter-self is likely to be working without a clear focus, writing songs that will be difficult to place.

When multiple personalities can be a plus!

You need to be able to wear two hats—but not at the same time!

Everybody knows that two heads are better than one. In this case, both heads happen to belong to you. You can even think of yourself as two people, each with a separate set of responsibilities. Get a couple of baseball caps; write "publisher" on one and "songwriter" on the other. Literally change hats—depending on which one is on call—to get into the habit of viewing things from both perspectives. Just like officemates, your two selves can get on each other's nerves and be disruptive, so be clear about what you expect from each of them and encourage mutual respect. Once you have them working together, they will be an unstoppable team.

> **Use your publisher-self to research the market.**
> Look, listen, and learn. Watch TV series and movies that use songs. Notice how the songs are used and what genre they're in. Keep a log of the song, artist, style, name of the film or show and any songs you have that are similar. Find out more information about the film or show on the Internet Movie Database (www.imdb.com), such as the name of the production company and music supervisor. Read Shortcuts 97 through 99 for more on pitching songs.

➤ **Have your songwriter-self follow up on the research.**
Complement your publishing research by looking at the information from a songwriter's perspective. Choose a song you like from the list of songs in your research log. Take a look at the song structure, the lyric theme, the way the melody is constructed, and the production. Could you write a song with similar characteristics? Be a knowledgeable craftsperson. Read Parts 3, 4, and 5 of this book and work on strengthening those skills that will help you write successful film and TV songs.

➤ **Give your songwriter-self the freedom to create.**
When you're in the midst of writing lyrics, humming a new melody, working on a chord progression, you're fully immersed in your songwriter-self. This may not be the appropriate time for your publisher-self to give input. Figure out a timetable that works for both of you. Maybe something like this:

Before you begin:
Let your publisher-self suggest a genre or style to write in. Play several songs by artists who work in that style, especially those songs that have been used recently in films and TV shows.

After you have a first draft:
Take a step back and let your publisher-self suggest some changes that might add marketability. Try out the suggestions. If you don't like them, go back to what you had, then try the process again.

When you finish:
A final rewrite and polish may make the difference between a song that doesn't quite make it and one that hits a home run. Give yourself a breather, maybe take a day or two away from the song then invite your publisher-self to listen. Play it underneath a couple of scenes, imagine a music supervisor auditioning it for a director. Try making changes that would strengthen the song for a particular type of scene or song use.

Songwriter and publisher: Each one has a job to do. Respect the team!

➤ **Use your publisher-self to keep things in perspective.**
Of course your songwriter-self falls in love with every song you write and, just like a proud parent, thinks it is a completely unique, special, never-to-be-equaled accomplishment and you should immediately rush out and spend tons of money recording it with choir and orchestra. Stop! Your publisher-self should take a hard look at the song and decide whether it's likely to pay back the investment. Let your publisher side make decisions on whether to demo or not and how much to spend.

➤ **Meet in the middle.**
You don't need to make every song you write a marketable monster. However, encouraging your songwriter side to create songs that take into account the needs of film and TV will give your publisher-self something to really work with. There's nothing more discouraging than trying to sell a product that no one wants. Both sides might agree on "one for you and one for me."

> **Don't buy into the myths about either self!**
> There are plenty of stereotypes and misconceptions about our creative and business sides:

"Creative people can't understand contracts."
"Business people don't know anything about good songs."
"Marketable songs are mediocre songs."
"Inspiration is all you need to be successful."

When you buy into one of these myths, you disrespect your creative or business side. Take a moment to do a reality check. These myths can't be true: every day, successful independent artists are writing and marketing good music. You can, too!

Do It Now

Have your publisher-self and songwriter-self each write a list of their goals and desires. Where do they overlap? How can one help the other? Where do they conflict? Try to work out any conflicts by finding a compromise that respects both sides.

Shortcut #95

Copyright Your Songs and Recordings

Protect the hard work, time, and money you've invested in your music.

You've invested a lot in your song. It takes time, energy, and money to write a strong song and make a broadcast quality recording. Now that you're holding it in your hands and you're ready to pitch it to music users in the film and TV industry, it's a good idea to put in just a little more effort to make sure it's protected.

In the United States (and many other countries) the writer of a song owns that song from the moment the melody and lyric are written down or recorded in a tangible, permanent form. For example, if you record yourself singing the melody and lyric (no guitar or piano accompaniment needed) and put that on a CD or cassette tape, your song exists in a tangible, permanent form and you own it. If you write out the melody line and lyrics, again, that's a tangible, permanent form of your song.

Protect your hard work and investment.

But—and this is a very big "but"—until you've registered your song with the U.S. Copyright Office, you can't enforce your claim of ownership in a court of law. If someone steals your song, there's really *nothing* you can legally do about it. Although the Copyright Law says you own the song, without the registration, it's like owning a house without a deed—there's no way you can *prove* it's yours.

Copyright both your song and your recording

Because you made a broadcast quality recording of your song, there are, in fact, two copyrights involved—one for the song (words and music) and another one for the sound recording, which consists of the recorded instrumental and vocal performances. Whether you performed the song yourself or you hired performers to sing and play, you are considered the owner of the sound recording copyright. (Read Shortcut 82 to learn more about performers and Work for Hire agreements.)

Public Domain songs

In the United States, any song written before 1922 is in the public domain. If you created an original musical arrangement of a song in the public domain, you can copyright it. If you wrote original lyrics to a public domain melody, you can copyright those, too. If you live outside the United States, check the copyright laws in your country to find out when a song enters the public domain.

Filing your registration

The Copyright Office now uses a single form—Form CO—to copyright both songs and sound recordings, among other creative works. You'll find Form CO on the Copyright Office website at www.copyright.gov. Under "Publications" click on "Forms." Scroll down until you see the link for "Form CO." You'll also see additional links to "Form CO Instructions" and a "Form CO FAQ," as well. Print out the instructions so you can refer to them easily as you fill out the form. If you choose the electronic filing option, use the Help links; they're invaluable! You'll find answers to many common questions, like "What is a publication date?" and "What does 'Made for hire' mean?" If you're registering music and lyrics, choose "performing arts work." For registering the recorded performances, choose "sound recording."

Here are two tips that can save you a lot of money:

Save money by copyrighting a group of songs.

➢ You can register multiple songs on a single form as long as each one is written by the same person and is owned by the same copyright claimant. In other words, if you wrote 10 songs, you can register all of them on a single Form CO. However, if you collaborated on two songs with another writer, you'll need to copyright those on a separate Form CO. The filing fee for each *form* is the same no matter how many song titles you include. Check the Copyright Office website for the current fees.

➢ You can protect your songs and sound recordings on a single form as long as the copyright claimant is the same for both. In other words, if you wrote 10 songs and paid for or created the performances on all 10, you can register all of them on a single Form CO. Under "Author created" check all the boxes: Sound Recording, Performance, Production, Music, and Lyrics. (If you collaborated on some of the songs, again, you'll need to copyright the songs and then the sound recordings separately.)

The Copyright Office accepts submissions both by mail and online. To submit by mail, fill out Form CO online then print it out and mail it together with your filing fee and a copy (or copies) of your work. Paper forms—Form PA, TX, and SR—are still available on request. The filing fee for paper forms is higher than for Form CO. Check the Copyright Office website for the current fee.

Your copyright registration goes into effect on the date the Copyright Office receives the completed application form, the filing fee, and a copy or copies of the work you are registering.

Put them on notice

Although no longer required by law, it's always a good idea to include a copyright notice on all CDs, digital music files (in the metadata), and lyric sheets, if only to let people know that you're aware of your rights.

For music and lyrics, your notice should contain the copyright symbol © or the word "Copyright" followed by the year in which you copyrighted the work and your name. The "C" in a circle refers to your copyright in the *songs*. For sound recordings, use the symbol ℗ for "phonorecord" followed by the year in which you copyrighted the sound recording and your name. The "P" in a circle protects your *sound recording*. Because we don't use the word "phonorecord" very much these days, it might be helpful to think of the "P" as the anti-Piracy symbol. It says, "Don't steal my recording."

Include your copyright notice on lyrics, digital files, and CDs.

For more information

The U.S. Copyright Office has an excellent overall FAQ page on their website at www.copyright.gov. While you might think that reading it would be about as exciting as watching paint dry, fortunately that's not the case. The questions and answers have real relevance to your business as a songwriter, publisher, and record label. Besides, "How do I protect my sighting of Elvis?" is a must-know! (Yes, it really is on the FAQ page.)

If you live outside the United States and want to know more about your intellectual property rights, check to see if your country is a signatory to the Berne Convention, Universal Copyright Convention or other intellectual property right agreements. These agreements have helped to standardize copyright protection around the world. You can find these documents on the Internet along with a list of signatories.

Do It Now

Go to the U.S. Copyright Office website at www.copyright.gov and click on "Frequently Asked Questions." Read the questions and answers that are relevant to you as a songwriter, publisher, and record label.

Shortcut #96

Get to Know the Music Pipeline

How does your song get to the final decision maker?

Every film or TV production that uses songs has a pipeline that funnels a large amount of material through a decision-making process, one that whittles down many possibilities to an ever-smaller number until, finally, one song is chosen for each available music spot.

The music supervisor

The most common pipeline leads to and through the project's music supervisor who works with the producer or director to determine which scenes could be strengthened with a song. The music supervisor then gathers songs from music libraries, publishers, and record labels, as well as his or her own personal research and music collection.

Find out more about music libraries in Shortcut 98.

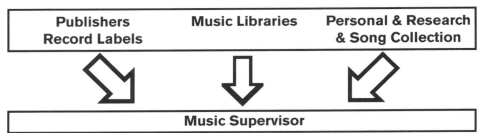

The supervisor then auditions dozens, sometimes hundreds, of songs for each spot. There will be a constant stream of new songs to listen to. He must have a good memory for the songs he has heard in the past that might work. In a very short time, he must sort through all these songs and find the few that will add an intangible extra depth to a scene. Once he has narrowed down his choices, he'll play them for the final decision maker—the director (if the project is a film) or the producer (if it's a TV series)—who may or may not agree with his choices. This is a risk the music supervisor takes with every song he presents. If the songs are not strong or if he fails to interpret what the director or producer is looking for, he may not be hired on future projects.

Once a song is chosen, the music supervisor contacts the rights owner to begin negotiating clearances and fees. The search, audition, and negotiation processes must all be completed within a short time, often a matter of one to two weeks.

The music editor and more

Of course, there are other ways a song can reach the producer or director. Music editors play an important role in the music pipeline. The music editor works closely with the music supervisor, preparing the supervisor's song choices to be presented to the director or producer, and eventually editing the final choices to give them the maximum impact in a scene. The music editor is present at all meetings in which decisions about songs are made. He may also assemble a temp track, music that is temporarily used during the making of a movie. If your song is in the temp track, it has a better chance of making the final cut.

The music composer who creates the instrumental underscore may collaborate with a songwriter or write songs herself. Film editors, staff members, attorneys, and friends all have their own favorite songs. They might suggest songs to the producer or director and they often do!

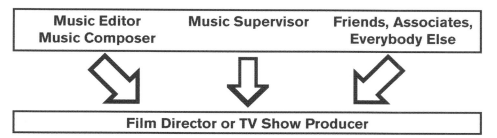

Music Editor Music Composer	Music Supervisor	Friends, Associates, Everybody Else

Film Director or TV Show Producer

Songs for TV commercials have a similar pipeline. The creative director at the ad agency acts as music supervisor. The client, the company who paid for the commercial, makes the final decision.

With so many songs bombarding a project, it's important that yours have some extra muscle. This is where the Shortcuts in the Lyric, Music, and Foundation sections of this book can be invaluable. A song with a clear emotional focus and strong sense of energy or atmosphere will quickly stand out from the crowd. Even if it isn't right for a particular project, it has a better chance of being remembered for future productions!

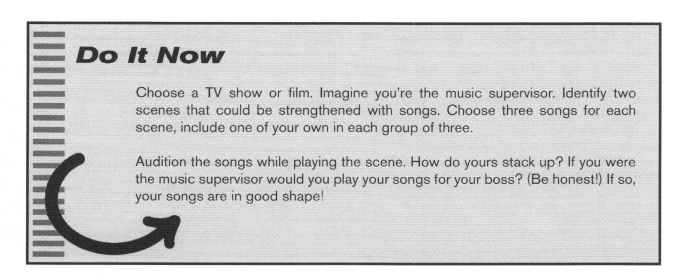

Do It Now

Choose a TV show or film. Imagine you're the music supervisor. Identify two scenes that could be strengthened with songs. Choose three songs for each scene, include one of your own in each group of three.

Audition the songs while playing the scene. How do yours stack up? If you were the music supervisor would you play your songs for your boss? (Be honest!) If so, your songs are in good shape!

Shortcut #97

DIY: Reach Out to the Industry

Do your research. Know what the market is looking for.
Then make your move.

"Do It Yourself" in the film and television song market means that you reach out to the music user directly, whether that's a music supervisor working on a production, a creative director at an ad agency, a film director, TV show producer, or any of the other people listed in the music pipeline in Shortcut 96. You pitch your song for projects the music user is working on and, should you get a placement, you negotiate the licensing deals yourself.

DIY takes time, research, resources and patience.

Because there's no music library or publisher involved, you end up keeping *all* of the fees and royalties earned by the song. Now *that's* appealing! On the downside: doing all of this on your own requires a huge investment of time in research and networking plus the ability to keep going in the face of negative responses or no response at all. However, you don't have to do it completely on your own; there are professional services that can help you get the job done. I'll tell you more about those in the following Shortcuts.

Getting names and contact information

While music supervisor names and contact information are available, it's important to keep this information in perspective. Music supervisors are bombarded with material from many sources. Their position is much like that of A&R executives at major labels. Because they can make an artist's career take off overnight, they're targeted by publishers, record labels, and managers, as well as unsigned artists and songwriters. An unsolicited CD or email has an extremely low priority. In addition, even though you may have the contact information, you still don't know what project the supervisor is working on. Sending a CD or link to a song in an email without that information is like tossing a snowball onto a bonfire. There's not much chance it will make an impression.

Directories

That said, there are directories that list the contact information for music supervisors and other music users. The *Hollywood Music Industry Directory* (www.hcdonline.com) lists address, phone, and email information for music supervisors, editors, and the music departments at film studios and TV networks. The *Film & Television Music Guide* (www.musicregistry.com) and *Music Supervisor Guide* (www.musicsupervisorguide.com) provide similar information. Once a year, *Music Connection* magazine puts out an issue that includes a list of music supervisors with their contact information. You can buy the issue on their website at www.musicconnection.com.

Industry trade publications

Instead of simply mailing out CDs or emailing links to a list in a directory, you can focus your efforts by checking out *Variety* (www.variety.com) or *The Hollywood Reporter* (www.hollywoodreporter.com). These are the two major entertainment industry trade magazines. Their Film and TV Production Charts list movies and TV shows that are currently in production along with the telephone number and address of the production company. You can contact the company to find out who's handling music for them. A subscription to either of these publications costs in the hundreds of dollars per year, so try this inexpensive work-around: subscribe to the online or print version of *The Hollywood Reporter* for one month at a cost of around $30, which will give you access to the Film and TV Production Charts. *Variety* will give you free access to its production charts just for registering online. IMDbPro is another good resource with a low monthly fee (www.imdb.com).

<= Try this cheap work-around!

Use the Internet to put it all together

Of course not every production will be using songs. To narrow your search even further, go to TuneFind (www.tunefind.com) and browse through TV series. Look for shows that use songs in a style similar to your own. No matter how you pitch your songs, this is good information to have. You can look up the name of the show's music supervisor in the Internet Movie Database (www.imdb.com), which provides detailed information on movies and TV shows. (You can also check their credits there.) You can then look at the industry trade publications' TV production charts to find out if the series is in production. Use the contact information in the trade publications or a directory to follow up.

You've got contact information, now what?

Contact by email:
If you have a telephone number, there's a real temptation to call a music supervisor and have a chat. Don't do it. Unless you've already developed a relationship and gotten permission, they won't appreciate your call. Try an email instead; it doesn't interrupt the flow of work the way a telephone call does and you can include a link that allows the supervisor to check out your songs.

Be considerate. Get to the point. Make it easy to listen to your songs.

Send a very succinct three or four sentence email that includes:

- Your name and contact information.

- A brief description of your music. The most useful description consists of your genre plus two known artists who are similar in style.

- Any notable film or TV placements you've had.

- A link to a web page where the supervisor can hear your music.

Before you send the email, be sure the link works! Test it! If it's a link to a web page, make certain the page is easy to navigate, that your song titles are clearly indicated, and the play buttons are easy to find. Some music supervisors will take the time to click on a link and listen to the first twenty seconds of a song. Put your strongest song *first* on the web page. Keep the song's intro short. Music users are very interested in hearing the vocal. Get there as quickly as possible. Do not attach an mp3 file to your email, not even a sample! If the supervisor replies requesting a CD, send one promptly. Read on for suggestions on how to label your CD.

By mail:

If you're contacting a music supervisor by mail, send a CD and a cover letter that includes the information listed above for an email. Put your contact information on the CD case and on the CD. Trust me, your CD will get separated from the case at some point; if you don't have your contact info on both, you're sunk. Put your CD in a jewel case with a bold, readable label on the spine to make it easy to find on a shelf with hundreds of others. (Don't send slim cases or clam shells.) Be sure to list the songs by track number and name on the case cover. If you control the rights to the song and recording (and you should), write that on the case cover, too. (See Shortcut 100 for more on song and recording rights.)

Then what?

One of three things will happen:

1. If the music user is interested, you'll be contacted by email or phone. If you've got something that will work for a current project, they'll be in touch.

2. If they hear something they like but it's not right for the current project, they may get in touch later on. It could be many months later, even a year depending on their needs.

3. If there's no interest, you'll hear nothing. How do you know anyone even heard your CD or mp3? You can't be sure. Music supervisors do their best but they can't keep up with the amount of music they receive. Listening to unsolicited music is at the bottom of their "To Do" list.

If you don't hear back, don't get discouraged. Keep writing and recording new songs based on your film and TV research. Study the types of shows the music supervisor works on and, if the music is similar to your style, write new material with that in mind. Then email again in a few months when you have the new material ready.

Shortcut #98

A Music Library Can Take Your Song to Market

From pitching songs to making the deal, they handle it all.

Simply put, a music library is a collection of songs and instrumental music that can be auditioned and licensed by music users. Anything in the library can be licensed and placed in film and TV productions. It's a time saver—and sometimes a lifesaver—for busy music supervisors and creative directors.

- Music libraries provide easy access to the vast array of affordable music created by independent songwriters, artists, and bands like you.

- Music libraries streamline the process of licensing by offering both a license to use the song and a license to use the master recording in one place. (Read Shortcut 100 to find out more about licenses.)

- Music libraries sort songs by genre, mood, tempo, and similar artists to speed up the search process for music supervisors. They may do the search themselves and offer their choices to the music supervisor, provide a searchable music database, or they may have custom music created to fit a specific need.

What a music library does.

This aspect of the industry is evolving very quickly. By the time you read this, there may be a new wrinkle in the auditioning process, music delivery system, or licensing deal. The industry can't even agree on what to call these companies: "source track library," "film/TV publisher," "song broker," "licensing company," "independent artist catalogue," and "music vendor" are all used to cover variations of the same core idea.

A variety of library types

Music libraries range from mega-giants with hundreds of thousands of instrumental and song tracks to boutique libraries with a hand-picked assortment of carefully chosen songs to "production music libraries" that offer custom music. Each provides a different type of service to the industry. If a TV series or entire cable network requires a large amount of music cues, a big library can issue a "blanket license" (one that covers all the material in their library) and the music user can search for whatever is needed. A boutique library generally has a one-on-one relationship with music supervisors and can cater to the specific needs of a production or single scene.

Mega libraries: In large libraries like Pump Audio (www.pumpaudio.com), the music tracks reside in an online database that is searchable by genre, tempo, mood, instrumentation, male or female vocal, similar artists, etc. In some cases, the music owner (the person who is submitting the song) does the initial categorizing which may not be particularly accurate. Music supervisors searching this database will end up with a large amount of music to listen to, more than they can handle on a busy schedule. In order to help them, big libraries often have a two-tiered system. Music supervisors and other music users can receive special access to an area of the database that has been screened by the company for accuracy and quality. This is where you want to be. It's like a library within a library. If you're not there, you're in Siberia. Whether you'll be included is up to the library.

Boutique libraries: Boutique libraries are discriminating about the music they sign right from the start. They take in only those songs they feel have a very good chance of being placed and earning money for them (and you). They keep in touch with music supervisors and other clients, gathering information about their current needs. The library will send only the songs that fit those needs—great for a music supervisor with a tight deadline!

What they need from you

You must control the rights to the song and your recording. If a music supervisor shows an interest in your song, the library will grant a license and negotiate fees to use both the song and the recording in a specific production. In order to do that, they first need to make a deal with you, the owner of the song and recording. You are the owner, right? If you wrote the song and recorded all the parts yourself, then there's no question about it—you're the owner, which means you control all the rights and can make a deal with the library. However, if the song is a collaboration, then you and your co-writer share the song rights. Read the section on collaborations in Shortcut 100 to learn more. If you hired singers or musicians to perform on the recording, be sure you have a signed Work for Hire agreement from each of them (Shortcut 82) so there are no questions about whether or not you're free to license the recording.

Your song needs to be strong from beginning to end. Music libraries look for songs with the maximum possible uses. If a project can use your entire song, or any part of it, it's more likely to get a placement and earn money. Your song may be edited down to 30 seconds or less, but you never know which 30 seconds, so be sure the whole song is strong! Here's what music libraries look for:

- Universal lyrics (Shortcuts 47 through 50)

- A strong chorus or refrain that sums up the emotion (Shortcut 56)

- Music that evokes energy or mood (Shortcuts 38 through 40)

- A compelling vocal on target for the style (Shortcuts 79 and 80)

- A broadcast quality mix that puts the song across (Shortcut 83)

You must control the rights to both the song and recording.

Your entire song must be usable. They won't look for the good bits!

Proceed with caution

Music libraries keep a portion of the fees they negotiate and visually capture a share of the song's performance royalties, making this a potentially lucrative field. There's a bit of a "gold rush" mentality in the area of film and TV songs today and it has attracted its share of newbies who would love to get a piece of the action but may not have the knowledge and experience needed to be successful.

Any time you're offered a deal by a music library, be sure to check them out thoroughly. What song placements have they had? In what kinds of TV shows and films? If it's just a few cable TV shows, you might want to wait until they have a stronger track record or look for another library. Most libraries will post their success stories. Contact some of those songwriters and artists and ask them about their experience with this company.

Shortcut 103 has more information on music library deals.

Where to find music libraries

➢ **Visit music library websites or use a directory:** Some libraries offer contact and submission information on their websites. Research the library to make certain it's reputable before submitting, then follow the directions carefully and submit in the form requested. *Film & Television Music Guide* (www. musicregistry.com) includes contact information for music libraries. Some libraries will not accept unsolicited material. Once you have the contact information, send an email to find out if they accept submissions and in what form. Be sure to find out about the types of deals they offer before submitting. If you're not interested in the deal they offer, don't submit!

➢ **Use a pitch service:** Many established, A-list music libraries use TAXI, a pitch service, to find new music. The library tells TAXI what they need for current projects and the information is passed on to the membership along with the type of deal the library offers. Submitted songs are screened by TAXI to ensure they match the style and quality the library is looking for. Read Shortcut 99 to learn more about using TAXI.

Cultivate a relationship

Once you've made contact with a library and they've signed a few of your songs, you can let them know that you're willing to write "on spec." This means that you'll write and record a song or instrumental track to fill a specific need for the library. You'll have to do this at your own expense and there's no guarantee that it will be placed, but if you can give them what they need quickly, the library will funnel more work to you.

Shortcut #99

Use TAXI: Pitch Your Songs and Learn What Works

Build your skills and knowledge. Strengthen your catalogue. Reach your goal.

Pitching your songs is a tough, time-consuming job. Locating contact information, researching current productions, figuring out the style that's wanted, all of these jobs take time. Then, once you send off an email or CD, you may not hear back. You have no idea why your songs didn't make the cut or how you could improve your pitch. Worst of all, marketing your songs this way can eat up the time you have available to create and record new material and improve your skills, an essential component of a successful film and TV music career. It would sure be helpful to have a knowledgeable, experienced guide to help you out.

Disclosure time!

Before we go any further, I need to be honest with you: I've worked closely with TAXI (www.taxi.com) for a number of years, first as a member, then as a screener, and finally as head of the A&R Screener Team. TAXI Music Books is the publisher of this book. Over the years, I've seen how TAXI provides a unique solution for the DIY songwriter who wants to break into the film and television market. I believe you should be aware of this resource so I'm going to take this one Shortcut to give you an insight into how TAXI works, what it can do for you, and how you can get the most from this service if you decide to join.

TAXI is a resource for music supervisors, music libraries, and publishers looking for broadcast quality songs.
Many highly respected companies in the film and TV market use TAXI's service to help them find songs and instrumental tracks to fill their needs. They give TAXI a description of what they're looking for and TAXI, in turn, shares that information with its members in the form of a listing. Members submit their music if it fits the listing description.

TAXI is a resource for the industry.

TAXI screeners listen to the submissions.
Screeners with extensive knowledge and experience in the music industry listen to every submission, compare it with the listing requirements, and decide if it fits the style and quality asked for. If it does, it's forwarded to the listing company. These companies depend on TAXI's screening process to give them just what they requested.

The listing company receives music from a trusted source.
The selected music is sent to the listing company along with the member's contact information. At this point, TAXI steps out of the picture and the listing company picks up the ball. Like all busy music supervisors and libraries, they have priorities. If the music is needed for a project that's pending, they'll review

the music quickly and contact the member directly to work out a deal. If a project has moved to a backburner or is scheduled in the future, they'll review the music later and make their decision. Deals can happen quickly or over many months, sometimes a year or more. Over time, some music libraries sign as much as 95% of the music that's forwarded to them from TAXI.

How you can use TAXI to break into the film & TV market

➤ **Submit your music to established music companies.**
TAXI's pitching opportunities come from highly reputable film and TV music companies, including music libraries, ad agencies, and music supervisors, as well as publishers and record labels that pitch songs in this market. The TAXI staff maintains personal contacts with each company, discussing their current projects and needs before running a listing.

➤ **Tighten up your pitches.**
Each TAXI listing includes a genre and usually several artists who are "in the style of..." the music the company needs. This is where your knowledge of similar artists (Shortcut 6) will be a big help. The screening process will let you know if your submission is on target stylistically or not. As you learn more, you'll find that you hit the style target more frequently. There's also a description of the song or production elements the company wants to hear. Learning how to read this information and apply it to the songs in your catalogue is a skill you'll need when you deal directly with any library or music supervisor.

Think like a pro.
Pitch like a pro!

➤ **Get feedback on your music and your pitch.**
Whether your music is forwarded or not, you receive feedback. Often that feedback includes suggestions for bringing your music closer to the listing requirements or generally strengthening the song or recording to make it more commercially viable. The more you learn about what it takes to be competitive, the more successful you'll be.

➤ **Build a track record.**
Pitching songs directly to the industry when you don't yet have a track record can be frustrating. It's difficult to get the attention your music deserves. TAXI is good way to get past that hurdle. When a TAXI screener forwards your music it's an industry recommendation. It gives your music added weight and credibility.

No track record?
No problem!

How to get the most from TAXI

TAXI can bring solid industry opportunities to you that can get you through the door and help you build your career. *However,* you have to do your part. If the music you're submitting isn't at the level needed, there's no magic wand that will make it better. Learn from the feedback you get from TAXI's screeners. Listen to the artists referred to in the listing and compare them with your material from a songwriting and production standpoint. Ask yourself:

- Am I submitting to the right listings?

- How can I get closer to the level of these artists?

- Should I rewrite this song or move forward with new songs?

To get the most from TAXI, keep writing and recording material based on what you learn. This is what successful film and TV writers do!

> **Think of yourself as a "mini music library."**
> Unlike a music library, TAXI doesn't keep a collection of music on hand. Instead, it relies on each member to read the listing and pull from his or her own catalogue of songs the tracks that best fit the requirements. Learning to think like a music library, categorize your songs correctly, and write your songs with the end-user in mind will help you move ahead rapidly with your career and strengthen your professional songwriting and marketing skills.

Fill your music library with good, usable film & TV songs.

> **Attend the annual TAXI Road Rally.**
> The Road Rally is a four-day songwriting conference packed with workshops, panels, and seminars. It's free to TAXI members and a guest. The Road Rally alone is worth the price of membership. You can find out more at TAXI.com.

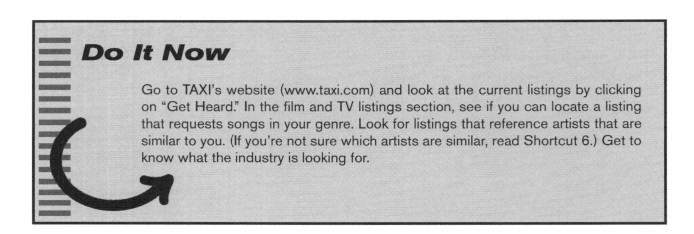

Do It Now

Go to TAXI's website (www.taxi.com) and look at the current listings by clicking on "Get Heard." In the film and TV listings section, see if you can locate a listing that requests songs in your genre. Look for listings that reference artists that are similar to you. (If you're not sure which artists are similar, read Shortcut 6.) Get to know what the industry is looking for.

Shortcut #100

License Your Songs and Recordings to Music Users
Learn about Synchronization and Master Use licenses.
It's simple. Really!

Okay, so words like "licenses" and "synchronization" can make just about anyone's eyes glaze over, but these ideas really aren't that hard to understand. A few minutes spent learning the jargon can pay you back many times over. Remember, *you* are your own publisher and, for the purposes of licensing your recording, you are also your own record label! So put on your business baseball cap for this one.

The first thing to remember is that unlike radio, which can play just about any recording it wants, a TV or film production must get permission to use a recorded song. In fact, they must get *two* permissions: a "synchronization license" giving them permission to use the composition (words and music) and a "master use" license giving them permission to use the sound recording (the vocal and instrumental performance). Often, they must pay a fee for both. (You'll learn more about fees in the next Shortcut.)

Film and TV must get permission to use your song and recording!

In the mainstream, commercial music industry, these two licenses—the synchronization license (usually shortened to "sync license") and the master use license—are frequently controlled by two different companies. The publisher controls the rights to the song (sync), while a record label owns the specific recorded version of the song (master). So, for example, if a low budget cable TV series wants to license Madonna's recording of "Material Girl," they'll need permission from both the publisher and the record label. The publisher might grant a sync license to use the composition but demand a big fee for the use, while the record label may simply say "No way!" to the use of the master recording.

So, what happens? Music users turn to someone like you, an independent songwriter with a broadcast quality recording that would work just fine in that very scene. Why? Because you're going to be affordable and you're a one-stop shop: you can grant licenses for both the song and the recording in a snap. Cape up, people! *It's you to the rescue!*

Be sure you control the rights to your song and recording

Before you can grant permission to use your song and recording, you must control all the rights. Here are some cases in which you might *not* control all the rights:

> **You do not have signed release forms:** You should get Work for Hire release forms signed by the singers, musicians, and producers who worked on the

recording waiving any ownership in the recording. Read Shortcut 82 to learn about works made for hire and see a sample form.

> **You are using uncleared samples:** If you've copied any part of another artist's recording and you're using it in your own without permission, then you've got an uncleared sample. Clearing a sample for use on your CD (for sales and digital downloads) does *not* cover film and TV uses. My advice is just don't do it. Replace the sample with something original to you.

Do you control the rights to your songs?

If you're using samples, loops, and sounds from a commercial sound library that you bought, read the agreement that came with it. Most will grant you the right to use the sounds as part of a music production of your own. Be sure there are no limitations on the use of your final recording. To be safe, make copies of the agreement and keep it on file in case anyone asks.

> **You are signed to a publisher or record label:** If you have a publishing or record label deal, chances are you do not control the rights to your songs or recordings. Because the film and TV song market is so hot, these companies are likely to have someone on staff pursuing these deals for you. Check in with them and see if you can create a little synergy.

Collaborations

Whether you wrote the song with one other person or your whole band, it's important that you have a collaboration agreement and that you understand what each collaborator can and can't do when making deals. If you're offered an *exclusive* deal from a film/TV publisher, then all of the collaborators must agree to the deal. However, each individual collaborator has the right to enter into *non-exclusive* deals. Make certain your collaboration agreement states that your share of any sync and master licensing fees will be paid directly to you. Then, if your collaborator forgets to inform you of a non-exclusive licensing deal, you'll still get paid!

What's in the license?

> **The title of the film or TV show for which the license is being issued:** You're granting a license to use your song and recording in the specific film, TV episode, or commercial named in the agreement. They can't just use it in any old thing. There is, however, a type of license, called a "blanket license," in which you give a company, such as MTV, the right to use the song in any production.

Licenses: Here's what you'll find in them.

> **The term of the license:** This is the length of time the license will be in effect. Most projects want a license "in perpetuity" so they don't have to come back in ten years to renegotiate if the film or TV show is still airing in reruns or being sold on DVD or newer visual technologies.

> **The territory:** The production will want a license to use the material in all the places where it might be aired or sold, for example "U.S. and Canada." These days, they aren't shy about asking for "the universe."

- **The fee:** Fees are negotiated for both the song and the recording. (Read Shortcut 101 for more on the range of fees for these uses.) Low budget indie films may request a deferred fee or "step deal." In this type of deal, you could be paid a specified fee if the film makes a distribution deal or receive a share of the profits on box office receipts and DVD sales.

- **Look for these...** There will be additional clauses that describe how the production can be aired (free TV, pay-per-view, etc.); a requirement that the production company provide "cue sheets" to the performing rights society with which you are affiliated (Shortcut 102); and a list of the visual media in which your song, in conjunction with the film or show, can be used, such as DVD and Blu-ray.

- **Extras you should ask for:** If the license includes any CD rights, try to limit these to a soundtrack album only. You want to be free to sell the song on your own CD! Also, be sure to request that a cue sheet be sent directly to you. Don't forget to ask for credit for your song and yourself as the writer wherever credits are customarily given.

- **Other license types:** A "festival license" is a limited-term license, usually for one year, which allows an independent film to be shown at film festivals for the purpose of obtaining a commercial distribution deal. An "ephemeral license" allows live shows, such as sports events, news programs, and awards shows, to use music *one time* without obtaining a license. However, if the program is aired later as archival footage, on the Internet, or as part of a "highlights" compilation, master and sync licenses will be needed.

FYI: When you license a song, you are NOT giving away any ownership.

Understand what you're signing

It's always a good idea to get as much information as you can before you sign any license. Check with someone who's been around the block before you. You'll find a good resource on the "Biz Talk" forum at TAXI (http://Forums.Taxi.com/Biz-talk-f12.html). A music attorney who has experience with deals of this type can advise you. See Shortcuts 105 and 106 for more on finding and working with an attorney.

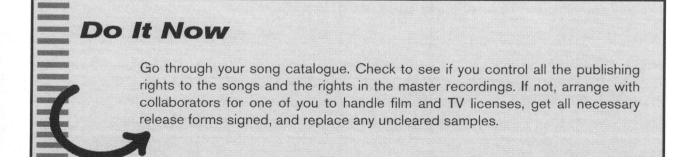

Do It Now

Go through your song catalogue. Check to see if you control all the publishing rights to the songs and the rights in the master recordings. If not, arrange with collaborators for one of you to handle film and TV licenses, get all necessary release forms signed, and replace any uncleared samples.

Shortcut #101

Fees for the Use of Your Songs and Recordings

Know what they pay and how to build your negotiating skills.

When your song is used in a film, TV show, or commercial, it can generate income in two ways: fees and performance royalties. Simply put, a fee is a lump sum that is negotiated and paid by the production company when you give permission—that is, when you issue a license—to use your song and your master recording. Performance royalties are paid after the film or TV show is broadcast and the money is collected by a performing rights organization such as ASCAP, BMI, or SESAC, sometimes as much as a year later.

Understanding fees and royalties isn't rocket science, but it can be a little confusing. Not only are there two types of payments—fees and royalties—but there are two things that are being paid for: the use of the song (the "sync fee") and the use of the recording of the song (the "master use fee"). So I've split fees and royalties into two Shortcuts to help keep things sorted out. For a look at royalties, read Shortcut 102.

How much can you make from a licensing fee?

There's a wide range of fees for different uses.

Sync and master use fees are negotiable. There's no list of standard fees for the use of a song or recording in the film and TV market. You (or a music library negotiating on behalf of your song and recording) can get whatever you can get! A successful negotiation is the result of both skill and knowledge. Doing your research, becoming familiar with the market, can help you build up a strong knowledge base for negotiations.

Based on a survey of industry professionals, here's an idea of the range of fees that an unknown song by an unsigned songwriter or band might command for a placement, followed by a list of factors that can influence the final figure. You'll typically be offered an "all-in" fee, that's one fee for both the sync and master use rights. I've separated them here.

Use in a national TV commercial:

Sync fee:	$15,000 to $100,000
Master use fee:	$15,000 to $100,000

Use in a feature film with distribution by a major studio:

Sync fee:	$7,500 to $17,500
Master use fee:	$7,500 to $17,500

Use in a one-hour episode of a primetime series on TV:

Sync fee:	$500 to $2,500
Master use fee:	$500 to $2,500

Use in a promotional trailer (theatrical):

Sync fee:	$4,000 to $7,500
Master use fee:	$4,000 to $7,500

Use in a promotional trailer (TV):

Sync fee:	$2,000 to $2,500
Master use fee:	$2,000 to $2,500

For more info on trailers, read Shortcut 13.

Use in an independent film with distribution:

Sync fee:	$250 to $750
Master use fee:	$250 to $750

Use in a daytime drama on network TV:

Sync fee:	$100 to $500
Master use fee:	$100 to $500

Use in a basic cable TV program (MTV, Lifetime, etc.):

Sync fee:	$0 to $250
Master use fee:	$0 to $250

Film festival use:

Sync fee:	$0 to $250
Master use fee:	$0 to $250

Remember, these figures refer to an unknown song by an unsigned songwriter or artist. Established artists and known songs can command much higher fees. Also, keep in mind that if a music library negotiates a deal on behalf of the song, they'll keep the portion of the fees agreed on in their deal with you, usually 50% of the sync and master use fees. However, if you're negotiating directly with a music supervisor, you keep all the fees.

What factors influence the amount of the fee?

➤ **Type of production and the size of the budget:** As you can see from the list of fees, television commercials are willing to pay for what they want. If you've got a song that they feel will connect with consumers, the money will be there! A feature film from a major studio has a larger music budget than a

Keep these factors in mind when negotiating.

primetime network TV series, a film that has a distribution deal in place has a larger music budget than one that will be shot on a shoestring with hopes of finding distribution later on, so adjust your expectations accordingly. In addition, if a film or network TV show has already licensed a couple of hit songs by known artists, there may not be much money left in the budget. They'll be looking to independent artists like you to help them fill their needs at a low cost.

> **The value of your song and recording to the production:** A well-known song is worth more than one that's unknown. A song by a band or artist who is signed to a hip indie label is worth more than one by an unsigned artist. Nevertheless, if your song is so unique they simply must have it or if your hook sums up the emotion of a scene and the music enhances the mood, you may be able to ask for more money. When you talk with the music supervisor, listen for verbal clues. Small bits of information can add up to a bigger picture.

> **The type of use:** If your song will be featured at the end of a scene with a portion of it "in the clear" (not under dialogue), it could be worth more than a song that's played in the background at a party or one that's buried underneath dialogue. Find out as much as you can about the way the song will be used.

> **The amount used:** A use of 30 seconds or more could push the fee toward the higher end of the range; less than 30 seconds, toward the lower end. The licensing request will include this information.

Ultimately, a film or TV show may not be willing to negotiate with you, especially if you don't have a track record. They'll offer you the fee they feel is appropriate and tell you to take it or leave it. The decision is up to you. Remember, you're not giving away any ownership of your song. You can continue to license it to other productions. But what if they don't want to pay you anything at all?

Why would you license your song for zero dollars?

Would you let them use it for nothing?

Some cable TV shows have very low budgets with little or nothing set aside for music. Others, like MTV's *Real World* and *The Hills,* carpet their shows with original songs, using anywhere from ten seconds to a minute of each. It isn't financially feasible for these shows to pay a fee for every song, so you might have a decision to make. Here are some reasons why you might make a deal for no fee.

> To build up your track record

> To establish a good relationship with a music supervisor

> To earn performance royalties

> To increase your artist CD sales and downloads

Shortcut #102

Performance Royalties:
A Long-Term Income Stream

Learn how much you can make and how you'll get paid.

While a fee is a one-time payment, royalties can pay off for a lifetime. A song used in a primetime TV drama earns a royalty the first time the show is aired, and again when it airs in reruns. It can earn money yet again when the show is broadcast on cable channels, or picked up by groups of local TV stations (syndication). If a show is popular in the United States, it's likely to be aired in foreign markets as well. *Dawson's Creek,* for example, has aired in more than 40 countries.

How much can a song make in performance royalties?

The amount of the royalty is determined by several factors but, in general, a good rule of thumb is: The larger the audience, the bigger the royalty.

Time of airing: A song that airs in primetime (8 p.m. to 11 p.m.) will earn more than a song that airs in the early morning hours.

Type of station: A broadcast on a major network (ABC, CBS, or NBC) is worth more than one on a local station or cable channel.

<= Factors that affect how much your song earns.

Type of use: A "feature performance" is worth more than a "background vocal." (More about feature performances in a minute.)

Duration of use: A song that plays for 45 seconds or longer will earn more than one that's played for less than 45 seconds. In fact, 45 seconds is an important length to remember. A feature performance of less than 45 seconds receives 50% of the full royalty rate; a feature performance of less than 15 seconds is paid at 25% of the full royalty rate.

Traditionally, a "feature performance" has been defined as an on-screen performance of a song, say, Carrie Underwood appearing on *Saturday Night Live* to sing her current hit. For this reason, it's also referred to as a "visual vocal" or "VV." However, with the increasing use of songs as a means of communicating emotion or generating energy, the definition of featured performance is widening. When a song sets the tone for a montage of scenes, or expresses a character's feelings instead of dialogue, or provides the accompaniment to a spotlighted dance (as on *Dancing with the Stars*), it's often treated as a feature performance. In other words, if the song is a focal point of the scene, it's a featured use. When a song is played at a low level, adding realism or atmosphere to a scene, but isn't the focal point, it's a background vocal. The following royalty examples are for a single use of 45 seconds or longer in the U.S. market and are approximate. PROs such as ASCAP, BMI, and SESAC arrive at their final royalty payments using complex formulas with many variables.

Primetime network TV (ABC, CBS, NBC):

Feature performance:	$1,750 - $2,000
Background vocal:	$300 - $350 per minute

Primetime on smaller networks (CW or Fox):

Feature Performance:	$1,200 - $1,500
Background vocal:	$200 - $250 per minute

Daytime drama (network):

Feature Performance:	$500 - $750
Background vocal:	$100 - $125 per minute

Basic cable and Syndication:

Feature Performance:	$300 - $750
Background vocal:	$50 - $100 per minute

Each additional broadcast pays you a royalty.

Most TV shows are aired at least once in reruns so you can safely double the network figures. A successful show will be syndicated, that is, sold to groups of local stations where it is likely to be re-broadcast several times. The royalty will depend on how many stations participate and how many viewers they have. Generally you can make $2,000 to $4,000 or more if the show is aired multiple times in syndication. If the show is sold to a foreign market, depending on how large that market is, you can earn from hundreds to thousands of dollars.

Keep in mind: If you got a placement on your own and you control all the rights to your song, then you keep all the royalties as both the writer and publisher of the song. If a music library got the placement, depending on your contract with them, they may participate in the royalties as a publisher. Be sure to read all contracts carefully and understand them before signing.

Join a PRO and get paid

Performance royalties are collected by PROs, performing rights organizations, which then pay them out to songwriters and publishers. Each PRO collects and distributes royalties only for those songwriters and publishers affiliated with it. In the United States, there are three PROs: ASCAP, BMI, and SESAC. Internationally, royalties are collected by a number of different PROs: for example, PRS in the United Kingdom, SOCAN in Canada, JASRAC in Japan. Reciprocal agreements between PROs allow royalties to be collected in one country and distributed to a songwriter who may live half a world away.

As a songwriter, you can join only one PRO. Because you're acting as your own publisher, you'll be joining the PRO as a writer *and* as a publisher. Both the songwriter and publisher must be affiliated with the same PRO. (If a collaborator belongs to a different PRO, he will need to set up his own publishing company with that PRO to collect his share of the royalties.) You can find information and answers to many of your questions on PRO websites like these, or the PRO in your country:

U.S.A. . . . . . . ASCAP.com, BMI.com, SESAC.com
U.K. . . . . PRSforMusic.com
Canada . . . . . . SOCAN.ca
Australia . . . . APRA-AMCOS.com.au

Attend events and showcases, talk to members, and ask about their experiences. Joining a PRO is a big step. Take your time; do your research.

➢ **When should you join a PRO?** If a music library offers you a deal or a music supervisor licenses a song or master recording from you, they're going to ask for your PRO affiliation. Go ahead and apply for membership when you have broadcast quality song recordings and you're ready to start pitching. Membership fees are nominal for most PROs and the requirements for membership are minimal.

Join a PRO when you start seriously pitching broadcast quality songs.

How do they know if your song has earned royalties?

➢ **Cue sheets:** The production company will file a "cue sheet" with your PRO. It lists the song title, writer and publisher information, the type of use, duration, and name of the production. As a precaution, you should also notify your PRO of song placements in case the cue sheet doesn't arrive or the information is incorrect. However, even with a cue sheet, if your song is played for 30 seconds on a local TV or cable show, there's a good chance your PRO may miss that use. Just add the placement to your track record and keep writing!

➢ **Theatrical releases:** Performance royalties are not paid when a film is shown in theaters in the United States but they are paid for theatrical performances outside the United States. If you have a song in a film that's released widely in foreign countries, the performance royalties can be substantial, especially if you put some extra effort into collecting them. It may be worth your while to talk with a music attorney about sub-publishing deals in foreign countries.

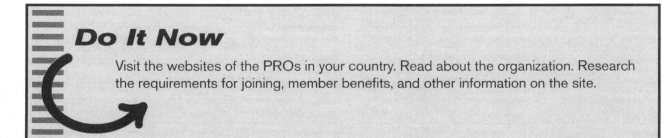

Do It Now

Visit the websites of the PROs in your country. Read about the organization. Research the requirements for joining, member benefits, and other information on the site.

Shortcut #103

Know the Basics of Music Library Deals

What rights will you give them and for how long?

For decades, the traditional music publishing deal was the only game in town for songwriters. These exclusive, long-term deals focused on royalties from album sales (mechanical royalties) and sheet music. Sync fees were often an afterthought and, of course, master use fees were never even mentioned. But, with the sudden, explosive growth of the film and TV song market, came a variety of publishing deals offered by music libraries and publishers who focused solely on film and TV placements. The field is still new and going through rapid changes. Deals are constantly evolving. There are, however, some areas that are addressed in all deals:

The basics of a music library deal.

Rights: When you make a deal with a music library, you are granting rights that give them some degree of control over the licensing of your song and master recording to film and television productions for the duration of the contract term. Having these rights allows film/TV publishers and music libraries to make deals easily, resulting in an income stream that pays for their time and creates a profit for both them and you.

Exclusivity: In the traditional publishing model, the publisher was the sole representative of the song in all areas: albums, film, TV, video games, and sheet music. The publisher was the only person empowered to make deals for the song in all those areas. Publishers, who focus solely on the film and TV market, may ask for exclusive representation of both the song and master recording but be willing to exclude your artist CD and digital download sales. A third type of deal doesn't ask for any exclusivity. We'll look more closely at exclusive and non-exclusive film and TV deals in a moment.

Termination: Every deal includes something about ending the deal. Some will have a "reversion" clause, stating that the rights in the song and the master recording revert to you under certain circumstances after a certain amount of time. Other deals will simply request notification from you of your intent to terminate the deal. Read these clauses carefully. How hard or easy will it be for you to exit this deal if you decide that's the best course?

Licensing fees: The library will keep a portion of both the sync and master use fees generated by each placement they get, usually 50%. This means that half of the fees for a placement will go to the library and half will be paid to you. In Shortcut 101, you'll find a general idea of the amounts that are paid for different uses. The amount you receive will depend on the terms of your contract. If the contract gives you less than 50%, be sure you understand what your share will be and whether you're comfortable with that.

Performance royalties: The majority of music libraries will insist on participating in the performance royalties earned by the song, just as a traditional music publisher would. The question is how much will they participate. Let's say that they get your song a featured performance in an hour-long network TV drama. The performance royalty for the initial broadcast will be around $2,000. Your performing rights organization pays 50% of that royalty to the writer ($1,000) and the other 50% to the publisher ($1,000). In their deal with you, a music library could ask for the full publisher's share or they may offer to split the publisher's share of the royalties with you (a co-publishing deal). In all cases, you (and your collaborators) keep the writer's share. Only the publisher's share is in play.

Exclusive film/TV publishing deals

Simply put, an exclusive film/TV publishing deal with a music library gives that library, and only that library, the right to issue synchronization and master use licenses for a particular song or songs. The library may also insist on participation in any soundtrack albums that result from their placements. Make sure, though, that you're not giving up any rights to your artist CD or digital download sales.

The reversion clause: The amount of time your song will be tied up in an exclusive deal before the rights revert back to you is an important consideration. Some music libraries (and traditional publishers) ask for a three- to five-year reversion clause. They can make a valid argument that they invest time and money in promoting your song and circulating it to their many professional contacts. Find out if there's any room to negotiate. If not, weigh the library's track record and prestige against a long reversion clause. Any publishing deal is a serious commitment, so be sure to research the library before signing. Find out where they've had placements and how long they've been in business. Contact other writers who have signed deals with the library and get their feedback. Check with your PRO to see if they've had any experience with them.

Research a music library thoroughly before signing.

Non-exclusive deals

A non-exclusive music library deal allows you more freedom when making decisions about your song's publishing rights. You can keep 100% of the royalties if you get a placement on your own, make other non-exclusive deals, or find new outlets for your music without worrying about getting permission from a music library that's only pitching to film and TV. You can often exit the deal simply by notifying the library of your desire to do so. From a songwriter's point of view, a non-exclusive deal feels safer, less of a commitment. And, if you can sign with five non-exclusive libraries, isn't that five times better than signing with one? Well, maybe not. But before we go there, let's take a look at something called "re-titling."

The word "re-titling" refers to the practice of giving a song a new title when a non-exclusive music library registers that song with a performing rights organization, such as ASCAP, BMI, or SESAC. When the song is pitched to music users by that music library, it will be under the new title. If it's placed in a show, it will be entered on the cue sheet under the new title and when performance royalties are generated by that particular placement, the music library will receive a share. In this way, several music libraries can register the same song under different titles and each can track the royalties generated by their specific placements.

The problem with re-titling is this: Let's say a music supervisor has heard a song she likes and is considering it for a project, but the same song was pitched to her by three different music libraries, each of which has a non-exclusive deal for that song. Which one should she license it from? She could try to figure out who sent it first or call all three libraries to see if they can work something out amongst themselves. But she probably won't. The truth is, a music supervisor on a tight deadline who wants to avoid any possible conflict might just put that song aside and look for another.

Treat a non-exclusive deal like a relationship. Make a commitment.

While there's nothing inherently wrong with non-exclusive deals (and there are some non-exclusive libraries that don't use re-titling), consider signing with only one library at a time even if the deal is non-exclusive. Good libraries all have the same contacts. They can all get top music users to tell them what they're looking for. If you're with a solid, established library, you don't need to add two or three more. It doesn't improve your chances for a placement and it could be harmful.

"Take it or leave it"

Some music libraries have a "take it or leave it" attitude when they offer you a contract. They're busy doing what makes them money: getting song placements. They don't have banks of lawyers available to negotiate the many song deals they offer to songwriters and artists. You may have to accept the deal as is or walk away. Of course you should never sign anything you're not comfortable with. On the other hand, sometimes you need to have a serious talk with yourself about what's realistic and what a deal is really worth. Look at the big picture. Establishing a track record and a relationship with a good music library is definitely worth something! Figure that in when you're looking at the bottom line.

Shortcut #104

Write Songs "on Spec"

Quick delivery of quality, on-target material is the key to success in this field.

When the great songwriter Sammy Cahn was asked which came first, the music or the lyrics, he replied, "The phone call." If Sammy were working today, he might say, "The email." This is especially true for songwriters and composers who work "on spec." These writers have no idea what they'll be writing until they're contacted by a music supervisor or music library asking for a specific type of song or background cue. It's a great opportunity but you'll have to be able to meet deadlines, write and record quickly, and there's no guarantee your music will be used.

Getting in the door

To get in on this opportunity, begin by building a relationship with a music library or music supervisor. Provide a steady stream of broadcast quality, usable material. Once they know what your strengths and capabilities are, they'll contact you when they receive word that a project is in need of music in your style. For instance, if you write and record strong Alternative Rock songs and instrumentals, you might get an email asking you if you have an Alt Rock song with a specific lyric theme or overall mood, feel, or energy level. If you do, you can send a link to a website or attach an mp3 file. If you don't have a song that fits their needs, you might decide to write and record one. *That's* writing on spec.

The assignment

It's 10:00 p.m. and you're just settling in to watch your favorite TV show. You check your email one last time and find a message from a music supervisor who has used one or two of your songs. It begins something like this: "Help! I need an XYZ-style song by tomorrow at noon." The thought of shutting yourself up in your home studio and working until the wee hours isn't very appealing. Not only that, there's no guarantee that what you write will be used. If it isn't used, you may not make any money for the time you put in. However, being the dedicated, career songwriter you are, you decide to take on the challenge.

A request from a music user can come in at any time.

The description in the email is brief. It includes a few specific details about the characters and situation, as well as the energy and mood being looked for. It might read something like this:

"Wanted for network TV episode, closing montage. Fun Rock/Alternative songs about getting something you've always wanted or making a dream come true. Positive vibe with lots of upbeat energy. Must sound contemporary! They like The Locarnos' "Don't Give Me a Hard Time." Scene: Teenage boy buys his first car, a real wreck. Engine trouble getting home. Sweating over it in garage. Final shot: boy stands grinning in front of shiny, tricked-out ride. $1k to $1500 all-in. Songs must be cleared within 24 hours at this rate. Need to give producers some options by noon tomorrow. Send mp3 files asap.

If you decide to write a song for this pitch, it's gonna be a long night! Here's what you need to keep in mind:

> **Give them what they ask for.** As you can see from this example, time is of the essence. The music supervisor has to make the best use of every minute. If you submit a retro car song that sounds like Jan & Dean, if you send a Country song or a thoughtful ballad, you'll be wasting the music supervisor's time and you will not be asked to submit on future projects. Read the request carefully and send *exactly* what they're asking for.

> **Capture the energy and feel.** Listen closely to any songs and artists referenced in the request. This is the level of energy, the music style, and the mood the project is looking for. You must give them a song that has a similar energy, style, and mood. For instance, the upbeat, high-energy feel of "Don't Give Me a Hard Time" is largely the result of a fast tempo (164 BPM) and a driving, syncopated drum track. You might want to use something similar in your submission. It will certainly give your song a contemporary flavor—you won't hear *this* drum style in a retro Jan & Dean car song. But avoid playing the *same* drum track—aim for the off-kilter *feel* only.

> **Chords and music should be on target for the genre.** Again, look to the referenced artists or songs as your guide. Don't copy any of the melody! Instead, try using some of the techniques you hear. How is the referenced song using interval jumps, contrast, and creating dynamics. For more on writing "in the style of" a song or artist, read Shortcut 6.

> **Avoid lyrics that are too on-the-nose.** Don't write a lyric that tells the story that's on the screen. Leave that to the scriptwriter. A lyric that's too literal will take viewers out of the immediate, emotional experience, which is exactly what you don't want to do. In other words, if you write a song for the scene described in the request, *don't* write a lyric that begins "The day I bought my first car." You might not want to mention "car" at all. Instead, focus on the emotion of the moment: the feeling of achievement, independence, or the excitement of endless possibilities. Make the audience feel what the character is feeling.

> **Don't submit if you don't like the deal.** If you're not prepared to accept $1,000 to $1,500 in fees "all-in" (total for both sync and master use) then think twice about submitting. The music supervisor has a budget and is on a tight schedule. If she auditions your song for the producer and the producer likes it but you want to start negotiating a higher fee, it could put her in a tough spot. She's likely to take you off her email list in the future.

Demo fees

Sometimes, a demo fee will be paid for spec demos. This means you receive a modest fee whether the song is used or not. Demo fees are generally limited to the advertising field but they're also paid to established acts that are asked to write a song for a film. Demo fees are rarely, if ever, paid for a spec song for a TV series.

Production music libraries

The "music library" label, as I've mentioned before, is applied to a wide range of song and instrumental music catalogues that are available to be licensed to film and TV. Some music libraries offer only pre-existing songs; you could think of these as artist or song catalogues. Other libraries will contact a shortlist of songwriters or composers asking them to create material on spec to fit the needs of a specific project. These libraries are generally referred to as "production music libraries" or "custom music libraries."

In some cases, a production music library will get a request for an original song that comes very close to an existing work. It's up to you whether you want to take on this type of writing assignment. If you're asked to create a song that "sounds like" another artist's song, get as much direction as you can from the library and be sure the library itself takes on any liability for copyright infringement. For all other uses, capturing the energy, mood, and style are all that's needed.

Do It Now

Give yourself an assignment similar to one you might get from a music supervisor or music library. Write a song "in the style of" an artist that might work for a TV commercial or series. Avoid copying anything in that artist's songs. Instead, try to evoke the energy, feel, and mood.

Shortcut #105

Get the Most from a Music Business Attorney

Be prepared. Know what you need and how to follow up.

Like any small business, there are times when you'll want to call on an attorney for information and advice. You'll get the best results if you consult with a qualified music business attorney with experience in the film and TV field, someone who has worked with independent artists and songwriters. Licensing fees for your songs are likely to be low initially, so be sure you get the most bang for your legal buck by being well prepared and consulting an attorney who knows the field.

When to ask for advice

Have an attorney look at these documents and discuss them with you.

Here are some of the film and TV music agreements, contracts, and forms you'll be dealing with:

- Synchronization and master use licenses (Shortcut 100)
- Music library and publishing deals (Shortcut 103)
- Collaboration agreements (Shortcut 100)
- Work for Hire forms for music producers, singers. and musicians who work on your recordings (Shortcut 82)

In the beginning: As with all new business ventures, you'll need more advice when you're getting started than you will later on. In the case of the Work for Hire form, you'll need to create this form only once; after that, you can use the same waiver form "as is" or with small changes.

Multiple deals: As you gain experience with sync and master use licenses, you'll find that certain clauses become old, familiar friends; you may not need to consult with an attorney for each one. If you make more than one deal with the same music library, you'll probably be asked to sign the same contract. Past experience will tell you whether this library is open to negotiating or not. If not, then compare the new contract with the previous contract you signed to ensure the two are identical. (A change in a single word can make a big difference.)

Can an attorney shop your music to film and TV? Unless an attorney has a personal contact with a music supervisor, film producer, or TV director, the answer is no. An attorney has no more pull with a music supervisor than you do.

Get the most from your music attorney

Whether you talk to your attorney on the phone, communicate by email, or drop in to the office for a visit, if you want to get the most from your consultation, come prepared.

- As you read through a contract on your own, write down a list of questions to ask your attorney. Don't count on remembering these later!

- For phone consultations, send your contract or deal memo ahead of time so the attorney can read it over before or during the call. If you're having a face-to-face meeting, bring at least two copies of the contract: one for the attorney and one for yourself

- Take notes during the discussion. If it's a phone consultation, record it for your reference. After the meeting or phone call is over, go through your notes while the information is still fresh. Organize your notes. Transcribe the phone call. It will help you remember and understand the information and provide an easy reference in the future.

- Educate yourself before your consultation. Do your research. Find out as much as you can. Read books like Donald Passman's *All You Need to Know About the Music Business*. Visit the business section of TAXI's forum (http://forums.taxi.com/biz-talk-f12.html) where you can ask questions of songwriters and composers who've signed these deals.

Do your research and prep your questions. You'll save money and learn more!

Keep things in perspective

Before you ask an attorney to negotiate a deal for you, check to see whether the terms of the deal are negotiable. If it's an offer from a music library, it may be of the "take it or leave it" type or they may be willing to make only very small concessions. An attorney might not be able to help you get a better deal or the improvements in the deal might not be worth the cost of hiring the attorney. Before you involve your lawyer in negotiations, balance the cost versus the income you're likely to receive from the deal. Sometimes an attorney's most valuable service is helping you understand what you're being offered. A simple phone or email consultation between you and your lawyer can be very useful—and cost effective!

Shortcut #106

Find an Affordable Music Business Attorney

Five resources for finding an experienced music attorney you can afford.

As you start your search for an affordable music attorney, remember this: You don't want U2's lawyer. That's right. A music attorney who handles big money contracts may not be the best person for your situation. You want someone who gets down in the trenches, someone who works regularly with film and TV licenses for unknown songs and understands the realities of busy music libraries offering take-it-or-leave-it deals.

"I have a friend who's a lawyer."
Asking an attorney friend to advise you is rarely a good idea unless that friend has recent experience with contracts and licenses in the film and TV music business. If she practices real estate law, she won't have the specific knowledge and expertise you need. It my be an affordable solution, but I don't recommend it.

Finding a music attorney

So, how will you go about finding such an exotic animal as a music business attorney? And if you're making music on a tight budget, how will you be able to afford one? Fortunately there are some very helpful resources.

➤ **Directories:** You'll find a list of attorneys in the *Hollywood Music Industry Directory* (www.hcdonline.com). This list is particularly useful because it includes the areas of music law in which these attorneys practice. Look for those that mention "film and TV law" and "licensing." Some of these attorneys can be pricey. Be sure to ask for their rates and prepare carefully before meeting with one to make the best use of the time.

Five ways to find a music attorney.

➤ **Volunteer Lawyers for the Arts:** There are organizations in many states that offer free or low-cost legal advice to artists working in a wide range of fields, from graphic design to dance to music. Many of them incorporate the phrase "volunteer lawyers for the arts" in their name. To find them, do an online search for the exact phrase "lawyers for the arts." To narrow your search, add the name of your state. If you use their *pro bono* (free) service, you may not be able to choose an attorney with experience in the specialty you want. However, you should be able to ask for a referral to an attorney in the music field if you are able to pay.

> **Personal referrals:** If you live in an area with an active music community, ask local bands and songwriters for recommendations, especially those with a thriving music career.

> **Bar Associations:** A search for the phrase "Bar Association" along with your state or city will take you to a website where you can search for a local attorney by their field of specialization. The general heading of "entertainment law" includes attorneys in the music field.

> **Legal Zoom:** LegalZoom's "Attorney Connect" service can help you find an attorney in your local area. When asked to choose your legal issue, select "Publishing, Licensing, and Royalties" under "Entertainment Law." If you want more results, try a location with a larger music industry presence, such as Los Angeles, New York, or Nashville (www.legalzoom.com).

Then what...

When you have a list of names and contact information, write or call with the following questions:

- Have you negotiated synchronization and master use deals for film or television projects? Which ones?

- Have you negotiated contracts with music libraries that represent independent songwriters and artists?

- Who are some of your clients? How long have you been practicing music law?

- How much do your services cost?

An attorney who gives you satisfactory answers to these questions, fits your budget, and has a good attitude could be just the person you're looking for.

Shortcut #107

Five Tips for Thriving in the Film & TV Market

*Pace yourself. Be yourself. Stay inspired.
Keep learning and growing.*

Like all creative businesses, writing for the film and television market can be exciting, challenging, rewarding, and, yes, sometimes frustrating. To survive and thrive in this business, adopt a professional outlook that will see you through the tough times as well as the good ones.

Pace yourself

You're in it for the long haul!

Everyone knows the story of the tortoise and the hare. The hare sprinted for the finish line and ran out of steam before he reached his goal. The tortoise kept up a steady pace and made it all the way to the end. Even though the tortoise obviously didn't have the speed of the hare, he had one important skill the hare did not: he knew how to pace himself, managing his resources so that he was able to keep going and going and going. That's what you need to do in order to reach your goal.

There's always a temptation to pin all your hopes on your latest song, investing everything in it: production money, time, and energy. You're excited; you know the song is great. But what happens if it doesn't pay off right away? Film and TV songs take time to get placed and begin earning money. There can be a real letdown when those fast, early laps around the racetrack turn into a test of endurance.

The most important resource you have is *you*. Your energy and commitment to your music are essential to your career. If you pour everything into one song or one album, you could find that you've exhausted yourself. To win this race, remember that the song you're writing now is only one of many strong songs you will write. Each one will get you closer to your goal. Each one will require your skill, resources, and energy. Always keep something in reserve.

Stay true to yourself

Authenticity isn't automatic!

In the interviews in Part Nine of this book, top music supervisors and executives talk about the importance of authenticity, uniqueness, and honesty in your music, as well as song craft and universality. It's important to remember that "authenticity" doesn't mean singing the first melody or lyric that comes to you. Often, some of your first musical ideas are the result of habit or musical styles that were embedded when you were younger. A first draft of a song can, in fact, be very derivative and not your authentic self at all. Discovering your authentic self is a process. It unfolds as you discover and deepen your insights and learn to use song craft in ways that support your unique vision. Take time to explore your voice and vision rather than assuming it's something that just happens to you.

Inspiration and marketability can be allies

Fundamentally, songwriting is about expressing what you feel. When those feelings come through in an initial burst of inspiration, don't hold back; go for it! Afterwards, you can decide whether the song is complete as it is or could be strengthened with rewriting for the film and TV market. Keep your original inspired idea at the heart of your song and let it guide you as you shape and strengthen it with the kind of craft that will help listeners understand you and feel what you feel.

Go through the music and lyric checklists (Shortcuts 44 and 64). With some rewriting, you might be able to give the song a stronger focus, clearer mood or atmosphere, or a better chance of enhancing the memorability of a scene. You can (and should) do all this without losing your original inspiration, the heart of your song.

Build a catalogue of songs

Creating a substantial income from the film and TV market is the result of placing *many* songs and instrumental tracks. With each placement, you invest in the future. At first the money may be only a trickle, but it will grow over time as you place more and more of your music in productions that are re-run, syndicated, and sold into foreign markets. I wrote and produced hundreds of songs for two cable television series. These shows didn't pay much for each individual airing, but both series ran for over a decade and eventually the performance royalties added up to tens of thousands of dollars.

Look at the big picture!

When you get a placement, in most cases, you'll receive a licensing fee up front. The performance royalties could take nine months to a year to start coming in, so don't waste your time waiting by the mailbox! You've got more important things to do. Study the market, improve your skills, and keep writing.

The best you can do keeps getting better

Even though you and I have never met, I know this about you: You always push yourself to do the best you can do. That's the kind of person you are and your music deserves nothing less. That's why it can be discouraging if your song or production doesn't rise to the level needed by the film and TV market. After all, how can you do better if you're already pushing yourself as hard as you can? The answer is simple: Today you'll learn something new, acquire an additional skill, and practice a technique until you improve. Tomorrow, "the best you can do" will be better!

<= Remember this!

Shortcut #108

When You Get a Song Placement

Call your Mom! Break out the champagne! Write another song!

You've done it! A music supervisor has found a great spot for one of your songs and everyone agrees that it's a perfect fit. It could be a 45-second feature performance in a primetime drama. It could be a 30-second TV commercial. Maybe it's a one-minute edit of an instrumental version that's being used as underscore. Whatever it is, you've achieved all of this:

√ **You wrote a competitive song.**

√ **You produced a broadcast quality recording.**

You did all this!

√ **You invested time and money in yourself and your talent.**

√ **You researched the film and television market.**

√ **You copyrighted your song and sound recording.**

√ **You joined a PRO and registered your songs.**

√ **You got your product to a music user.**

√ **It fit the needs of the film and TV music market.**

√ **You stuck with it and believed in yourself.**

Now, *that's* impressive! You deserve a healthy dose of self-congratulation. Hold onto this feeling of achievement.

What's next?

The money: Sync and master use fees negotiated by you directly with the music supervisor should be paid to you on signing the final agreement. Initially, you'll receive a short deal memo outlining the major points on which you and the music supervisor have agreed: the name of the song, the name of the project, type of use, duration of use, etc. A final agreement will follow, one that includes more details. This can take several weeks. If a music library got the placement for you, they'll have to go through the same process before collecting any fees. You'll receive your portion of the fees after the music library has been paid.

Your share of the performance royalties will be paid directly to you by the performing rights organization with which you're affiliated. The payment covers performances that were logged at least six to nine months earlier so be patient. In the case of foreign royalties, the time frame will be longer.

Sales: Be sure people can buy your song. While researching this book, I came across two beautiful songs that weren't available for sale anywhere. I wasn't the only one looking for those songs, either. What a missed opportunity! Release a CD single through CD Baby (www.cdbaby.com) and give them permission to make it available at iTunes. Do it ahead of time because the process can take up to eight weeks.

Bragging rights: Once you know when the film or TV show with your song will be released or broadcast, call your friends, call your mom, post it on Twitter, and on your web page. Don't keep it a secret!

Post your track record where you can see it. Tack a sheet of paper on a bulletin board headed "Placements." Start your list with your current placement. Leave plenty of room for more!

Sometimes stuff happens

You're smart; you know that nothing is done until it's done. Things can change right up until the very last minute. The final cut of a film might drop the scene with your song in it or be cut so short it's hardly recognizable or the volume level of your song is so low it's hard to hear. It's not the best outcome you could have hoped for but that doesn't change the fact that your song stepped out from the rest of the pack and got that placement. It's a contender! Keep putting it out there and you'll get another chance.

Grow your song catalogue

This is the time to push forward. A successful publisher thinks in terms of a whole catalogue of songs. Look at the song that got you the placement. What worked? What could you do to build on that one? How about another one in the same style?

So... what should you do when you place one of your songs?
Go write another one!

PART NINE

Get It from a Pro

Read these interviews with some of the top music users

in the film and television song market.

They'll give you insights and information

that can help you give your songs a jumpstart!

Shortcut #109

Get It From a Pro: Tanvi Patel

The President/CEO of Crucial Music tells you what she looks for in film/TV songs.

Tanvi Patel describes Crucial Music as an "independent artist catalogue." It's a highly regarded resource for music supervisors, ad agencies, and other busy music users who want to license broadcast quality, pre-recorded songs by talented, unsigned artists and songwriters. Crucial Music has placed songs in dozens of top network TV series and numerous successful movies from 21 *to* Brokeback Mountain.

What is the role of songs in film and television?
Tanvi: In film and television, a song is there to support another message. It's not there to deliver its own message. It's there to support what's going on in the visual and deliver a concept. In advertising, it's there to deliver a brand, not necessarily for the pure enjoyment of the song itself. For me, when I'm picking songs to bring into the catalogue, I look to see if it's a well-constructed song with a strong lyric and I ask, "Is this going to support a visual?"

Would you say that the reason for using many of these songs is to create an atmosphere or enhance a mood?
Tanvi: A lot of the music by independent artists is used to create a mood. But there are some supervisors that, even if they're wanting to create a mood, they still want the song to relate to what's going on in the scene.

I notice they'll often bring up the chorus of a song at the end of a scene to turn a spotlight on an emotion or theme that's in the scene.
Tanvi: That's correct and that's one way of telling part of the story and that's why it's so important for the hook to be strong because that is what gets used and not necessarily the verses. The hook needs to be a focused one-liner like a movie tag line for the song. That's why it should be universal, catchy. It's like writing copy for a movie tag line. *[Note: A movie tag line is a single, compelling sentence or phrase, used in trailers and print ads, that conveys the feel and content of a film.]*

Make your hook a strong "one-liner."

Would you say you look for songs that have a range of possible uses or placements?
Tanvi: Yes, most of the time. About 80 to 90 percent of the time I'm looking for songs that can be used in a variety of ways.

Can you give me an idea of what is meant by "universal lyrics"?
Tanvi: For example in Country music, there's a very specific story that is told in the lyric and that doesn't work for film and television most of the time. If you're telling a very specific story how many times is there going to be a scene that's going to match exactly what your lyrics say? So, if you're talking about love, which is the most common theme that people write about, a universal love theme would be "Let's celebrate our love," or "It's a great day because you love me," but

not "I'm marrying this woman and now we're at the altar and now we're at the reception."

The [songs] that get placed the most are the ones about having a great time, partying, celebrating. You can't write enough songs about that. How many times have you heard the Black Eyed Peas' "I Gotta Feeling"? That song is being used everywhere right now because it's about having a good time, I'm feeling great. The idea that "tonight's the night," a line from "I Gotta Feeling," it can be used for the Oscars, party scenes, at a dance, or in a bar in the background. So that's what I mean by a universal lyric. It has the ability to be used in so many instances as opposed to once or twice.

You're suggesting that the lyric focus on an emotion?
Tanvi: Exactly. Focus on the emotion rather than the specific incidents that are occurring because those incidents are very limiting and when you're trying to pitch a song to hundreds of shows a year, that one song needs to apply in many instances.

A vocal that's in tune could make the difference.

Is there anything about a vocal performance that you consistently like to hear?
Tanvi: It has to be in tune. A lot of times we get songs where the production is great, the lyrics are great, but the vocal is so out of tune it just ruins the track. Then we don't take that track.

If you're somebody that sounds like Tom Waits or Leonard Cohen, artists that aren't necessarily always in tune, that's okay if there's a whole different vibe going on with the production, sort of a barebones, gruff, edgy vocal. There are uses for that. For instance, [the Showtime cable TV series] *Californication* uses a lot of that style of music because the main character is sort of an intellectual writer, comes from that world of gruffness, so a song where the vocal may not be completely in tune can get used but that, again, is the exception. It has to be a great song where the emotion is coming across in the vocal. But most of the time I'm looking for songs where the vocalist is in tune.

Do music supervisors call you looking for songs or do you approach them?
Tanvi: It's a combination of both. They reach out to me and I reach out to them so we stay in touch quite a bit.

How much information do they give you?
Tanvi: It can be anything from "I just need a Rock track" to someone who describes the scene, they tell you what they want in the lyric of the song, they give a general direction of the types of artists that they think would fit in that spot, and then you can basically search based on the details they give you.

If an artist or band has a sound that's similar to or in the style of an established artist, is that a plus or a minus for them?
Tanvi: For film and television, it can be a plus because in our lexicon of how we identify music, we're used to hearing name artists. For example, a producer will say, "Here's a character and he listens to this kind of music and we'd love new bands that are in this style." Of course, "new bands" means that they want undiscovered bands but they don't know those bands' names. So how do they

describe those bands? Well, they can only describe them in terms of bands that they're aware of.

Do you ever come across artists who say they sound like someone else when they don't sound like that at all?
Tanvi: Yes, we find that a lot. Self-perception does not always match reality. They don't know what their genre really is. If it's a Blues style, they may say they sound like Stevie Ray Vaughan when they really sound like B.B. King.

How do you find new songs?
Tanvi: People submit to us online. We also run TAXI listings. Labels find out about us and pitch directly to us. We work with independent labels that own their own masters and publishing.

You have a large number of songs in your library. How do you organize those songs so you can find what you need?
Tanvi: In our search engine we can pick male or female vocal, mood, and lyric theme. We can pick tempos, genres, sub-genres. If somebody wants something like the Cherry Poppin' Daddies, we can search for Swing meets Boogie-woogie meets Rockabilly and come up with tracks that match what they're looking for.

Do you ever sort by "in the style of" or "artists similar to"?
Tanvi: Yes. You have to be kind of careful about that, though. There could be copyright issues Be careful not to rip off that person.

So when you say "in the style of" or "sounds like" you don't mean "sound alike"?
Tanvi: Right. It means referencing the energy and the vocal style and the genre. It's relating to all the elements that make up a sound and not necessarily a specific artist's songs.

If the title of the song is descriptive of the content or feel does that help you when you're searching?
Tanvi: Yes. The best thing is to use the hook as the title. For instance, if the hook is "A Great Day" then the title of the song should be "A Great Day." I think it's important for the song title to give you an idea of what the song is about.

Where do you think the film and TV market is headed in terms of song use? Do you feel it's increasing or do you feel we've peaked in terms of numbers and kinds of uses?
Tanvi: I think it's increasing. Even though budgets for television are getting smaller and smaller, I think song use has increased and it's because of the success of shows like *Grey's Anatomy* and *The OC* and *Gossip Girl* where songs are used to really enhance and support the visuals. And also these shows have become a place where people can discover new music. The networks all have websites where they list the titles of the songs that have been used in the episodes, so it's also driving traffic to their websites.

You can find out more about Crucial Music by visiting their website at www.crucialmusic.com.

Know your genre, style, and artists you're similar to.

Shortcut #110

Get It From a Pro: Chris Mollere

This in-demand music supervisor discusses placements in high profile TV series.

Chris Mollere is a successful music supervisor whose TV credits include The Vampire Diaries, Kyle XY, Greek, *and* Pretty Little Liars. *He has helped to create a musical identity for such films such as* The Box, The Haunting Of Molly Hartley, I Hope They Serve Beer in Hell, *and* Miss Nobody. *Whatever project he undertakes, Chris brings a strong sense of song-as-underscore as well as a wide ranging musical taste that introduces fans to exciting, new artists and bands.*

Can you walk us through the process of choosing music for a show like *The Vampire Diaries?*

Chris: We start with the script about a week out from production starting on that particular episode. I'll read the script, break it down, and make sure there are no musical issues, like a band playing live on camera or one of the actors singing. Then, I look to see if there's a party or a bar scene that will need kind of a vibe. For that type of scene, I'll send some music over to the set. They'll play it before they shoot to create the mood and give the actors the tempo and feel.

The process of choosing songs for a TV episode.

After the scenes are shot, there will be a series of cuts—a cut is the episode pieced together. There's an editor's cut, then a director's cut, then the producers' cut, then the studio cut, then the network cut. The producers' cut alone can be three or four cuts. I start working with the editor's cut. I watch a scene and it may look *nothing* like what I thought it was going to look like when I read the script! I work a little differently from some people because I use Final Cut Pro and Pro Tools to drop in music and songs to picture. I actually edit music myself for people to check out. I'll even make little QuickTime movies. That way there's a better representation, more of a feeling about whether the music is going to work or not. It's hard to just imagine how a song is going to work. When you edit the music, you can hit different points, create a build. In TV, the director gets his say during his cut, but ultimately it's up to the producers and showrunners to decide what is sent to the studio and network for the completed episode pending the studio and network's notes. *[Note: The showrunner is the executive producer/writer of a TV series.]*

What is it you're looking for the song to do for the scene?

Chris: It depends on the scene. When we have a bar or party scene, we're adding source music to create some energy and make it as realistic as possible. Or, sometimes, especially on *Vampire Diaries,* we start off with source music but then weave it in and out because musically, vibe-wise, it might play into what's on the screen. So we'll start it off as source music and then bring it up as being more of a score-type song or what we like to call "scource" which is a song that plays kind of like score in a scene or sequence.

So do you think of songs as being underscore?

Chris: Yes. Definitely. We have big montages with songs that are all about trying to accentuate the scenes, add strength to them, give you that extra feeling, and pull on the heartstrings.

How many songs will you go through sometimes?

Chris: For *Vampire Diaries,* it seems like every third or fourth episode there will be a huge scene that we're trying to find the perfect song for. I'll go through hundreds of songs. I'll probably pitch 15 to 20 songs for a montage like that.

Does the director or do the producers ever say, "No, none of those work. Go back and find some more"?

Chris: Of course. Everybody's got their own opinion and we just keep going until we find the song that we feel is strongest for that episode.

You go through a lot of songs before you even pitch to the director or producers. Are you out there looking for music all the time?

Chris: I receive music from every major label, pretty much every indie label, every major publisher, every indie publisher, music reps, managers, bands; basically music comes in from everywhere. I listen to satellite radio in my car. I go to music festivals. I go to SXSW, Coachella, Austin City Limits Festival, Lollapalooza and Bonnaroo. At "All About Music," an indie showcase in Nashville, Tennessee, I saw mostly indie, up-and-coming artists—26 artists in three days.

Do you go to companies like Crucial Music?

Chris: Yes, I work with them all the time. On an episode of *Greek* recently we had a scene where we needed '30s and '40s type music and they had some great stuff for that.

How can you tell if a song fits a show?

Chris: There are no rules. Once you start choosing music for a show, then that becomes the sound of the show. If you chose different music it would be a different show. You have the opportunity at the beginning of a show to establish a musical identity and after that you just go with it.

Do you ever hear a song and know it will be good for a show even though you don't have a particular scene in mind for the song?

Chris: Yes, definitely. I make playlists. That would be a song that would go on my playlist for that specific show. It would be a song that's got the right vibe, the right lyrics, and the right feel for the show.

You mentioned lyrics. Are there some lyrics that don't work well for film and TV?

Chris: A lyric with too many specifics. Using a name in a song makes it difficult. Unless the character in the scene has the same name as the one in the song—and sometimes even if it is the same name—I can't really use it. Using precise events also doesn't work. If a song has a very specific religious theme it won't work. But I do use Christian artists who are basically singer-songwriters, like Mat Kearney. His songs are open to interpretation, which allows them to have more possibilities for being worked into a scene. So, if you're writing about a relationship, keep it

Hundreds of songs may be auditioned for a spot.

non-specific, open to interpretation. Maybe it could be about a friendship, a parent, a sibling, a girl, a guy. The more you keep the specifics open, the less likely the song will end up being too on-the-nose. I hear this from producers a lot: "It's such a great song but it's too on-the-nose. I'm just not feeling it." I feel that way, too, when the song is too blatantly in your face, when the song is trying to tell the story.

So keeping the lyrics focused on the emotional content—what the singer is feeling—works better?
Chris: Yes, I think so. Take more of a broad view of things.

Is there anything else that helps make a song more useful for you? In the production, melody, lyrics?
Chris: Yes, it's just a small thing but it's probably one of the most important things an artist can do. At the end of a song, if you have a "definitive out" that's going to give you a better chance of having an end-of-episode song, one of the big emotional montages. Make two mixes if you have to. If you have a definitive out, like a ring-out drum hit, that's going to give you a lot more possibilities, as well as the possibility of being used as a transition to another scene. I've been in situations where I really wished a song had a different ending. A fade out at the end into the final credits can be kind of boring. When I use a natural out, a definitive out, the response is so much better. It just feels like the end of an episode now. It's crazy how that one little thing can make a huge difference.

A "definitive out" is a button ending.

Is there any advice you'd like to give artists, bands, and songwriters about something that stops you from using their music?
Chris: Low production value. I know it's expensive to go into the studio and record, but you can do incredible things in a home studio. I've heard really fantastic things and I can't believe what they're recording with. But if the quality's not there, if it's got pops and hisses in it, it's not mixed properly, or the band says they're planning to go in and change something but they wanted me to hear it anyway... You know, send it when it's done. Spend some extra time actually making a mix you're proud of. You don't have to master the track.

First impression is the most important impression. If my first impression is that the recording is low quality, then that suggests that maybe the clearance process won't be easy. Do they own their publishing? Do they know what they're doing? The paper is only as good as the person who signs it.

So if you hear a music presentation that's not professional, it alerts you that maybe the whole process will be unprofessional?
Chris: Yes, if you're not going to present yourself in the best possible manner on the creative side when the opportunity arises, why would I expect you to have all your ducks in a row on the business side? Take the time to get everything in order. Make sure there are no licensing issues. Have your fee and royalty splits broken down beforehand.

When you use a song in a TV show or film, do you get a strong response from viewers?
Chris: Yes. People really want to know. I have a Twitter account for *Vampire Diaries* and *Pretty Little Liars.* I'll list all the songs on the episode right after it airs. Then, on the CW website and on the ABC Family website, they'll list the songs the next day.

Can a good placement, say, under a closing montage, help an artist's career?
Chris: Jason Walker, whose song we used in *Vampire Diaries* in a big break-up scene, right after the airing of that, people were asking, "What is that? It's so good!" And, next thing, it sold over 20,000 downloads.

Film and TV is a great place to get very quick exposure, a good way to make some extra money and, because budgets have gone down, producers have opened their minds to the idea that they don't have to use Coldplay; it doesn't have to be a big name band. They're now open to the idea that it's all about the right song. It's taken people a little while to figure out the value of music, how it can raise a production, the emotional quality of it. Music is one of those things that can make or break a show. A good scene can be great with the right song, a great scene, amazing. But you can make a great scene just okay with the wrong song.

Is there anything else you'd like to add?
Chris: Probably the most important thing is: Know who you're pitching to. Know what type of music is being used and whether your music fits. Don't overload people. I'd rather hear two songs that are in the ballpark than hear twenty songs with only two songs in the ballpark.

Songs get a strong response from viewers!

Shortcut #111

Get It From a Pro: Stephan R. Goldman

Read these insights from a music supervisor
for Academy Award-winning motion pictures.

Steve Goldman has supervised the music for over 65 major motion pictures, including The Godfather: Part III, A River Runs Through It, Mercury Rising, Full Metal Jacket, Lolita, A Walk on the Moon, *and many, many more. Whether he's using a song by a Top 10 major label band or an unknown, independent artist, he understands the interplay of picture and music and knows how deeply the right song can affect an audience.*

Do you feel that a song can increase the impact of a scene for viewers?
Steve: Absolutely. It can have a tremendous impact on the emotional fabric of a film or teleplay.

What are some of the ways a song can be used in a scene?
Steve: The right song can tell the viewer about motivation, enhance story development, and impact the emotion of the story being told. It can also be an effective tool to propel a storyline, provide information, and help develop characters by using the song to suspend time as it is played over one set scene to another. This is a very effective use of songs. A wonderful way to provide the audience a deeper insight into who the characters are and what they might be feeling internally. You can create memorable montages this way as songs play over cut footage. It's very entertaining and informative at the same time. You see this in film and TV all the time when you want to propel the storyline or even suspend action.

So what you're telling me is that these songs have uses, they need to do something.
Steve: Yes, exactly. There's a wide variety of uses for songs in filmed entertainment.

When you're looking at songs to put in a scene, you're looking at whether the song fulfills the needs of the scene, is that correct?
Steve: Yes, I've done films where I've used almost an entire song-score. Using the tracks to help tell the story. In the movie, "A Walk on the Moon," for instance, which was set in the Catskill mountains in New York in 1969, I used songs from that era to tell a story set against the time of the Woodstock Music Festival, exactly when our astronauts first walked on the Moon. This was a story of the heart wrenching effect an illicit affair had on a working class family. A young wife met a man who sold blouses from his van, an affair ensued and it tore the family apart. I used many different kinds of songs that were popular during that period; some of them were used in completely different contexts than you would expect.

There are uses in dramatic pieces where the song helps set the period and you are taken back to what was going on. And there are songs that underscore emotional, internal feelings unexpressed by the dialogue of the story. Sometimes a song is used in a context that the songwriter didn't even consider when they wrote it. Most times the songwriter is telling one story but the song used in the film tells a completely different story, one that the filmmaker is trying to convey.

When you're looking for a song to set the time period, how important is authenticity in the instrumentation, vocal performance, and song style?
Steve: It's very important when you're trying to set a place and a period. It's less important in terms of working with emotion. You always want to be accurate and concerned with the time frame. There's a little leeway when it's really more about the emotional feel of a particular song. You can take a contemporary song and use it in a period piece if it supports the emotional fabric of the scene and doesn't fight with the period. "Shakespeare in Love" is a great example of this. And vice versa, you can take an old song and use it in a new context in terms of time and place if it works with the scene. Tarantino and Scorsese are masters at this.

Do you look for songs with a strong, clear emotional focus?
Steve: I look for great honesty and songs that are well crafted, that are not cliché. I love originality, genuine feeling, and really strong lyric content.

What things do you look for in a vocal performance and what things might be negatives for you?
Steve: I look for authenticity and a genuine heartfelt delivery of the lyric. It's best when the singer isn't trying to sell me, when they're actually performing from their heart.

Are there times when the performance is genuine but there are, say, vocal pitch problems that detract too much for it to work?
Steve: Occasionally you come across music that is kind of sloppily done. A crack in the voice here and there, can add to the genuineness of a performance. Bob Dylan comes to mind, for one. Within that style there's a lot of room, but if there are glaring pitch problems or performance problems, then it's not usable. It has to be professional and it has to be real.

Do you find that there are some songs that tell a story that might make them too specific for use in a film or TV scene?
Steve: That's a good point. Sometimes you see a film where the song used is so specific to what you are seeing on the screen that it actually takes you out of the movie. It's too darn close; too spot on. Aspiring composers and songwriters tend to automatically submit music that's too closely related to the project. And then there are the filmmakers, amateurishly sometimes, using a piece of music that is telling the story. It's actually distracting. A song is underscore; you shouldn't use a song as dialogue. That's the worst thing you could do. It's manipulative and the audience knows it right away. It's always better to be a little oblique.

What works ...
Honesty
Good song craft
Originality
Emotion

Were you ever in a situation where the budget wasn't big enough to afford a major act so you went looking for a lesser known artist with a similar sound or energy?

Steve: Many, many times. That's normal. Some of these big artists command such huge fees especially now, there's no budget for these big artists.

So when you go looking for a band to fill a slot, maybe the project can't afford U2 but they really want that sound, how would you describe what you're looking for?

Steve: I still look for authenticity along with excellent playing and well-constructed songs and tracks. In terms of U2, I'd look specifically for their kind of sonic richness, swirling guitars with masterful rhythm tracks. U2 has their own distinctive instrumental sound. It's very rich and textured.

Would you look for the same propulsive drive, maybe pace, tempo, and energy?

Steve: Exactly.

Do you have a music/song collection of your own?

Steve: I do. I have an enormous library of music from all genres and periods.

How do you organize it so you can quickly find what you need?

Steve: I have everything broken down by genre, artist, and mood.

Does it make a difference to you whether the artist is well known or unknown?

Steve: Not at all. The quality of the music is the most important element for me.

Shortcut #112

Get It From a Pro: Paul Antonelli

An Emmy Award-winning music supervisor
for daytime dramas shares his knowledge.

For more than 25 years, Paul Antonelli has contributed to the sound of daytime dramas—General Hospital, Santa Barbara, All My Children, Sunset Beach, Passions, and As the World Turns—choosing songs to accompany weddings, break-ups, and montages of memorable moments that helped to keep viewers in touch with the lives of their favorite characters.

What do you feel a song can do for a scene?
Paul: It enhances it in every way. That would be the biggest thing that I look for in a song, that it enhances the scene, or scenes if it's a long montage. You really want a song that has a lot of emotional impact.

Can you describe how a song works with a scene to create that kind of emotional impact?
Paul: What I try to do is ascertain what the scene is trying to say. For instance, if there's a montage of a couple who have been together and we see pictures of their life together, I need to know what do we want the audience to feel? Is it poignant? Are we rooting for a couple to stay together? Do we want them to split up? Do we want the audience to make their own judgment about what's going to happen? I always speak with our executive producer and sometimes the director to see what it is they're trying to get across.

And you're relying on the song to help you express that?
Paul: Oh, absolutely, it's integral. Especially when you're doing a montage. The song has to express the point of view, the message.

The song expresses the message.

When you're listening to CDs that are submitted to you, is the vocal performance important?
Paul: Extremely important! This is going to be the version that hits the air and everything that I use is a direct reflection on me and the show—so I want to make sure the tune I'm using is the very best it can be.

Is there anything about the lyrics or music that is usually a plus or minus for you? For instance, does the lyric need to have a strong emotional focus?
Paul: Every situation I'm looking to score with a song has some kind of focus, whether it's a Thanksgiving montage between a group of families with a broader focus on the importance of family and togetherness, or a more specific focus on a particular star-crossed couple who have come back together again. That focus would be more specific—true love that was lost, but is now found again.

I usually find it difficult to use a song that has too much focus. Take, for instance, the example I gave of a love that was lost but was found again. If the writer is getting the point across in more general terms, it could prove to be quite useful for me. But if the writer is mentioning that she runs into her old love on West Main Street in Des Moines on her way to the early-bird special at Appleby's, it's going to be next to impossible for me to use because our couple is from Manhattan and they happen to be jet-setters who consume little else other than beluga caviar & Cristal champagne.

A simple, poignant track can do the job.

Do you prefer a song with a big chorus and a lot of dynamics over a more intimate, more singer-songwriter style song? Or is there a place for both?
Paul: Oh, without a doubt, there is most definitely a place for both! It's all dependent on the content of the visual I'm working with or simply the tone I'm trying to convey through the song. I've found that there are times when there's nothing more powerful than a simple, poignant piano/vocal or acoustic guitar/vocal. Of course, the song itself has to be killer! Rip my heart out, toss it on the floor and stomp on it for good measure!

Do you use a lot of songs in daytime drama?
Paul: It is really dependent on the show. On *Passions,* we used a lot. Probably 20 percent of all music used was songs. It's different for different shows. On *As the World Turns,* we use less. It depends on the style, on the sensibility of each show.

Do you ever use music libraries to help you find songs?
Paul: Yes. There was one in particular. When I was working on *Passions* until late at night on the west coast and I needed a song, I would call them on the east coast and they would always pick up at two or three o'clock in the morning. At *Passions,* since I was the only music guy there, I couldn't put it off. I had to get it wrapped up; it had to be finished before I went on to the next show the next day. Sometimes things have to move really fast.

Do you use material by independent artists or songwriters?
Paul: Yes. Sometimes an executive producer might want a song to be something the audience can relate to, a better-known artist, but I get more personal satisfaction when I can use a song or an artist that nobody has heard before. Because, to me, anyone can look in Billboard or on iTunes and find out what the popular things are but I've found over the years that there are just so many undiscovered gems. I love to be able to let one shine because we've got millions of viewers and they respond to music so well, which makes my gig so rewarding. I love when they're emailing and phoning in, wanting to find out what the song was.

You have a lot of CDs in your own personal collection. How do you organize it so you can find what you need? Do you sort by title? Lyric theme? Mood? Genre?
Paul: Aha! For myself, I find that generally I put most everything commercially available in alphabetical order. Soundtracks and Classical have their own sections, as do International cuts. I also have specific sections for Blues, Dance, Religious, Children, and Christmas.

I keep notes on specific songs I want to keep in mind for the future like... Love: love lost, love found, love lost but found again. Dying: friend, lover, father, mother. These notes have saved me countless hours of research when I'm faced with scoring a scene quickly. It's so important to keep these notes due to the sheer amount of music that crosses my desk on a daily basis. It can become quite overwhelming otherwise.

Do you ever describe or categorize an artist as being "in the style of" an established artist or band? Does the executive producer ever do that when describing the type of music he or she wants to hear?
Paul: Absolutely. You often come across an executive producer who has very specific tastes in music, artists or bands. I can't tell you how many times I've heard something along the lines of, "I want the moodiness of Bryan Ferry or Chris Rea..." or "Get me the angst of Patti Smith..." or "You *know* how much I love Sarah McLachlan...." That's the feel, the general direction of what they want and I have to find an artist with a sound like that.

Why he might look for artists "in the style of...".

How do you find new artists and songs?
Paul: I'm listed under Antonelli Music in *Billboard, Music Connection,* and various other music publications. People email me and I encourage them to send in their music and I listen to as many as I can. Sometimes something just resonates in somebody's email that makes me really want to check this out when the CD gets in. I get so many CDs; that's the big frustration. So much material comes in there aren't enough hours in the day. I have stacks of CDs. Sometimes I'll be going through CDs and I'll see a title that piques my interest so I'll throw that CD on.

I'll also make a note if somebody sent me an email that really stood out. You can tell that they've done their homework. You can tell it's not a generic form letter which was mass emailed. I really am more inclined to listen to product sent by someone who's put some time and thought into their email.

For instance, if somebody says, "I saw that episode where you used such-and-such a song. I have a song that might work for you."
Paul: Yes, that person more than anyone because that person is more likely to send me what I need.

Shortcut #113

Get It From a Pro: Marianne Goode

Let a leading music executive give you the big picture.

Most recently serving as Senior Vice President in charge of Music for a major cable network, Marianne launched her own company, ALL MEDIA MUSIC GROUP in early 2010. Her clients include Lifetime/AETN, independent content producers, recording artists, record labels and artist management companies. Marianne began her career in music publishing at Rondor Music International, the esteemed music publishing company started by A&M Records founders, Herb Alpert and Jerry Moss, where her last position held was Vice President, Television Music.

When you look for a song to put with picture, what is it that you want the song to add to the scene?
Marianne: Usually it's the same thing you want a song to provide when you're listening to it; the emotion. You want it to evoke a certain feeling in the viewer. For me, some of the best uses of music with visuals have a "counterpoint" element to them, the juxtaposition of the song with picture that allows the viewer to get to the emotion on their own without being led or pushed into a specific thought or feeling. One of the most widely known examples is the use of Louis Armstrong's recording of the song "What a Wonderful World" (written by David Weiss and Bob Thiele) in the film Good Morning, Vietnam—it provides the backdrop for the audience to create their own experience.

Read Shortcut 59 for ideas on how to add a fresh angle to your theme.

A great song can also provide depth to a common theme. One of my favorite songs in this regard is "I Can't Make You Love Me" written by Mike Reid and Allen Shamblin and first recorded by Bonnie Raitt. The lyric covers a familiar subject—loving someone, having feelings for someone who has fallen out of love or doesn't feel the same for you—but written and performed with such authenticity and powerful honesty—you ache for the person who is losing the love of the other.

Montages are such an important part of today's TV dramas. What are you looking for a song to do in a montage?
Marianne: I think there is a greater burden on songs that are featured in montages because often there's little to no dialogue, so there is more focus on the song. This is in contrast to a song that is used as background source to establish a scene in a bar or club that is not front-and-center the way it is if it's the foundation for a montage sequence.

For montage sequences, I look for songs that create a strong emotional reaction when you put them up against the picture. When you find the right song for a montage, you know it by the way it makes you feel when you watch it.

So, a scene that's as simple as two people looking at each other, do you mean that a song can create a reaction in the viewer when it's played under that scene?

Marianne: A song can do that if the scene calls for a song, rather than underscore. If the director and/or producer decides to leave the audience with the feeling that something is unresolved between those two people—that's one kind of song. If he or she wants to leave the audience with the feeling of happiness and contentment, that's a different song. If you ever were to watch the same scene synched with three very different songs presented by the music supervisor, your reaction would be different for each song. It's the same visual, but the song can make you feel something completely different!

Do you sometimes hear a song and feel it will be good with picture even though you don't have a specific use in mind for it?

Marianne: Yes. Most of the people I know who are in a position to use music in a supervision capacity hang onto a great song. They categorize it, catalogue it and they go back to it when they have the right scene. It's common for supervisors to place songs months and even years after they first hear it.

So a songwriter should aim for something that resonates with the music supervisor or director or producer, something that really moves them and is memorable for them?

Marianne: I'm glad you asked this question. With so much focus currently on film and TV placements as a way for writers to have their music heard and earn income in the process, I think there is a danger in trying to target that market too specifically. First and foremost, I think a songwriter should focus on writing a great song. When a song is well crafted and well recorded and there's a very moving performance, I think that's what grabs people. That's what I would aspire to do if I were a songwriter. I would stay true to my authentic artistic style first and then, if there's a home for it, trust that it will be found.

Does it make any difference to you whether an artist is well known or unknown or is it always the song?

Marianne: For me, it's always about the song and the performance over the marquee value. I think one of the reasons we've seen such a proliferation of independent and lesser known artists having success in this area is because, again, when you see it against picture and it works, you know it. No one is asking, "Is that X band or Y artist, but they may ask, "Who is that artist I've never heard before?" Music supervisors get a lot of gratification in creating awareness for an unknown artist and I think viewers are interested in discovering new music in this way.

What are some of the avenues that you use to find new music?

Marianne: There are many good and well-respected people who act as placement agents on behalf of writers and artists. If a supervisor trusts that person and their ears, they'll listen to what they pitch because it's been pre-screened and there is a relationship there. Placement agents serve as a way to streamline the process.

I also have a lot of relationships with managers and songwriters that I have maintained from my time spent in music publishing, which is where I started out

A song can determine the viewer's reaction to a scene.

in the business. Then there are the major and indie label and publisher contacts, the independents, etc., but I don't accept unsolicited material.

You must have a lot of music that you've heard, that you've thought "I might use that for a show in the future." How do you organize that so you can go back and find a song that you've got under your umbrella somewhere?
Marianne: Everybody does it a little differently. I usually use playlists: female singer-songwriters, male singer-songwriters, bands, different genres, a combination of all that. Then I might also enter key words that sum up the general lyric or broader message, because I can then search for a song later using those key words. But, a lot of it is also just hearing something, loving it, and becoming a fan. It's sort of etched in your consciousness depending on your level of enthusiasm and your passion for that particular song or artist. I have a lot of artists that I'm just a fan of in general and I love their body of work so I won't think of a song necessarily; I'll think of *them*.

So it comes back again to how memorable you are. How unique, how authentic, how much of an impression do you make with your music.
Marianne: That's right, yes. That's why I think it's so important to stay true to who you are artistically. And hone your craft to the best of your ability rather than trying to fit into a description of what somebody is looking for at the moment.

Make a unique, memorable impression.

Shortcut #114

Get It From a Pro: Peter Greco

This top advertising executive offers an inside look at songwriting for commercials.

As Executive Music Producer/Senior Vice President at Young & Rubicam Advertising, Peter Greco made his mark producing award winning music tracks for accounts such as AT&T, Jaguar, Sony, Bacardi, Citibank, and Xerox. He has helped these companies, and many more, find just the right song—whether it's by an iconic Rock band or an unsigned singer-songwriter— that will create an identity, add new life to a brand name, communicate a message, and connect with viewers.

What do you feel that a song can do for a commercial?
Peter: A song can serve a multitude of purposes. It can deliver an emotion. It can deliver a message, tell you how to think or how not to think.

How about the perception of the product? Can a song connect certain emotions or thoughts with a product?
Peter: Yes, it can definitely reinforce branding. For example, I worked on a commercial called "Beaches." The overall concept was a mom taking her little girl to the beach and because the mom has a cell phone she can still stay in touch with the office, be part of a meeting. We used Cyndi Lauper's "Girls Just Want to Have Fun."

And the upbeat message and feel of that song attached to the cell phone, to the brand?
Peter: Exactly.

When you look for a song for a commercial, are you looking for a song that creates a strong emotional impression on you?
Peter: When you look for a song for a TV commercial, it goes through a different lens than it would for a film or a TV show or a game. You're connecting to a product and/or a client. So there's a slightly different thought process that goes into it.

Do you look for songs that have an obvious association with a product?
Peter: There's a misconception, a mistake that a lot of songwriters make. I used to get this phone call all the time saying: "I just wrote this great song about 'connecting' and it would be great for AT&T" or "I just wrote this great song about taking a ride in an airplane and it would be great for Jet Blue." Nine hundred and ninety-nine times out of a thousand, it doesn't happen that way. In the 20 plus years I worked at ad agencies, I don't know if I can even point to a time where somebody went running around with a song in their hands saying, "We have to write a commercial to this!"

So, how does the song fit into the process of creating a commercial?
Peter: There are two ways. In the "old days," people actually wrote songs for a commercial; that's where the word "jingle" comes from. The jingle itself was the concept. The lyrics were written to convey a specific marketing message. Rather than have a voiceover actor or narrator deliver those marketing points, it was fashioned into lyrics and given to a music production house that would then write a melody to them. The images in the commercial were crafted around the jingle.

Jingles were a very effective selling/branding tool. However, that's precisely why they've become almost extinct—save for some funny parodies, and really hip jingles like some that McDonalds has done. The traditional jingle has lost its cool. Advertisers want to reach a younger audience and that audience wants music that sounds like what they listen to on their iPods. Whatever it is, it's *gotta* feel real or they will tune out. The word "jingle" is taboo in advertising these days.

In today's world, music is usually retrofitted to the concept. Licensing a real song, whether it's a Mary J Blige tune or one from an indie band, gives a commercial a different sensibility than a jingle might. A song like that isn't trying to *sell*. It's either lending its caché, its cool factor, its emotion, its energy, its attitude, its elegance, or its edge—as long as it's *not* doing the selling! That's why it's so important for songwriters to understand that it's always best to write from the heart. If you start getting cute or too clever, if you sound like you're trying to impress, you're toast. They will smell it a mile away. When you're given direction by the client or agency, *use the adjectives* to guide you. They'll use words like "indie," "speed metal," "moody," "bright," "fun," "simple," "dense," and so on. Let those lead you. My favorite quote: It's better to be smart than clever. Write smart music. When you try to get clever, that's when you get cute and it doesn't work.

Focus on the adjectives when you're given direction.

Who goes looking for those existing songs by artists and bands?
Peter: It happens in many different ways. I came from a culture in which ad agencies had people like myself, in-house music producers, who would typically search for those songs. Now, there is so much musical content out there, and there are fewer people like me at ad agencies. Typically, the agency's creative director or the music producer will reach out to record labels, music publishers, song libraries, and A&R companies like TAXI, who find songs within the brief that's provided.

When a songwriter gets a chance to write and pitch a song or instrumental for a specific commercial, what's the best way to approach that?
Peter: When someone's giving you a project, the most helpful thing you can get is good direction. Ask as many questions and get as much information as possible. Everybody will interpret direction differently. Follow wherever the direction leads you as a musician. Direction is going to help you more than anything.

If you're given a piece of film to work with, really study it, get inside of it. A lot of times, when composers and songwriters are watching a piece of film, they forget to listen to the dialogue or voice-over copy *[scripted lines spoken by a narrator]*. More often than not, the copy will lead you better than the visual itself. With commercials, many times, there's a problem/solution aspect to it. If you follow the copy, it will generally lead you to that transition point where the solution happens. The logic path of the copy is much clearer than the picture.

And that will affect what you're writing?

Peter: Of course. You have decisions to make. You might decide in the problem area to take a simpler approach to the music and then when the solution comes, the music might be fuller. You might start with something that is somewhat dramatic and foreboding and then change that attitude to triumphant.

You're a composer yourself. Do you have any advice for songwriters about what works and what doesn't?

Peter: Do not write songs about soup. Do not write songs about cars. Do not write songs about telephones. It's really all about authenticity. They don't want anything that smacks of any sort of pre-meditated commercialism. They want to be able to find a song that speaks to their audience and speaks to their product in an almost coincidental way—a *uniquely* coincidental way. Mostly because it's just cooler that way! I might find a song that's talking about "throwing out the garbage" and that might work for a computer commercial that's talking about how you trash your files. There's a real spark—and it's happened many times—where you find a song that was written with one thing in mind and it found a completely new meaning when combined with a visual.

They want a song that speaks to the audience, not one that sells.

So, you suggest just writing the best songs you can?

Peter: I think the best advice is "Do what you do best" with the realization that there are millions of people out there competing and you can only do best what it is you do best. You'll be found out really quickly if you try to do something out of your league because there are people in that league who are really brilliant. Being true to yourself is the best tack that you can take on all levels and as it relates to advertising, TV, and films—absolutely.

Shortcut Resources

Studying how songs are used in a TV series or film is easier to do when you can fast-forward to an exact spot, play the scene over and over, or stop the action while you look up the lyrics. Thus, it's a good idea to focus on shows and films that are available to buy, rent, stream or download. Try these resources to get your film and TV songwriting career in gear! You've got plenty of choices, so pick those that work best for you.

➤ **Use the "Film & TV Song List" on page 310.**
The Film & TV Song List includes all of the songs used as examples in this book, plus the TV shows, films, commercials, and promo spots in which they can be heard.

➤ **Choose your favorite TV shows.**
Most of the popular TV series that aired within the last decade are available to buy or download, whether they're currently running or not. So if *Scrubs* was your favorite show and you want to study the songs that were used in the first season of the show, it's easy to do. If you're not sure whether your favorite show used songs, try searching for the series title at Tune Find (www.tunefind.com).

➤ **Choose your favorite films.**
Films from the silent era up to the present are available on DVD and video to rent or buy. While there are cable stations that air the latest releases, you're better off with a DVD, Blu-Ray, or VHS that allows you to replay a particular scene and note the time at which it occurs for later reference. Movies are usually released on DVD six to eight months after theatrical release.

Resources for TV shows and films

Rent or stream: Rent DVDs or stream movies and TV shows at these sites:
Netflix – www.netflix.com
Blockbuster – www.blockbuster.com

Watch for free: To see many of the TV series referred to in the book, go to the network on which the show airs. Look for "Full Episodes" or "Shows" to see if the show you're looking for is available. Avoid websites that offer free downloads unless you're sure the files are free of viruses. Here are a few trusted websites to get you started:

ABC – http://abc.go.com
CBS – www.cbs.com
NBC – www.nbc.com
Fox – www.fox.com
MTV – www.mtv.com
Lifetime – www.mylifetime.com
E! – www.eonline.com

More...

Hulu – www.hulu.com

Fancast – www.fancast.com

Public Libraries – Most public libraries have a selection of DVDs and VHS tapes. Check to see if they have the movies and shows you want.

Buy: Buying an individual episode from a TV series is easy and inexpensive. Both iTunes and Amazon.com offer a large selection. While streaming and downloading work well for TV shows, if you want to acquire movies that way, you'll need a fast connection and a lot of space on your hard drive. Therefore, I recommend buying movies on DVD, VHS, or Blu-Ray. Consider buying gently used DVDs at Amazon.com to save money. Here are a few sources where you can purchase inexpensive movies:

Amazon – www.amazon.com

Walmart – www.walmart.com

Barnes and Noble – www.barnesandnoble.com

Buy.com – www.buy.com

… even your local supermarket now sells inexpensive DVDs!

What was that song? – TV shows

To find out which songs were used in a TV episode, or whether the show used any songs at all, try these helpful websites:

Tune Find – www.tunefind.com

TV Show Music – www.tvshowmusic.com

Heard On TV – www.heardontv.com

You can look through the song lists for various episodes of a show until you find one that looks interesting, then buy it at iTunes or rent the episode at Netflix.

Find a song that was aired in a TV episode: If you watched a TV show and want to know the name of a song that was played, note which network or cable channel was airing the show, the name of the TV series, and the date and time of the broadcast. Then check your local TV listings or go to a website that carries TV listings to look up the episode title. Here are two websites with TV listings that include the episode title:

TV Guide – www.tvguide.com

Yahoo! TV – http://tv.yahoo.com

You can then take that information and look up the show and episode at Tune Find, TV Show Music, or Heard On TV to find the song list. There are also fan sites that carry song lists. An Internet search using the series title plus the phrase "song list" will usually give you good results.

What was that song? — Films

You can find the songs that were used in a movie by looking for a soundtrack album or searching the Internet using the word "soundtrack" followed by the title of the film. Here are more resources:

The Internet Movie Database (www.imdb.com): This is an excellent resource for film song information. On the website, search for a film title then look for "Soundtrack Listing" under "Fun Stuff." You'll find all the songs listed in the film's credits, including those that are not on the soundtrack CD.

Amazon (www.amazon.com): A search of Amazon's website using the word "soundtrack" plus the movie title will bring up a page for the soundtrack CD, assuming that a soundtrack was released. You can either purchase the CD or buy and download individual songs.

Academy Award winners and nominees: You can find a list of all Oscar nominees and winners from 1934 through the present in the Academy Awards database. The easiest way to get to the database is to do an Internet search using the exact phrase "official Academy Awards database." In the database search form, choose the category "Music (song)" for the complete list. You can narrow your search by adding the film title or year.

Wikipedia (en.wikipedia.org): Type in the name of the movie plus the word "soundtrack" for a list of the songs in the film.

Resources for commercials, film trailers, and promos

You can watch many commercials, film trailers, and promo spots online for free. Check out these websites.

Fan Cast – www.fancast.com
Coming Soon – www.comingsoon.net
YouTube – www.youtube.com (For commercials, search by product name. For trailers and promos, search by movie or TV series name.)

Find the songs: If you don't know the name of the song or artist used in a commercial or trailer, try an Internet search using the product name plus the words "song" and "ad" or "commercial." You can also visit these websites for more information.

Ad Music Database – www.admusicdb.com
Splendad – www.splendad.com
AdTunes – www.adtunes.com

Film & TV Song List

The timings given here for all movies and TV shows are either for the commercially released DVD or iTunes download. These may vary by up to one minute. Commercials can be found online by doing an Internet search for the product name and song name. YouTube.com is the best resource for watching commercials online.

SONG TITLE (ARTIST)	FILM: YEAR OF RELEASE TV SHOW: SEASON / EPISODE TITLE COMMERCIAL: PRODUCT / BROADCAST YEAR	AT TIME hrs:min:sec	USED IN SHORTCUTS
1 2 3 4 (Feist)	TV Commercial — *iPod Nano* 2007	00:00	11
1901 (Phoenix)	TV Commercial — *2010 Cadillac SRX* 2009	00:00	86
99 Times (Kate Voegele)	TV Series — *One Tree Hill* Season 6: "A Kiss to Build a Dream On"	05:45	28, 30, 39
After Hours (We Are Scientists)	Film — *Nick & Norah's Infinite Playlist* 2008 (PG-13)	38:01	9, 19, 20, 38, 54
All I Need (Mat Kearney)	TV Series — *Grey's Anatomy* Season 3: "Time Has Come Today"	39:49	60
All I Want Is You (Barry Louis Polisar)	Film — *Juno* 2007 (PG-13)	01:44	13, 22
And I Am Telling You I'm Not Going (Jennifer Hudson)	Film — *Dreamgirls* 2006 (PG-13)	1:02:20	42, 61
Apologize (OneRepublic)	TV Series — *Smallville* Season 7: "Hero"	38:29	28, 32, 53, 56
At Last (Etta James)	TV Series — *Alias* Season 4: "Authorized Personnel Only: Part 1"	00:10	9, 19, 40
Be Here Now (Ray LaMontagne)	Film — *27 Dresses* 2008 (PG-13)	1:26:56	77
Be Prepared (Jeremy Irons)	Film — *The Lion King* 1994 (G)	28:06	62
Beautiful (Christina Aguilera)	TV Commercial — *The Foundation for a Better Life* 2010	00:00	20, 40
Beautiful Tree (Rain Perry)	TV Series — *Life Unexpected* Theme song	00:00	13, 48, 59, 65

Song (Artist)	Usage	Time	Pages
Before I Knew (Basia Bulat)	TV Commercial "Lost Sunglasses" — *Subaru Outback* 2009 - 2010	00:00	11
Bennie and the Jets (Elton John)	Film — *27 Dresses* 2008 (PG-13)	1:08:27	8
Best of Both Worlds, The (Miley Cyrus)	Film — *Hannah Montana: The Movie* 2009 (G)	04:29	62
Break Me Out (The Rescues)	TV Series — *Grey's Anatomy* Season 5: "Sweet Surrender"	39:55	55
Breathe In Breathe Out (Mat Kearney)	TV Promo Spot — *Grey's Anatomy* Season 4 promo	00:00	13, 19, 32, 53
Bring On the Day (Vaughan Penn)	TV Series (MTV) — *The Hills* Season 4: "Boys Make Girls Cry" (instrumental)	00:00	86
Butterfly Fly Away (Miley Cyrus & Billy Ray Cyrus)	Film — *Hannah Montana: The Movie* 2009 (G)	1:18:07	61
Can't Go Back Now (The Weepies)	TV Series — *Life Unexpected* Season1: Pilot	37:49	24, 28, 48, 77
Cannonball (Damien Rice)	TV Series — *The O.C.* Season 1: "The Rivals"	38:43	20, 21, 31, 32, 40, 49, 57, 59, 75
Climb, The (Miley Cyrus)	Film — *Hannah Montana: The Movie* 2009 (G)	1:28:00	25, 32, 36, 42, 48, 55, 57
Come Back When You Can (Barcelona)	TV Series — *The Vampire Diaries* Season 1: "History Repeating"	40:11	22, 73
Dance With Me Tonight (The Wonders)	Film — *That Thing You Do!* 1996 (PG)	49:01	63
Day Before the Day, The (Dido)	TV Series — *Grey's Anatomy* Season 5: "Wish You Were Here"	35:34	57
Daydreamer (Adele)	TV Series — *90210* Season 1: "We're Not in Kansas Anymore/ The Jet Set"	1:17:02	75
Don't Give Me a Hard Time (The Locarnos)	Film — *Post Grad* 2009 (PG-13)	18:43	9, 38, 104
Down (Jason Walker)	TV Series — *The Vampire Diaries* Season 1: "Lost Girls"	40:42	23, 25, 31, 51, 110
Everyday Is a Winding Road (Sheryl Crow)	TV Commercial — *Subaru Outback and Impreza* 2006, 2008	00:00	11, 20, 36, 38, 56

Song	Type	Time	Pages
Everything I Can't Have (Robin Thicke)	Film — *Step Up 2: The Streets* 2008 (PG-13)	55:49	17
Eye in the Sky (Jonatha Brooke)	TV Series (MTV) — *The Hills* Season 4: "Boys Make Girls Cry"	10:20	53
Fallin' for You (Colbie Caillat)	TV Series — *Ghost Whisperer* Season 5: "Excessive Forces"	28:28	20, 30, 31, 39
Falling Slowly (Glen Hansard & Markéta Irglová)	Film — *Once* 2006 (R for language)	15:45	15, 40
Flying High (Jem)	TV Series — *Grey's Anatomy* Season 2: "Band-Aid Covers the Bullet Hole"	38:44	31, 48
From the Morning (Nick Drake)	TV Commerical — *AT&T* 2010	00:00	75
Full Moon (The Black Ghosts)	Film — *Twilight* 2008 (PG-13)	01:51	46
Good Life, The (Miley Cyrus)	Film — *Hannah Montana: The Movie* 2009 (G)	10:50	61
Gravity (John Mayer)	TV Series — *House M.D.* Season 3: "Cane and Able"	41:40	48, 49, 55, 60
Hands (The Count voiced by Jerry Nelson)	TV Commercial— *Delta Faucets* 2009	00:00	11
Hero (Regina Spektor)	Film — *(500) Days of Summer* 2009 (PG-13)	1:07:34	75
Hide and Seek (Imogen Heap)	TV Series — *CSI: Miami* Season 5: "If Looks Could Kill"	42:28	75
High Noon (Do Not Forsake Me) (Tex Ritter)	Film — *High Noon* 1952 (NR)	00:12	10
Hoedown Throwdown (Miley Cyrus & Cast)	Film — *Hannah Montana: The Movie* 2009 (G)	51:33	42
I Am the Unkown (The Aliens)	Film — *21* 2008 (PG-13)	40:41	9
I Gotta Feeling (Black Eyed Peas)	TV Series — *Melrose Place* Season 1: "Nightingale"	18:38	20, 39, 48, 109
I Just Can't Wait to Be King (Weaver, Williams, Atkinson)	Film — *The Lion King* 1994 (G)	15:53	62

Song (Artist)	Source	Time	Pages
I Need to Wake Up (Melissa Etheridge)	Film — *An Inconvenient Truth* 2006 (PG)	1:29:40	17, 60
I Want It All (Ashley Tisdale & Lucas Grabeel)	Film — *High School Musical 3: Senior Year* 2008 (G)	24:14	42
I'll Be There for You (The Rembrandts)	TV Series — *Friends* All episodes: theme song.	00:00	13
I'm Yours (Jason Mraz)	TV Series — *90210* Season 1: "We're Not in Kansas Anymore / Jet Set"	1:05:39	20, 40
Idumea (Sacred Harp Singers)	Film — *Cold Mountain* 2003 (R)	11:34	12
In Your Eyes (Peter Gabriel)	Film — *Say Anything* 1989 (PG-13)	1:16:45	8, 59
It's Hard Out Here for a Pimp (Terence Howard feat. Taraji Henson)	Film — *Hustle and Flow* 2005 (R)	1:01:15	42
Janglin' (Edward Sharpe & the Magnetic Zeros)	TV Commercial — *Ford Fiesta* 2010	00:06	86, 89
Jungle Drum (Emiliana Torrini)	TV Series — *Grey's Anatomy* Season 5: "Dream a Little Dream of Me" — Part 1	40:31	19, 20, 38
Keep Breathing (Ingrid Michaelson)	TV Series — *Grey's Anatomy* Season 3: "Didn't We Almost Have It All"	46:45	2, 20, 24, 26, 54, 55, 56, 65, 77
Kiss from a Rose (Seal)	Film — *Batman Forever* 1995 (PG-13)	2:00:17	53
Last Day of Your Life (Glass Pear)	TV Series — *90210* Season 1: "We're Not in Kansas Anymore/ Jet Set"	41:35	23
Let Go (Frou Frou)	Film — *Garden State* 2004 (R)	1:33:33	10, 48, 59
Let Your Love Flow (Petra Haden)	TV Commercial — *Toyota Prius* 2009	00:00	11
Let's Not Pretend (16 Frames)	TV Series — *Kyle XY* Season 3: "The Tell-Tale Heart"	39:30	77
Live to Be Free (Griffin House)	TV Series — *Kyle XY* Season 2: "Balancing Act"	36:31	20, 21, 25, 28, 52
Love Remains the Same (Gavin Rossdale)	TV Series — *90210* Season 1: "Okaeri, Donna"	00:44	39

Song (Artist)	Media	Timecode	Pages
Make Me Believe (Angel Taylor)	TV Series — *90210* Season1: "The Party's Over"	39:28	46
Man Who Can't Be Moved, The (The Script)	TV Series — *Ghost Whisperer* Season 4: "Heart & Soul"	41:21	23, 28, 32, 36, 59, 60
Mine, Mine, Mine (David Ogden Stiers & Mel Gibson)	Film — *Pocahontas* 1995 (G)	25:53	42
Mister Sister (The Tender Box)	TV Commercial — "Self Expression" — *Sharpie* 2010	00:00	88
My Heart Will Go On (Celine Dion)	Film — *Titanic* 1997 (PG-13)	3:07:31	13, 40
My Mathematical Mind (Spoon)	Film Trailer — *21* 2008	00:25	13
Never Say Never (The Fray)	TV Series — *The Vampire Diaries* Season 1: Pilot	39:33	10, 21, 25, 32, 40, 67, 77
Now or Never (The Cast)	Film — *High School Musical 3: Senior Year* 2008 (G)	04:00	15, 42
One (Tina Dico)	TV Series — *Grey's Anatomy* Season 2: "Band-Aid Covers the Bullet Hole"	33:10	20, 39, 52, 54, 60
One Day (Jack Savoretti)	Film — *Post Grad* 2009 (PG-13)	1:25:10	49, 73
Perfect (Michelle Featherstone)	TV series — *Smallville* Season 7: "Arctic"	31:01	10
Pink Moon (Nick Drake)	TV Commercial — *Volkswagen Cabrio* 2000	00:00	11
Poker Face (Lady Gaga)	Film — *Percy Jackson & the Olympians: Lightning Thief* 2010 (PG)	1:13:37	39
Pretender, The (The Foo Fighters)	TV Series — *CSI: Miami* Season 6: "Dangerous Son"	39:24	9, 26, 38, 48
Razzle Dazzle (Richard Gere & cast)	Film — *Chicago* 2002 (PG-13)	1:19:20	63
Reasons to Love You (Meiko)	TV Series — *Kyle XY* Season 3: "The Tell-Tale Heart"	01:37	28, 32
Rescue Me (Sarah Bettens)	TV Series — *90210* Season 1: "The Party's Over"	36:55	20, 24, 36, 39, 52

Song (Artist)	Source	Time	Tracks
Right Here, Right Now (Zac Efron & Vanessa Hudgens)	Film — *High School Musical 3: Senior Year* 2008 (G)	10:50	15
Rise (Eddie Vedder)	TV Promo — *Deadliest Catch* Season 6 Promo spot	00:00	17, 75
Save Me (Remy Zero)	TV Series — *Smallville* All episodes, theme song	00:00	13, 23, 39, 46, 51
Say It to Me Now (Glen Hansard)	Film — *Once* 2006 (R for langauage)	3:33	75
See the World (Gomez)	TV Series — *House M.D.* Season 3: "Half-Wit"	42:16	19, 57
Shattered (O.A.R.)	TV Promo — *90210* Season 1 Promo Spot	00:00	20, 32, 39, 54
She's Got You High (Mumm-Ra)	Film — *(500) Days of Summer* 2009 (PG-13)	1:30:34	13
Songbird (Fleetwood Mac)	TV Series — *Alias* Season 1: "The Box: Part 2"	41:42	26, 48, 75
Stayin' Alive (The Bee Gees)	Film — *Saturday Night Fever* 1977 (R)	00:55	9
Sun Comes Up (John Legend)	TV Series — *Grey's Anatomy* Season 4: "The Heart of the Matter"	39:32	39, 48
Sweet and Low (Augustana)	TV Series — *Kyle XY* Season 3: "The Tell-Tale Heart"	35:53	20, 23, 25, 26, 40
That's How You Know (Amy Adams)	Film — *Enchanted* 2007 (PG)	47:43	42
This Is Me (Demi Lovato & Joe Jonas)	TV Movie — *Camp Rock* 2008 (TV-G)	1:25:01	15, 25, 39, 42, 60
Top of the World (The Pussycat Dolls)	TV Series (MTV) — *The City* Season 1: "He Never Said He Had a Girlfriend"	01:35	13, 20, 38, 51, 60
Turn Back Around (Lucy Schwartz)	Film — *Post Grad* 2009 (PG-13)	1:20:16	10, 20
Unwritten (Natasha Bedingfield)	TV Series (MTV) — *The Hills* All episodes, theme song	01:44	48
Violet Hill (Coldplay)	TV Series — *One Tree Hill* Seaons 6: "Touch Me I'm Going to Scream: Part 1"	38:50	24, 30, 50, 56

Song (Artist)	Usage	Time	Pages
Waiting On the World to Change (John Mayer)	Film — *Evan Almighty* 2007 (PG)	58:15	39
Walking In Memphis (Marc Cohn)	Film — *Finding Graceland* 1998 (PG-13)	1:10:26	63
We All Want the Same Thing (Kevin Michael)	Film — *Step Up 2: The Streets* 2008 (PG-13)	19:09	86
We're Going to Be Friends (The White Stripes)	Film — *Napoleon Dynamite* 2004 (PG)	01:26	20, 30, 65, 75
What Are You Doing the Rest of Your Life (Dusty Springfield)	TV Commercial — *Zales* 2006	00:00	11
Who Knows (Natasha Bedingfield)	Film — *27 Dresses* 2008 (PG-13)	37:00	10, 59
Who Let the Dogs Out (Baha Men)	Film — *Rugrats in Paris: The Movie* 2000 (G)	1:12:56	16
Winter (Josh Radin)	TV Series — *Scrubs* Season 6: "My Night to Remember"	19:22	53
World On Fire (Sarah McLachlan)	TV Series — *Alias* Season 4: "Authorized Personnel Only, Part 1"	26:00	49, 53
Worries (Langhorne Slim)	TV Commercial — *Travelers Insurance* 2010	00:00	11
You and Me (Lifehouse)	TV Series — *Smallville* Season 4: "Spirit"	39:00	20
You Will Be My Ain True Love (Alison Krauss)	Film — *Cold Mountain* 2003 (R)	09:16 2:31:40	12, 63
Youthless (Beck)	TV Series — *Grey's Anatomy* Season 5: "Dream A Little Dream of Me: Pt. 1"	27:15	20, 38, 60
Zydeco Gris Gris (Beausoleil)	Film — *The Big Easy* 1986 (R)	00:00	63

Glossary

Commonly used terms in the film and television song market.

Atmosphere: In film and television, the prevailing, overall emotional tone of an onscreen place, time, or situation.

Creative director: The executive at an advertising agency whose job it is to find the creative talent to create the commercial. If the music is to be an existing song, the creative director will search for, audition, and present a selection of songs for the client to choose from.

Cue: Any music (song or instrumental) played under a film scene, TV scene, movie trailer, or TV commercial to add energy, mood, or atmosphere.

Cue sheet: A form that lists information about the music cues used in a television show or film. It includes the name of the song or instrumental, name of the songwriter or composer, name of the publisher, duration of the cue, type of use, and the performing rights organization affiliation of both the publisher and writer. The cue sheet is compiled by the production company and submitted to the appropriate performing rights organizations.

Director: In the film world, the director is responsible for the tone and content of the entire film. If the director wants to use songs in the film, he or she will indicate the overall style and may suggest specific songs. In television, a director works on a specific episode but defers to the show's creator or producer for the overall tone. The director and music supervisor work together to "spot" the film or TV show, that is, determine exactly where a song is needed. (See "Spotting.")

Film/TV publisher: A music publisher who offers an exclusive publishing deal with the sole intent of pitching to film, television, and games. These deals usually exclude the artist's own CD sales and download royalties.

Master recording: In film and TV, the recording of a song or composition that is being licensed for use in a film or TV production.

Master use license: A master use license allows a specific recording of a song or instrumental to be used in a particular film or TV production in the manner described in the agreement. It often includes a negotiated fee.

Montage: A suite of short scenes edited into a sequence to compress time or information. In today's TV dramas, an ending montage often ties together the various through-lines of the plot, summing up the central emotional theme.

Music coordinator: The music coordinator ensures that the music budget for a project remains on track and helps to coordinate the many people involved in finding, creating, and licensing music for a production.

Music editor: The music editor is responsible for editing and syncing music and songs to the action on the screen to ensure a strong match that enhances the visual material.

Music library: A collection of pre-existing, recorded songs and instrumental tracks that can be licensed and used in film, television, and other visual media. This type of library may be referred to as a "source track library," "film/TV publisher," "music broker," "song placement company," or "artist catalogue" to distinguish it from a "production music library." See "Production Music Library."

Music supervisor: The person whose responsibility it is to search for and audition songs to be used in a film or TV production based on input from the project's director or producer. When the final decision is made on which songs will be used, the music supervisor negotiates licenses for those songs and generates cue sheets.

"On spec": Writing "on spec" refers to writing and recording a song at the request of a music library or music supervisor. There's no guarantee that it will be used. Demo fees are rarely paid to unknown, unsigned artists and songwriters for this work.

Performance rights organization (PRO): Performance royalties are collected on behalf of publishers and writers by PROs such as ASCAP, BMI, SESAC, PRS, and SOCAN. Royalites are paid out on a regular schedule according to each PRO's accounting system.

Performance royalty: The royalty generated by the broadcast of a song or instrumental track on television. Performance royalties are paid on theatrical performances of films outside the United States.

Pitching a song: Sending a song via CD or emailing a link to a song, accompanied by relevant information, to the appropriate person for consideration in a production.

Placement: The licensing of a recorded song or instrumental track for use with picture.

Producer (TV): In television, this is often the person who developed the show's creative concept. If the show uses music, the producer will generally set the tone for the style of the music as well as its role in the show. He or she may be involved in the music and song choices for all episodes.

Production music library: These music libraries offer custom, made-to-order music in addition to pre-existing music tracks in a variety of styles. They're sometimes asked to create songs and recordings that are very similar to hit songs or known songs by established artists.

Publisher (music): A publisher represents a catalogue of songs and controls the rights to those songs. These rights almost always include the right to license the songs to film and television productions unless specifically excluded from the song contract. Most publishers actively pitch songs in the film and TV market.

Re-titling: Re-titling occurs when a music library changes the title of a song in order to register it as a unique title with a performing rights organization and collect performance royalties for specific placements under that title. Sometimes referred to as "derivative publishing."

Song bed: A mix of a song minus the lead vocal and any background vocals with words.

Song-score: A pre-existing, recorded song accompanying a scene that enhances the scene by adding energy, mood, or atmosphere. This music originates *outside* the world of the characters; they don't hear it but the viewer does.

Source music: A music track or song that originates within the world of the film or TV show. It may come from a radio or jukebox in the scene, a live band, or a DJ, for example. The characters can hear this music in their world.

Source tracks: Pre-existing songs, selected from CDs, digital files, or from music libraries are sometimes referred to as "source tracks." The implication is that these tracks are not created by a composer specifically for a production but come from an outside source such as an artist's CD. Don't confuse this term with "source music." See above.

Spotting: The process of watching a film or TV show to locate the points at which a song will be used, the length of the use, and the type of song that will work best.

Stems: A sub-mix of a single instrument or vocal or groups of similar instruments or vocals, including any effects such as compression, reverb, or EQ that were applied to those tracks in the final, full mix.

Synchronization license: Also referred to as a "sync license." This license allows a film or TV production to use a composition—words and music or just music in the case of an instrumental track—in the manner described in the agreement. It often includes a negotiated fee.

Temp track: Songs and instrumental music used during the making of a movie to give the director and picture editor an idea of the pace and emotional feel of a scene.

TV mix: A mix of your song track that has no lead vocals, no background vocals, and no sound effects such as audience noise, spoken word, or nature sounds.

Underscore: Instrumental background music that does not originate in the world of the characters.

Work for Hire: Work that is done by request and is the subject of a written agreement. When a performance is a work is made for hire, the person who pays for the performance is considered the author and owner of the work.

INDEX

Made in the USA
San Bernardino, CA
19 November 2019